Making Smart Growth Work

PRINCIPAL AUTHOR
Douglas R. Porter

CONTRIBUTING AUTHORS
Robert T. Dunphy
David Salvesen

Bank of America

The Urban Land Institute would like to thank Bank of America
whose financial support made this publication possible.

**Urban Land
Institute**

About ULI–the Urban Land Institute

ULI–the Urban Land Institute is a nonprofit education and research institute that is supported by its members. Its mission is to provide responsible leadership in the use of land in order to enhance the total environment.

ULI sponsors education programs and forums to encourage an open international exchange of ideas and sharing of experiences; initiates research that anticipates emerging land use trends and issues and proposes creative solutions based on that research; provides advisory services; and publishes a wide variety of materials to disseminate information on land use and development. Established in 1936, the Institute today has more than 17,000 members and associates from some 60 countries representing the entire spectrum of the land use and development disciplines.

Richard M. Rosan
President

ULI Project Staff

Rachelle L. Levitt
Senior Vice President, Policy and Practice
Publisher

Marta V. Goldsmith
Vice President, Land Use Policy
Project Director

Gayle Berens
Vice President, Real Estate Development Practice

Nancy H. Stewart
Director, Book Program

Libby Howland
Manuscript Editor

Betsy VanBuskirk
Art Director

Helene Y. Redmond
Book Design/Layout

Meg Batdorff
Cover Design

Diann Stanley-Austin
Director, Publishing Operations

About the Author

Douglas R. Porter is known as one of the nation's leading authorities on growth management techniques and issues at state, regional, and local levels. In addition to his consulting on growth management concerns, he formed the nonprofit Growth Management Institute in 1992 to conduct research and educational endeavors in growth management policies and practices. His current work spans a wide spectrum of issued from infill housing programs to transportation/land use relationships, regional growth management, transit-oriented development, new town development, and local growth management. He consults with local governments, development firms, state and regional agencies, and national organizations and regularly speaks at national and regional conferences. From 1979 to 1991, Porter directed the public policy research program of the Urban Land Institute. He is a Fellow of ULI and has chaired the Maryland Transportation Commission. Porter has written or contributed to more than 30 books and 100 articles on growth management subjects. His recent publications include *The Practice of Sustainable Development* (ULI, 2000), *Managing Growth in America's Communities* (Island Press, 1997), and *Transit-Focused Development: A Synthesis of Transit Practice* (National Academy Press, 1997).

Recommended bibliographic listing:

Porter, Douglas R. *Making Smart Growth Work*. Washington, D.C.: ULI–the Urban Land Institute, 2002.

ULI Catalog Number: M40
International Standard Book Number: 0-87420-883-1
Library of Congress Control Number: 2002092265

Copyright 2002 by ULI–the Urban Land Institute
1025 Thomas Jefferson Street, N.W.
Suite 500 West
Washington, D.C. 20007-5201

Second Printing, 2004

Cover image: ©Jonathan Evans/Illustration Works

Contents

Foreword and Acknowledgments

nterest in smart growth was in full bloom throughout the nation when I started work on this book. ULI's commission to me to write this book challenged me to go beyond the usual generalities in describing the much ballyhooed tenets of smart growth and, perhaps more significantly, to define how the principles of smart growth could be applied in the everyday world of real estate and community development.

I discovered that smart growth is a moving target. New interpretations of the principles evolve daily as various interests propound their special views of what constitutes smart growth and as public officials and developers pronounce their pet projects to be "smart growth in action." The evolving state of smart growth (and my own perceptions of it) required constant rethinking of the information and ideas I was putting on the page—-and ultimately extensive reworking of the drafts of almost all the early chapters.

Several people have helped me to track and understand the changes taking place in the principles and practices of smart growth. First, I would like to thank David Salvesen and Robert Dunphy for their initial drafts of chapters 3 and 4, respectively. David, once my environmental right arm in ULI's public policy research division, was a "natural" choice for writing about open space. His compre-

hensive view of the subject helped me formulate the contributions of open space to growing smartly. Bob Dunphy and I have chewed over transportation/land use relationships more times than I can count; and his data-rich writing on travel modes helped me to discern the path to smart transportation. Although I have both trimmed and expanded upon their original chapter drafts, the information and ideas that they contributed remain essential to the final product.

Second, Marta Goldsmith, who initiated the idea of a ULI book on smart growth, provided constant and refreshing guidance in determining the content and direction of each chapter. Her focus on defining reasonable practices and her vigilance in identifying flaws in logic propelled my thinking about making smart growth workable.

Third, Libby Howland's heroic editing of the manuscript eliminated my wordiness and repetitions, squared away errant sentence structures, and reorganized the order of presentation where necessary to make the work both more sensible and readable.

Also I would like to thank the eight reviewers of the early draft, who are listed here. These reviewers labored over chapters that needed help—much help. Their cautions, criticisms, and contributions were helpful and are appreciated. And I owe special thanks to Don Priest, my former boss at ULI, whose skeptical analysis of where smart growth is heading prompted many of the ideas I offer in the final chapter.

Finally, I would like to take this opportunity to thank the staff and members of ULI who believe enough in smart growth to have commissioned this book.

Douglas R. Porter
ULI Fellow
President
Growth Management Institute
Chevy Chase, Maryland

Reviewers

Gary Binger
Director
ULI California Smart Growth Initiative
Oakland, California

James DeFrancia
President
Lowe Enterprises Community Development Inc.
Aspen, Colorado

Stephen Dragos
Former President and CEO
Business Partnership of Somerset County
Bridgewater, New Jersey

Alexander Garvin
ULI Fellow
Commissioner
New York City Planning Commission
New York, New York

Maureen McAvey
Senior Resident Fellow in Urban Development
ULI–the Urban Land Institute
Washington, D.C.

Anne Vernez Moudon
ULI Fellow
Professor, Department of Urban Design
    and Planning
University of Washington
Seattle, Washington

Robert Rhodes
Executive Vice President and General Counsel
The St. Joe Company
Jacksonville, Florida

Smedes York
President
York Properties Inc.
Raleigh, North Carolina

Smart Growth Defined

Growth means development. Smart growth means development that accommodates growth in smart ways, which is to say in economically viable, environmentally responsible, and collaboratively determined ways. Smart growth calls for building communities that are more hospitable, productive, and fiscally and environmentally responsible than most of the communities that have been developed in the last century.

Smart growth abides by a set of interrelated principles of community development. These basic principles seek to accommodate the different interests of all sectors of society with a stake in community development. ULI describes this underlying objective as follows: "Smart growth seeks to identify a common ground where developers, environmentalists, public officials, citizens, and others can all find acceptable ways to accommodate growth."[1]

Generally, the principles of smart growth are widely acceptable ideas about the desirable form and character of communities. Not surprisingly, which principles of community development make it onto an organization's list of smart-growth principles depends somewhat on the particular interests of the organization. Some self-styled advocates of smart growth emphasize protection of open space and natural resources. Others focus on giving developers and builders the flexibility to mix uses and increase the range of housing choices in their projects. Others stress wider participation

(and regional input) in decisions affecting future development.

This book considers the following six forms, qualities, and processes of community development to be the key principles of smart growth:

▲ compact, multiuse development;
▲ open-space conservation;
▲ expanded mobility;
▲ enhanced livability;
▲ efficient management and expansion of infrastructure; and
▲ infill, redevelopment, and adaptive use in built-up areas.

Development that is in accordance with these key principles should result in well-designed, multiuse communities that offer people a range of options for living, working, recreation, and travel. These principles can guide development in newly developing greenfields on the edges of urbanized areas as well as infill development and redevelopment in cities and suburbs. These principles can guide the siting and design of large and small projects, of single-use and multiuse projects, and of high-density complexes and lower-density residential neighborhoods.

There is mounting dissatisfaction with current forms of community development, or with many of its perceived consequences—chief among them, traffic congestion, the wasting of scarce resources,

1

environmental pollution, loss of open space and habitat, inadequate (or too costly) public services and facilities, lack of affordable housing, and lack of community variety and vitality. The smart-growth model of community building has emerged from the confluence of long-standing interests (ideas about community that have evolved over decades) and fresh perspectives (growing dissatisfaction with the way things are), and this dual provenance strengthens its appeal throughout the nation.

Smart growth offers a 21st-century, pro-growth path to creating livable communities. "Good Growth" signposts have replaced those saying "No Growth." Smart growth is growth that plays up the benefits of development and change and takes care to avoid and mitigate the negative consequences of community growth and change.

This chapter traces the emergence of the concept of smart growth, describes the aims and elements of the concept, and identifies the issues it raises for both public and private participants in the development process.

The Suburban Ideal—Dashed

Through the ages, scholars, philosophers, and religious leaders have sketched many models of ideal communities. Some have centered on spiritual enrichment, others on military protection, efficient physical patterns, or a rich civic life.

From the 17th century onward, North America provided Europeans a fertile field for experimentation in applying such ideas. Many settlers in America founded ideal communities, like those of the Moravians, Shakers, and Mormons, that prescribed community layouts and building forms serving their doctrines of religious conduct, social relationships, and economic survival.

Early planner/developers such as the founders of Savannah, Georgia, and countless other colonial towns laid out disciplined grids of streets and parks that defied the hazards of the surrounding wilderness. Planner/developer William Penn in Philadelphia and the designer/developer team of Pierre L'Enfant and George Washington in the District of Columbia borrowed European ideas of grand boulevards, formal parks, and stately monuments. Many of these ideas flowed also into

the design of the White City, the site of the 1893 World's Columbian Exposition in Chicago. The urban design of the Chicago fair and ideas propounded by the City Beautiful movement stirred community officials and community builders throughout the United States to build grand streets, parks, and public buildings.

The mix of form and function in pre-car living environments answered to the needs of the times. In cities, until rail transit came into being, the scale of housing and its location in relation to essential services respected the limits of walkable distances. Most people lived in neighborhoods that provided most of their needs for daily existence. The emergence of industrial cities in the 19th century depended initially on high-density worker housing within walking distance of industry clusters. Later, when employers could draw on labor pools in far-off neighborhoods linked to employment centers by trolleys and trains they could concentrate their factories and office buildings in larger districts.

The coming of the automobile broke the urban mold. No longer was it necessary to live cheek by jowl. The abundance of land made accessible by automobile encouraged lavish lot sizes for housing. Streets become conduits for cars and lost their quality as pleasant pedestrian spaces.

Americans soon became enamored of the suburban style of existence—building single-family homes on large lots, paying to extend public facilities and services into new territory, and traveling everywhere by car. The new lifestyle eventually wrought tremendous changes in the physical, economic, and social structure of urban areas. Undifferentiated housing spread over vast areas, business complexes grew ever larger, huge shopping centers sprang up drawing patronage from far and wide.

Already in the 1920s, the New York area's Regional Plan Association observed in its first comprehensive report that the growth of suburban jurisdictions was bringing about major shifts in population in the region. In 1959, not two generations later, Edgar Hoover and Raymond Vernon were predicting that this trend would accelerate:

> Freed from the need to be close to the centers of the old cities—unbound from spatial restraints by the wider use of the automobile and the truck

—the people of the [New York] Region and many of the enterprises on which they live will devour space at a faster rate than ever before.[2]

Even the large-scale master-planned communities, designed as paragons of good development, relied almost exclusively on auto-oriented patterns of development. Reston and Columbia (both in the Washington, D.C., region) featured inward-focused neighborhoods connected by pedestrian paths to community centers and schools. Laid out within a broad framework of highways, these protected residential environments were isolated from centers of employment and shopping as well as from the outside world and were thus dependent on automobile access. To the present day, most master-planned communities and other large-scale developments repeat variations of these design ideas.

▲ **The concept of smart growth arose from people's increasing concern about the downside of urban sprawl.**

While suburbs boomed through the postwar decades, the populations and economies of central cities dwindled, especially in older cities in the Northeast and Midwest. As the periphery of the urbanized area pushed farther into the countryside, many older suburbs joined their central cities in decline. In the 1980s and 1990s, western and southern cities discovered that, like older metropolitan areas in the Northeast and Midwest, they too had evolved declining inner cities and thriving outer cities—urban cores and outer suburbs with great differences in social and economic conditions.

Now, the residents of declining inner-city neighborhoods make do with rundown housing, poor services, and few job opportunities. Inner-city cores have become the last refuge of the have-nots, and lack of tax base and requirements for welfare drain the fiscal resources of cities. Infrastructure systems go begging for maintenance and replacement. Even the resuscitation of the commercial core in some downtowns has not halted the outflow of people and wealth.

Suburban jurisdictions today are numerous and powerful. The suburban population is growing twice as fast as that of cities, and suburban jurisdictions are attracting the bulk of new jobs. A metropolitan region's major retail concentrations, high-tech industrial corridors, and most desirable neighborhoods are generally found in suburban locations. Housing in metropolitan regions numbers 88 million units, with 54 million located in

suburbs and 34 million in central cities. Commuting flows are increasingly suburb to suburb rather than suburb to central city.

In state legislatures and in Congress, representatives from suburban districts have become more numerous than those from central cities. Within metropolitan regions, interjurisdictional competition is commonplace. Reaching regional consensus on growth issues becomes increasingly difficult as fiscal, social, and economic disparities widen.

Outward growth is not confined to the orbits of large cities. It is occurring as well in many remote areas—small towns, villages, and undeveloped rural areas—as people seek to escape the hustle and bustle of urban environments. In sufficient quantity, freelance workers, retirees, and commuters drawn to rural and small-town life can quickly alter the ambience of rural communities.

Americans' love affair with the suburban style has become less passionate and has even soured for some as certain problems caused by the forms of development it inspires have become more evident. Communities mired in traffic and dogged by fiscal difficulties have begun to look for solutions. People attracted to suburban locations because of their environmental and open-space qualities have become disturbed about the loss of environmental quality and open space.

A typical scenario: A few families move to a suburban enclave or rural village on the fringe of the metropolitan area. Other families follow right behind. New houses sprout along rural lanes. Subdivisions soon carpet the countryside. Strip malls and strip business centers spring up along the highways. Cars soon clog the roads. Buying a gallon of milk requires burning a gallon of gasoline. Too many kids overwhelm school capacities. Taxes go up to pay for sewer and water expansions. Planning and zoning conflicts mushroom. There is no relief in sight.

Many people feel that growth and change are out of control, that the charm of their communities is being eroded and their fiscal soundness compromised by indiscriminate and misguided development. Consider the following trends over the last two decades:

▲ Metropolitan regions large and small are converting farmlands and forests to (sub)urban uses at unprecedented rates and residents of urbanized areas are finding that open space is less and less accessible to them. Atlanta's suburbanization, for example, is now occurring 45 to 70 miles north of downtown and approaching the South Carolina border.[3]

▲ Commercial land uses are sprawling like housing. According to a study of office space trends by staff of the Fannie Mae Foundation, the suburban share of metropolitan office space increased from 26 percent in 1979 to 42 percent in 1999, with much of the suburban space located in highly dispersed, edgeless locations.[4]

▲ From 1978 to 1998, the U.S. population increased by 22 percent, while the number of vehicle-miles traveled (VMT) jumped by 70 percent. And VMT is still climbing. The number of motor vehicles increased by 41 percent during that same period.[5]

▲ Development is threatening essential environmental qualities and features of the countryside. The national list of threatened and endangered species grows longer every year. In many communities, water quality is diminishing and water supplies are increasingly undependable as aquifers are drawn down or polluted. Air quality has improved over the past two decades, but 100 million people live in areas where smog is a problem.

▲ The total cost of providing basic infrastructure is increasing disproportionately as it is extended far from existing service areas, as consumers demand higher service standards, and as engineering and construction standards rise.

▲ Existing infrastructure is given short shrift in the already inadequate infrastructure budgets of local jurisdictions because meeting needs for the construction of new systems is more politically popular than meeting maintenance and replacement needs. Thus, existing infrastructure is falling into disrepair.

▲ The economic disparities between jurisdictions within metropolitan regions is widening, with desirable communities capturing more value and wealth and less desirable communities, including many older suburbs, losing value and wealth.

Consider also the responses to growth encountered in many communities:

▲ Communities are putting more restrictions on development. Stricter rules reflect a desire to improve the quality of community design and buildings. And they also reflect slow-growth and no-growth attitudes on the part of local residents. Proposed projects are subjected to lengthy review processes, extensive exactions, and sharp reductions in scope.

▲ Proposed development projects face escalating (and costly) requirements for providing public facilities and amenities and higher standards for their design, regardless of the needs of the market to be served by the development.

▲ The residents of communities resist all new forms of development, especially if it exceeds average local densities—regardless of its design attributes, its conformance with adopted public policy, and its proven acceptance by the market.

▲ Many local residents who participate in the community decision-making process seek to preserve the quality of life in the community by exclusion rather than through constructive adaptation to changing circumstances.

All in all, conflict and dysfunctionalism seem to be more the rule than the exception these days in the community development process. In many jurisdictions, the community development process is failing to achieve broad public goals for community betterment and also failing to accommodate the private sector's development proposals to meet consumer demand in a reasonably profitable manner. Enter smart growth.

Why Smart Growth?

The concept of smart growth emerged during the 1990s, a reaction to worsening trends in traffic congestion, school overcrowding, air pollution, loss of open space, effacement of valued historic places, and skyrocketing public facilities costs—and a reaction as well to the apparent failure of traditional planning techniques to improve these conditions.

Local governments have attempted to deal with growing pains by planning and zoning. They have formulated brave goals and policies that promise —but seldom deliver—significant changes in the character of community development. Many communities have expanded and elaborated their planning and regulatory toolkits to include sophisticated growth management devices. They have, for example, circumscribed the areas in which urban development is allowed, conditioned pro-ject approvals on the availability of public facilities, disallowed development in rural and environmentally sensitive areas, and added requirements for developer contributions to community facilities and amenities.

In many cases, however, public policies encourage forms of development that make growth problems worse. Public policies promote or require too large sites for all kinds of land uses, even schools and churches, which eats up land and lengthens travel distances. Public policies limit the range of housing types that can be developed and travel modes that can be supported, and in so doing they frequently make communities unaffordable except to well-off households. In their competition for tax ratables, jurisdictions lose sight of siting and design concerns.

Jurisdictions that do try to make better choices often find it difficult to fight conventional forces of growth. What their neighboring jurisdictions do has consequences for them. Uncontained sprawl on the fringes of an urban region, for example, stresses regional commuting corridors and thus also deteriorates air quality throughout the region. Furthermore, the record shows that as inner suburbs learn lessons about smarter development, outer exurban and rural communities that are still low on the learning curve make counterproductive development decisions.

Meanwhile, attempts by developers to use responsible development practices are frequently frus-

trated. They seek but do not receive permission to design housing in clusters, provide a mix of uses within small areas, design narrower streets, and use natural systems of storm drainage and water conservation.

Clustered housing, for example, is a concept that ULI began espousing as early as 1961, and it has been promoted by the National Association of Home Builders and other key groups.[6] Urban planners have consistently supported the idea of clustering as a method for accommodating development while retaining land in farms, forests, and other natural areas. Cluster designs are mainstays of most master-planned community developments and the essence of many design prescriptions for subdivision development in rural areas.[7] Nevertheless, despite widespread support for clustering among the cognoscenti, local elected officials and resident activists often recoil from it because, they say, high-density housing attracts undesirables and adds to traffic congestion.

Smart growth offers a way out. It changes the public context of the development process from regulatory restrictiveness to collaborative planning for the community in process. Very often local resistance to development proposals stems from the lack of a clear vision of ways in which growth and change can be assimilated and guided to create livable communities. Smart growth promotes preferred types of development (development that contributes positively to the community) rather than proscribing unpreferred types of development. Smart growth puts community support behind public/private partnerships to build livable communities.

Smart growth is one of several new approaches to community development that have raised much interest, the notable others being sustainable development and new urbanism.

▲ Sustainable development. Initially, sustainable development tended to focus on conserving and recycling natural resources. In its present incarnation, sustainable development calls for preserving, enhancing, and interrelating economic prosperity, the integrity of natural ecosystems, and social equity—broad goals that apply to global and national as well as local development. Many sustainable development aims are reflected in smart-growth principles.[8]

▲ **New urbanism.** Concerns about the design of neighborhoods and cities are primarily what gave rise to the new urbanism movement. New urbanism absorbs and expands upon proposals for traditional neighborhood development rooted in the historical American hunger for utopian living. In 1991, a group of neotraditional architects and urban designers formulated new urbanism's basic principles, the Ahwahnee principles (named after the Ahwahnee Lodge in Yosemite National Park where they were meeting). New urbanism, says the preamble to the principles, aims to reestablish "the relationship between the art of building and the making of community through citizen-based participatory planning and design." The patterns of development espoused by new urbanists are similar to those promoted by advocates of smart growth. The focus of new urbanism is more on specific urban design relationships for buildings and uses, and less on some other key communitywide concerns of smart growth, such as regional transportation systems and regional open-space systems.

Elements of smart growth (along with elements of sustainable development and new urbanism) are already recognizable in the public policies and development regulations of a great many communities. And they are also evident in the practices of many developers and builders.

Smart Growth in Theory and Practice

The six key principles of smart growth listed earlier are embodied in three core themes:

▲ **Conservation of resources.** Three key principles of smart growth—compact and multiuse development, development that is contiguous to existing development, and infill and redevelopment in urbanized areas—are, not incidentally, resource-sensitive: they require less extensive infrastructure, make use of existing structures and facilities, use less land, require less VMT. Growing by these principles also reduces the amount of land needed to accommodate development and thus helps achieve open-space conservation, another key principle of smart growth.

▲ **Wider choices.** Smart growth seeks to widen people's options—for types and styles (and prices) of housing, for types of neighborhoods and lifestyles, for work locations, for modes of travel, and for recreational and cultural opportunities.

This theme recognizes the growing variety of types of households and jobs in the country, the need to open up opportunities for economic and social advancement, and people's preferences for more vital, livable communities.

▲ **Inclusive, public/private, multijurisdictional decision making.** Smart growth calls for working out the details of growth and development community by community and region by region through constructive collaboration—a real partnership of interests and accomplishments—among public officials, development interests, community interests (residents), and special interests (for example, environmentalists or advocates for affordable housing). Decision-making processes must recognize regional concerns and economic development concerns.

Smart-growth principles and themes may appear at once too general and too confining, vague ideals that can be interpreted in various ways to require or to prohibit certain forms of development. These qualities are their strength, however. The principles are meant to express targets and directions for community development. Smart growth does not mandate wholesale and overnight change. It proposes rather to bend the current course of development, to promote more compactness, for example, more open-space conservation, more infill and redevelopment, et cetera. Communities can take a variety of paths to the achievement of smart growth. Specific community priorities and circumstances will dictate a certain amount of trading off and compromising among the principles.

Smart growth envisions each community fashioning its own version of smart growth through a shared decision-making process, a version that accords with community interests and reasonably balances the various principles that make up smart growth in theory.

Sometimes, however, the principles of smart growth can be viewed too selectively by interests and interest groups involved in community development. Many public officials and civic activists support smart growth's advocacy of higher-quality development and more livable neighborhoods, for example, while they vigorously oppose proposals for more intensive development. Skeptics note that public opinion surveys consistently find overwhelming support for curbing urban sprawl coexisting with lack of support for higher-density development.

Developers adduce smart growth to validate projects proposing higher densities and mixed uses, but they oppose open-space conservation initiatives to restrict development in greenfield locations. On the other hand, environmentalists and residents seek to preserve more open space but fail to support offsets in the form of higher-density development and more infill development.

Some developers suspect that for many communities smart growth is an anti-growth concept in disguise. On the other hand, some community organizations and environmental groups view smart growth as an open invitation to public officials and developers to design unattractive and too-dense projects that violate the character of the community. In the view of many transportation officials and advocates, smart growth's advocacy of expanded travel options supports investment in transit and in pathways for bicycles and pedestrians in lieu of—instead of in addition to—investment in highway capacity.

Reaching consensus on specific applications of smart growth in individual communities will require education, discussion, common sense, and compromise. This book confirms that smart growth is not easy. Yet its advocates can take heart from the extent to which smart-growth principles are already incorporated in public policies and in private development practices.

Public Policy and Smart Growth

Smart-growth principles have been mainstream planning concepts for many years. The official statements of community objectives for future development in numerous jurisdictions across the United States sound themes remarkably similar to smart-growth principles. The planning goals of Wichita-Sedgwick County, Kansas, and New Jersey's statewide development and redevelopment goals provide examples.

In 1993, the county board of commissioners and the city council for the Wichita-Sedgwick County area (hardly a hotbed of radical planning) adopted the following comprehensive planning goals (shortened and paraphrased here), among others. Except for a lack of emphasis on conserving environmentally sensitive lands—possibly not a major issue for a slowly growing metropolis on the plains of Kansas—these goals closely adhere to the ideas of smart growth.

▲ Encourage orderly growth in order to meet future demand while considering cost to taxpayers, developers, and the environment.

▲ Guide future growth and development to areas that are served by existing public facilities and services, or that can be served economically; and promote compact and contiguous development.

▲ Provide for rural, suburban, and urban residential areas that provide a variety of housing opportunities; and develop and conserve housing and neighborhoods that will provide safe, decent, and affordable conditions for all residents.

▲ Insure that an adequate supply of land is made available to promote successful commercial activity and the expansion of the industrial base in appropriate areas throughout the county.

▲ Provide the highest-quality utility and public-safety services to the public at a reasonable cost.

▲ Enhance the quality of life and image of the city and county through the provision and proper maintenance of open space and natural resources.

▲ Protect and preserve the manmade and natural elements that support human habitation, add to the community's quality of life, enhance opportunities for greater cultural and educational experiences, and create a unique living environment.

▲ Increase economic wealth and opportunities for Sedgwick County citizens.

Adopted in 1992, the New Jersey State Development and Redevelopment Plan contains the following strategies:

▲ Revitalize the state's urban centers and areas by investing sufficiently in their human resources and infrastructure systems to attract private investment.

▲ Promote beneficial economic growth, development, and renewal by providing realistic growth opportunities through good planning and the provision of infrastructure in advance of or concurrent with the impacts of new development.

▲ Protect the environment by planning for growth in compact forms, at locations and intensities that make efficient use of existing and planned infrastructure, and by increasing infrastructure capacities and growth potential in areas where development will not damage water resources, critical habitats, or important forests.

▲ Provide adequate public services at a reasonable cost by planning locations and patterns of growth that maintain existing and planned capacities of infrastructure, fiscal soundness, and natural resource systems; and minimize the need for substantial public investment in new, unplanned infrastructure.

▲ Provide adequate housing at a reasonable cost by planning for concentrations of housing sufficiently close to both employment opportunities and public transportation so as to reduce both housing and commuting costs for low-, moderate-, and middle-income groups.

▲ Preserve and enhance historic, cultural, open-space, and recreational land and structures by using preservation, conservation, and other programs and techniques to guide growth in locations and patterns that protect them.

The aims for community development expressed in the Wichita-Sedgwick County and New Jersey plans come very close to describing the principles of smart growth. This comparability of goals indicates that smart-growth ideas build closely on a broad unanimity, at least in the public sector, on what forms of community development are most desirable.

Private Development and Smart Growth

Projects and buildings around the country exemplify smart forms of development. Developers do not have to start from scratch in designing smart and smart design is not pie in the sky. Many developers are experienced in the development of compact, mixed-use projects in built-up locations and greenfield locations. Many developers have completed attractive adaptive use and infill projects. Developers know from experience how to design projects to fit compatibly with existing development, how to preserve environmental features as community amenities, and how to design for mixed incomes and mixed uses. The developers of master-planned communities, in particular, have a long record of experience in developing projects that reflect many, if not most, smart-growth principles.

But smart growth needs to become a more prevailing ethic in the development business. Realizing smart growth requires most developers and builders to refocus some of their decisions and practices, but it does not require draconian changes in basic development approaches. Two essential qualities of smart growth make it workable, feasible, and profitable for developers:

▲ it is an evolutionary process; and

▲ its achievement relies on an expansion of market choices.

Smart growth is not talking revolution. It will be achieved over time out of incremental changes that occur as the development process adapts to new and future needs. Smart growth asks developers and builders to incorporate its principles into practice in ways that make good business sense, not just sound public policy.

Furthermore, the participation of developers in smart growth is not based on the adoption of abstract principles. Rather, it is based on needing to change product design and location in order to meet changing market demand. Documented demographic and economic trends support smart development. Only one-quarter of households today fit what was once the norm: a married couple with two children. In only 13 percent of households does a parent stay home with the children instead of going to work. The share of formerly unconventional households—one person living alone, a married couple without kids, unrelated adults, single-parent families—is projected to continue to grow. Already nonfamily households—persons living alone or with nonrelatives—account for 31 percent of all households.

Also, there is a growing mismatch between household incomes and housing costs. In particular, detached suburban houses are becoming less affordable to more households. And perhaps increasingly less suitable to more lifestyles as well. Immigrants, many with particular ideas on what makes a livable neighborhood, are adding a new dimension to housing markets.

Workplaces (and work locations) are changing too. The imbalance between jobs and housing in many areas is worsening, and many employees are forced to commute longer distances. More people work at least part time at home. In short, market forces—growing social and economic diversity—are supporting the development of more varied and more urban living environments, and making smart growth an idea whose time has come.

Support for Smart Development

Developers cannot achieve smart growth in a vacuum. They need reliable, positive, constructive, and predictable support from the public sector. As much as the principles of smart growth are a response to the needs of the time—demographic, environmental, social, and economic—smart growth will flourish only if the various forces—cultural, economic, and institutional—that are the foundation for conventional development processes and products are redirected, adapted, and adjusted.

Business as usual for everyone involved in community development has built up substantial inertia that resists change. Lenders recognize only stock, off-the-shelf products. Elected officials pay more attention to noisy NIMBYists than to the principles of smart growth. Developers recycle timeworn designs. Environmentalists are quick to protest and slow to show support for good development. Civic activists have obstruction tactics down pat but lack a development strategy. Fundamental institutional obstacles to smart growth can be overcome only by constant and committed collaboration among the interests.

In addition, smart growth requires regional understandings and regional development standards that reduce regulatory disparities across regions and provide a more certain public context for development. To practice smart growth in a competitive business and regulatory climate, developers need a level playing field. Doing the right thing developmentally in one jurisdiction may have cost and risk implications that makes the proposed project uncompetitive with lower-quality projects in other jurisdictions. Even the most committed developers who value high-quality design and community connections cannot survive the undercutting of their competitive position in the regional market.

Achieving smart growth, it seems, will require a new kind of collaboration and cooperation in managing and practicing development—a true public/private partnering for developing livable communities.

This Book

This chapter has argued that current development patterns generate a number of undesirable consequences—economic, social, and environmental. It has set forth six principles of smart growth that are intended to promote salutary changes in development patterns and functions. These principles are broad and generic. They must be translated into more specific goals by communities to reflect local interests and conditions.

This chapter has further argued that smart growth must be patient. The eventual goal is long-term modifications in the character of the market, consumer demand, industry practices, and public policy. Because such modifications will take time, the intent of the smart-growth principles is to guide incremental but lasting changes in the forms and processes of community development. The intent of smart growth is not revolutionary.

The next four chapters in the book address the broad aims of development in the smart-growth mode—compact and multiuse development (chapter 2), open-space conservation (chapter 3), multimodal mobility (chapter 4), and livable communities (chapter 5). The following two chapters describe applications of the smart-growth principles, first in greenfields (chapter 6) and then in urbanized areas (chapter 7). The final chapter discusses the regional imperative for smart growth and describes collaborative approaches to achieving smart growth (chapter 8). The main themes of each of these chapters are briefly described next.

Chapter 2: Compact, Multiuse Development

Achieving more compact forms of development with a greater mix of uses will reduce the impacts of growth on open space and sensitive land, contribute to the place-making qualities of development, reduce infrastructure investment requirements, and expand opportunities for multimodal travel.

Degrees of compactness and elements of mixed use can and should vary according to the context of specific regional and community practices. Smart growth does not insist on a one-size-fits-all approach. Moderate increases in current density patterns can achieve a beneficial increase in compactness. What constitutes a beneficial mix of uses can vary from place to place, depending on market and other conditions. To be most effective as a smart-growth tool, however, compact, multiuse development should provide a sizable area in which walking is convenient and transit service can be feasibly provided as the community matures.

Chapter 3: Open-Space Conservation

Current urban and suburban growth is converting land to development at a rapid pace, disrupting the natural functions provided by undeveloped land, and removing land from productive uses. The current land conversion process is unsustainable. Smart growth emphasizes open-space conservation because of the many values of open space (including farmland)—for recreation, for productive uses, and for sustaining environmental processes and protecting environmental quality.

Development planning to use land wisely and to retain its important natural features and hydrologic functions is an essential tool of open-space conservation. Communities should implement green infrastructure programs on a regional scale to provide sustainable, naturally functioning, connected green areas and corridors in urban and urbanizing areas. A variety of programs have been tested and proved successful in their ability to conserve many types of land—including farmland, forests, parks, and habitat and other environmentally sensitive land.

Chapter 4: Expanded Mobility

Car travel (vehicle-miles traveled, VMT) within metropolitan regions has been increasing at a faster rate than population, and highway and transit improvements have fallen well short of demand. Congestion is bad and projected to worsen. Its alleviation is possible only through a coordinated, multimodal approach—carefully selected highway improvements, the more efficient use of existing highway capacity, and the shifting of a significant share of travel to transit (of which there are a variety of available forms) and to walking and biking.

Shifting travel share to transit and to nonmotorized modes requires more transit-friendly and pedestrian-friendly patterns of growth. Evolving these patterns will take a long time, given the almost total dominance of auto-dependent patterns of development in metropolitan regions. For this reason, and because Americans will continue to favor the car for most travel, investment in new and improved highways continues to be necessary. More transit, even a lot more transit, cannot do the job alone. However, highway investment should go hand in hand with greater public commitment to transit investment and transit-supportive development.

Chapter 5: Enhanced Livability

Livability involves a community's quality-of-life features, such as housing choices, educational opportunities, employment and business opportunities, essential facilities and services, and a sense of community identity and shared regional experience. Improving these soft qualities of development for all current and potential residents is essential to smart growth. Raising the quality of amenities in wealthy neighborhoods and communities is not a substitute for providing affordable housing and employment opportunities throughout the region. Communities and developers have initiated programs and projects that demonstrate the feasibility and benefits of working to improve livability for all residents.

Chapter 6: Growing Smart in Suburban Greenfields

Suburban greenfields present the greatest challenge to smart growth. But also perhaps the greatest opportunity. Suburban greenfields are developing fast and furious in unsmart ways. Success in redirecting those patterns can help regions avoid some of the most serious consequences of continued unsmart growth.

Ingrained habits of development and public regulation thwart the application of smart development practices in suburban greenfields. Conventional approaches to development need to be changed, but doing so in this setting will be an uphill fight. Smart growth can be achieved over time in suburban greenfield areas only by creating opportunities for different approaches to development. Developer choices in site selection and project design, for example, need to be broadened. Systems of firm, predictable public guidance of development through innovative policies, incentives, and regulations need to be established.

The principles of smart growth should guide development in rural areas, small towns, and remote areas as well. In these settings, resorts sited in environmentally sensitive areas, retirement communities, and other large-scale projects should be particularly required to practice smart development.

Chapter 7: Growing Smart through Infill and Redevelopment

The contribution of changing demographics to the achievement of smart-growth goals in in-town locations is significant. Market interest in infill locations and nontraditional housing (units in adapted industrial buildings, for example) is strong.

While opportunities exist, serious obstacles remain. Securing financing can be difficult. Designing new development to be compatible with existing development can be challenging. Regulatory constraints, including opposition by local organizations and community groups, can be onerous. Maintaining momentum for the infill and urban redevelopment that is underway is made easier by various incentives such as the federal historic-preservation tax credit and state and local site assembly initiatives, and a growing body of demonstrably successful projects inspires imitation.

Chapter 8: Mobilizing Support for Smart Growth

Achieving smart growth will not be easy and it is not inevitable. Making the necessary changes in the process of community development will be difficult and controversial and will require leadership, a willingness to innovate, and collaboration among all the players involved.

For smart growth to work, special interests must put aside narrow views of what makes communities desirable, and public officials must find ways to invest more in and provide more incentives for the elements of good development. Smart-growth advocates have a large toolkit of time-tested programs and regulatory tools they can use. Trying out experimental approaches should be encouraged. Collaborative and inclusive processes that involve goal-setting can help communities reach decisions that support smart growth. The new kid on the block is project rating systems that can be used to secure endorsements for proposed developments from organizations that promote smart growth.

Making smart growth work ultimately will require securing commitments from public officials and interest groups to recognize regional needs, provide effective regional coordination of the development process, and fund the necessary public infrastructure. This is the hard reality that will test the will of smart-growth advocates.

Notes

1. Michael Pawlukiewicz, "What is Smart Growth?" *Urban Land*, June 1998, pp. 6–7.

2. Edgar M. Hoover and Raymond Vernon, *Anatomy of a Metropolis: The Changing Distribution of People and Jobs within the New York Metropolitan Region* (New York: Doubleday/Anchor Books, 1959), p. 245.

3. Christopher Leinberger, "The Changing Location of Development and Investment Opportunities," *Black's Guide*, 1996, p. 22.

4. Robert E. Lang, *Office Sprawl: The Evolving Geography of Business* (Washington, D.C.: Brookings Institution Center on Urban and Metropolitan Policy, October 2000).

5. Federal Highway Administration, *Our Nation's Highways: Selected Facts and Figures* (Washington, D.C.: 2000).

6. See, for example, *Innovations vs. Traditions in Community Development*, Technical Bulletin 47 (Washington, D.C.: ULI–the Urban Land Institute, 1963); *Housing America—the Challenges Ahead* (Washington, D.C.: National Association of Home Builders, 1985); and Welford Sanders, *The Cluster Subdivision: A Cost-Effective Approach*, Planning Advisory Service Report 356 (Chicago: American Planning Association, 1980).

7. See, for example, Randall Arendt, *Growing Greener: Putting Conservation into Local Plans and Ordinances* (Chicago: Island Press, American Planning Association, Natural Lands Trust, and American Society of Landscape Architects, 1999); and his *Conservation Design for Subdivisions* (Chicago: Island Press, American Planning Association, Natural Lands Trust, and American Society of Landscape Architects, 1996).

8. See Douglas R. Porter, ed., *The Practice of Sustainable Development* (Washington, D.C.: ULI–the Urban Land Institute, 2000).

Principles of Smart Growth
Compact, Multiuse Development

Smart growth entails more compact patterns of community development than those that have evolved in the United States over the past 50 or more years and a more fine-grained mix of activities within individual communities. This chapter considers the meaning of the terms "compact" and "mix of uses" in the context of community development and it describes the issues involved in achieving more compact, multiuse development.

Compact, Multiuse Development: What and Why

Smart growth proposes a return—modified to fit contemporary needs and market realities—to traditional development patterns that are more compact and integrated by use than is much of today's conventional development. There are a number of reasons for making compactness and a mix of uses basic principles of smart growth.

One benefit of compactness is that it permits the conservation of more land in open-space uses, such as farmland or forest, which, in turn preserves wildlife habitats, permits the continued operation of natural drainage systems, and enhances people's quality of life.

A second benefit of compact development relates to the cost of infrastructure. The cost of providing basic infrastructure systems for development generally increases as densities decrease. One study, for example, shows average per-unit capital costs in

1987 dollars for streets, utilities, and schools varying from $20,302 for a project at 12 units per acre to $44,410 for single-family houses on one-acre lots.[1] (These figures do not include the cost of extending facilities outside built-up areas.)

More recent studies by the Center for Urban Policy Research at Rutgers University show that low-density development typically raises per-unit road costs by about 25 percent, school costs by 5 percent, and utility costs by 15 percent.[2]

Infrastructure costs also can be reduced when compact development can build on existing infrastructure. This generally means when it is located in undeveloped (or greenfield) areas contiguous to areas served by infrastructure, allowing orderly service extensions, or in infill areas in which existing facilities may be tapped.

A third major benefit of compact development, particularly when it incorporates a mix of uses, is that it reduces commuting distances. It shortens distances between where people live and where they go on a daily basis—employment centers, schools, and stores. This enables greater use of mass transit, carpooling, and even walking and biking to satisfy everyday travel needs.

Concentrating community destinations in compact districts helps create walkable districts, and providing a mix of uses in these districts allows people to satisfy several needs in one location and also enhances walkability. Such districts expand opportunities for access by public transit as opposed to automobiles. (And transit's cost-effectiveness is improved by increased ridership.)

A fourth benefit is that the centers of activity created by compact, mixed-use development offer many opportunities for people to meet casually. They encourage neighborliness and the kind of social interactions that bind communities together. Also, an activity center can ideally become a memorable place that gives a community its special identity.

Traditional Development Patterns

From the founding of the first colonies in America until the 1930s, when zoning became popular along with the automobile, towns and cities were generally compact and land uses were intermixed. Developing in tight clusters provided security from marauders and, because most people had to walk to their destinations, compactness facilitated trade, government, socializing, and religious and cultural activities.

As cities grew larger, travel by horse and carriage continued to focus on centrally located activities. The advent of rail transportation allowed excursions to outlying resorts and commuting from towns in the countryside, and thus loosened activity bonds within communities. But until expanding automobile ownership freed people to live almost anywhere a road could be built, most residents of urban areas lived and worked in the central city, close to their primary destinations. Working-class neighborhoods clustered around industrial districts. Retail services operated out of the first floors of residential buildings. Wealthy people tended to live in enclaves concentrated near shopping districts and rail lines.

At the same time that the automobile was expanding location choices, many cities began adopting zoning restrictions to protect residential uses from industrial noise and fumes, commercial hustle and bustle, and other intrusive nuisances. Zoning normally designated districts in which only a few uses were permitted and others prohibited. Most ordinances avoided—and still do avoid—mixing uses.

Spreading Wave of Metropolitan Development

Automobiles and zoning restrictions became twin stimulants of urban sprawl. Sprawl was side-

tracked by a lack of development for the period of the Great Depression and World War II. When the war's end released the economy to respond to pent-up civilian markets, suburbs pushed into the countryside. In the strong postwar construction economy, large projects that could deliver housing and commercial and industrial space rapidly and in bulk were favored.

The spreading wave of metropolitan development was propelled by highway construction, guided by zoning that favored projects devoted to single uses, and supported by housing-finance policies that favored single-family homes. No longer were houses, factories, and stores arranged cheek by jowl. Developers built (ever larger) housing "communities" and specialized commercial centers and business centers—a few hundred houses on half-acre lots on one site, dozens of townhouses on another, a strip commercial center along the highway, a half-square-mile landscaped business park nearby, later a regional shopping center with a 5,000-car parking lot—accessible only by automobile.

This pattern of metropolitan growth brought many problems, including traffic congestion, overcrowded schools, growing backlogs of needed public facilities, declining water and air quality, and mounting frustration and conflict over development. Moreover, for central cities and many older suburbs, the loss of people and jobs has had serious fiscal, social, and economic consequences.

Compact Development

Compact development is simply development that uses less land than conventional development. It can occur on the urbanizing fringes of towns and cities or on infill parcels in developed areas. Some elementary math illustrates the results of compact development, as shown below:

	Land Needed To Accommodate 1,000 Housing Units*
1 unit per acre	1,000 acres
3 units per acre	333 acres
6 units per acre	167 acres

*Plus land needed for schools, parks, and other associated uses.

Developing townhouses (six units per acre) would save 1.3 square miles of land compared with developing houses on one-acre lots and it would save one-quarter of a square mile compared with developing at a density of three units per acre. Land saved can be used for open space.

The idea of compact development tends to scare people. Presented as more intensive or higher-density development, it is an approach that many people find unpalatable. City planners call "higher density" by other names— "concentrated development," "focused development," or "clustered development"—but by any name, "density" seems to signify to many people all that's bad in urban development.

To these people, density connotes high-rise apartment buildings that will bring in people who are "different"—whatever their socioeconomic status. It seems to be associated somehow with a number of unwanted conditions: unsafe streets, blackboard jungle schools, overcrowded schools, unsightliness. It is routinely blamed for traffic congestion. People tend to view the idea of density not as a relative condition but as an absolute one—like viewing all heavy traffic as gridlock without distinguishing levels of traffic. Perhaps "compact development" is a term that scares people less, but only slightly less.

Four important considerations affect thinking about compactness as a principle of smart growth:

▲ **Scale.** Compactness can promote smart growth at different levels, from the region to the community, the neighborhood, and the project.
▲ **Appropriate density.** Compactness is relative. The term connotes a reasonable intensity of development based on local circumstances, including average densities, site and area conditions, and market demands.
▲ **Incremental process.** Smart growth does not call for abruptly ratcheting up project densities throughout a community or establishing some uniform standard of density for all development proposals. Market, political, and project conditions require incremental approaches to density increases.
▲ **Accommodation of diverse demand.** Any density goal must recognize the multiplicity of demand for housing and other space. A variety of building forms is required to meet these needs.

These considerations are discussed more fully in the following sections.

Drawing used by permission of Roger Lewis.

▲ Architect and journalist Roger Lewis portrays some of the perplexing notions people have about density and compact development.

Scale

Compactness can promote smart growth at a variety of scales. On the scale of metropolitan areas, smart growth seeks to develop central places that concentrate economic, social, governmental, and cultural activities, and intensive forms of residential development. In most regions, central-city downtowns as central places are supplemented by other important nodes of activity, including inner-suburban business districts and outer-suburban edge cities. Such multiple nodes of activity can become focal points for the kinds of concentrated development that strengthen the aims of smart growth.

On the scale of municipalities, communities, and neighborhoods, smart growth seeks to achieve higher average densities in keeping with regional growth trends by allowing concentrations of development in appropriate locations. Small, built-up, single-family communities may not have suitable sites for higher-density development, but they can increase densities by allowing accessory apartments or group housing. Cities and towns often have sites —vacant or underutilized properties or land that can be annexed—appropriate for well-designed, higher-density development that can help meet regional housing or commercial needs.

▲ A regional activity center has grown up around a Metrorail transit station in Bethesda, Maryland, spurred by county plans and incentives promoting mixed-use development in this location.

On the project scale, smart growth seeks to encourage planning—both public and private—for greenfields development that uses land more efficiently than does conventional development. It also seeks to encourage developers and builders to incorporate compactness in planning and designing individual projects.

The transformation of Bethesda, Maryland, into a significant regional downtown over the past 20 years illustrates ways in which compactness can be introduced in growing areas. An unincorporated community in the northern suburbs of Washington, D.C., Bethesda consisted of neighborhoods of mid- to high-priced housing grouped around a sleepy commercial center and a few employment complexes, such as the National Institutes of Health.

In the 1960s, Montgomery County designated Bethesda's commercial center as a regional commercial node that would be served by the region's Metrorail system. Detailed plans and subsequent zoning allowed a considerable amount of intensive development and favored a mix of office, retail, hotel, and residential uses.

With a central and accessible location in an upscale market area, Bethesda soon attracted substantial

redevelopment that replaced the old one- and two-story commercial buildings with ten- to 12-story mixed-use projects. Single-family houses (many converted to professional offices) on the commercial center's fringe gave way to apartment buildings and townhouses. The most recent development, Bethesda Row, has transformed an area formerly in light-industrial uses into a neotraditional shopping area with buildings that are mostly two or three stories high.

Bethesda's transformation has been both praised and damned. Some long-time residents who cherished the individuality of the old shops resent the new buildings and traffic associated with the higher level of activity in the area. Other people find the new Bethesda an exciting place in which to live, shop, dine, and be employed. County officials appreciate the tremendous boom in tax revenues generated by the high-value development.

Appropriate Density

There is no universal "right" density. Smart growth calls for more intensive development than is generally provided in conventional development, but the appropriate degree of density or compactness is place-specific. Density must be tailored to conditions of development in the area and the general character of the community. In Bethesda's transformation, for example, 40- or 50-story buildings would have been out of scale with the suburban character of the area. From a market standpoint, moreover, the space provided by development of a ten- to 15-story building every year or two could be easily absorbed, but a much higher building would have added more space than could be marketed in a reasonable period of time.

Density variations within a community are perfectly acceptable. They should be based on the character of existing development, the range of market demands, and site conditions. For example, half-acre lots in one neighborhood may be considered large, while in other neighborhoods two-, three-, and even five-acre lots may be common. Small one- and two-story shopping centers may be the rule in some neighborhoods, while higher office buildings and mixed-use centers may be appropriate responses to the market and conditions in other locations.

In many areas, land can be used much more efficiently without significantly changing the overall feel of the area. In outer-suburban locations with large residential lots, cutting lot sizes in half, for example, could reduce the conversion of open space to urban uses without significantly affecting the relaxed lifestyle desired by large-lot homebuyers. In locations closer to town, downsizing lot sizes by 25 to 30 percent—say from a third of an acre to a quarter acre, or from 10,000 square feet to 7,500 square feet—could make a significant difference in retaining open land, again without changing the overall appearance of the residential environment.

Clustering a mix of housing types at a relatively moderate overall density—say six to ten units per acre in suburban locations or 15 to 20 or more units per acre in urban locations—would produce a more significant change in terms of the efficient use of land and resources. Raising densities need not decrease resident satisfaction. "From surveys," writes Reid Ewing, a proponent of better development practices, "residents are as satisfied with housing at six or seven units per acre as they are at three or four units per acre."[3]

Ewing also notes that site development costs are nearly halved at the higher densities. Much of this cost saving comes from per-unit reductions in pavement surface. With smaller lots, less street pavement is required per lot. If the width of streets is narrowed in accordance with the principles of new urbanism, the amount of pavement surface per lot is further reduced. Chapters 6 and 7 contain discussions of projects developed at these higher densities that show how they can be attractively designed to appeal to the market.

The reality is that large lots can consume an amazing amount of land. In Charles County, Maryland, an outer-suburban county of Washington, D.C., lots being developed within the county's designated growth area average about a half acre, while those outside the designated growth area average about 3.4 acres. If projected development continues to be divided as it is now, with three-quarters occurring inside and one-quarter outside the designated growth area, by 2020 the large-lot housing will have consumed 48 square miles of land, which is three times the amount of land that will be used by the three times as much housing that will be built in the designated growth area.[4]

In Lancaster County, Pennsylvania, where the planning commission tracked development from

1994 to 1997, a similar pattern of land use is occurring. During this period, 75 percent of new residential units were built inside local growth boundaries, but the 25 percent of units built outside the boundaries consumed 61 percent of the land developed.[5]

Standard single-family houses (6.7 per acre).

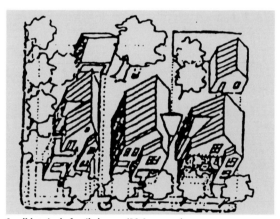
Small-lot single-family houses (10.6 per acre).

Townhouses (22 per acre).

Podium apartments (66 per acre).

Diverse possibilities for compact growth are demonstrated in Portland, Oregon's 2040 regional plan by depictions of a range of density levels for residential development.

The bottom line is that communities that zone large amounts of land for minimum lot sizes of one to three acres are facilitating sprawl and denying many households an opportunity to live at higher, affordable densities. Communities that zone large areas for minimum lot sizes of five to ten acres in order to preserve a rural or agricultural character are fooling themselves (or the voters). Experience has shown that lots of this size rarely restrain the forces of growth, which, when it comes, will certainly not be rural or agricultural in character.

Whereas reducing lot sizes and clustering can make residential development more compact, increasing the density of low-density commercial, office, and industrial development is more problematic. Parking is the usual suspect.

The industry standard calls for four to five parking spaces per 1,000 square feet of retail and office space. When this is provided by surface parking, density is drastically lowered. Almost two-thirds of a typical neighborhood shopping center site, for example, is used for parking spaces. A modest, two-story medical building with 20,000 square feet of floor space might require an acre of surface parking around it. Commercial buildings surrounded by a sea of parking are a common sight in both city and suburban neighborhoods.

Achieving higher densities in commercial and industrial development requires using structured parking. However, where land is relatively inexpensive surface parking costs substantially less to develop than parking structures. Structured parking is cost-effective only in areas that are sufficiently built-up and attractive as commercial locations. (These are the conditions that make public transit more feasible as well.)

Older business centers in developing areas are good candidates for a shift to higher-density commercial development—rather than being left to die on the vine as development occurs in new locations. The successful redevelopment of downtown Bethesda (described in the preceding section) was due in large part to the vigorous measures—zoning amendments, provision of public parking, organization of a business improvement district—that the county took to ensure that the small but well-located commercial center would grow.

Maintaining (and enhancing) the market attractiveness of existing regional centers, on the model of downtown Bethesda, is a necessary step in the direction of compact commercial development. This strategy involves also exerting some control over the spread of competing edge-city development in the region.

Incremental Process

Over time, incremental gains in the intensity of new development (and redevelopment) will start to make a difference in communities and regions. Achieving more compactness in most communities requires time for markets to mature and become accustomed to (and even desirous of) more compact, mixed-use forms of development.

Overall densities throughout metropolitan America, influenced by the vast amount of low-density development already on the ground, will continue to be low. But some forms of compact development are likely to attract considerable market interest across the country and become more widely accepted as desirable components of every community.

Even the most favorable public policies and enlightened development processes would fail to stimulate or support a massive, overnight increase in density. It took at least 20 years from the adoption of planning policies and construction of the Metrorail station for downtown Bethesda to mature as a regional center—and the makeover is still in progress.

Developers who aim for higher densities cannot get too far ahead of the market. Just as important, they need to consider the receptivity of neighbors to proposed projects. A project proposing a drastic increase in density beyond the norm for the area —even if it is supported by public policies and responsive to an identified market—would probably generate opposition from neighbors fearful of potential impacts on neighborhood livability.

Diverse Demand

Compact development recognizes that neighborhoods, communities, and regions all contain a diversity of demand for development, and that this diversity must be accommodated. Furthermore, compactness as a principle of smart growth can be applied to low-, medium-, and higher-density forms of development.

Whereas typical single-family residential subdivisions provide few choices of living and working venues, higher-density development allows a range of densities and uses and therefore can accommodate a greater variety of housing, employment, and service needs.

Bethesda demonstrates how compact development can serve diverse demands. In their planning for Bethesda's transformation into a regional downtown, Montgomery County planners understood that a critical mass of activity would have to be achieved to create an integrated downtown that would be competitive with similar concentrations of activity elsewhere. More than a large amount of floor space would be needed. Critical mass would require an intensity of development that would stimulate transactions among the activities within the downtown. The planners' goal was to provide a cross section of mutually supportive businesses that would allow the people who work in downtown Bethesda to also live there (or near there), eat in restaurants there, and satisfy their demand for services and cultural events there.

Issues Raised by Compact Development

Long-held practices and beliefs make compact development not an easy sell. The focus of attention for decades has been on low-density development in greenfields. The development industry has evolved routines and the public sector has established regulatory regimes that make spread-out development easy. Most Americans have become accustomed to the look and feel of low-density development.

At the same time, some people have become skeptical about the desirability of more compact patterns of development, based on their perceptions about the (non)livability and (non)functionality of higher-density development. The prevailing myths about compact development are addressed in the next sections.

High-Rise Hell

People frequently see high-rise buildings lurking behind every proposal for increased densities. In truth, the high-rise hell envisioned by many community residents protesting proposals for higher-density development ignores the essential idea that compact development can incorporate many forms of development at different density levels.

Opponents of planning for higher densities, including many homebuilders, often argue that the market wants nothing but low-density development. The truth is, however, that a considerable amount of compact development, residential and commercial, occurs throughout metropolitan areas—and it sells. Unfortunately, a fair number of compact developments, notably many residential projects in suburban fringe areas, are randomly scattered along major roads or located in isolated rural locations. Scattered high-density development fails to achieve the critical mass needed to create functional places that can support smart-growth principles. Moreover, such housing tends to be low rent or low cost because of low land costs, but it may cost local governments and state transportation agencies more in public services expenditures than it yields in taxes.

Portland, Oregon's 2040 regional plan, which proposes to promote compact patterns of development for the metropolitan area, responds to the idea of diversity in compactness. It puts about 8 percent of the region's housing growth within relatively high-density city, regional, and town centers. The other 92 percent of expected housing growth, consisting of single-family and multifamily dwellings, will be in residential neighborhoods that resemble Portland's existing neighborhoods. Even in the high-density centers, projected growth can be accommodated in two- to four-story apartment buildings or in a mix of townhouses, garden apartments, and some higher buildings.[6] This smart-growth plan can hardly be seen as promoting cramped clusters of high-rise buildings.

Bethesda's growth as a regional center (referred to earlier in this chapter) also demonstrates that urban compactness need not be uniform and oppressive. New construction in Bethesda features a number of 10- to 15-story buildings, some for offices, some for apartments. At the same time, many one- and two-story commercial buildings and two- and three-story townhouses and apartment buildings have been retained (and renovated) or newly constructed. Bethesda's mix of intermingled building types creates a varied and lively urban scene that is far from qualifying as overwhelmingly dense and depressing.

Traffic Congestion

Increasing the density of development attracts cars and exacerbates congestion. Most people assume that this is the case, but is it? Standard traffic projection methods, assuming that a fixed road network has only so much capacity, typically predict higher levels of congestion as density increases. But standard traffic projections usually discount (or fail to take into account) potential changes in travel behavior as congestion mounts.

At certain high levels of density, people will walk and use public transit for many travel needs. In 1990, the share of all trips to downtown that were by public transit was 36 percent in the Washington, D.C., area; 61 percent in Chicago; and 50 percent in San Francisco. There is some evidence that transit use in all these areas has been rising since 1990.

Furthermore, compact development increases the likelihood that people will live and work closer to destinations, so average driving distances will be shorter. No development—compact or conventional —is likely to decrease local congestion, especially if through traffic is on the rise, and compact development may increase local congestion under certain conditions. However, development that shortens trips usually translates into less time on the road for drivers.

While traffic congestion occurs whether the prevailing development pattern is high or low density, it can be more bearable and manageable in compactly developed areas that encourage and support nonauto travel. (Unfortunately, many Americans consider driving a car to be an important part of their lifestyle. They tend to worry more about the traffic effects of compact development than to welcome the opportunities that compact development might afford to walk or use transit instead.) Chapter 4 describes in greater detail how smart growth can improve mobility.

Ugly and Alien Landscapes

Some critics believe that compact development will appear ugly and alien to American tastes. But the most common version of today's compact development not at all resembles the kinds of urban development that such critics may have in mind— apartment buildings that look like everyone's idea of public housing, single-family houses crammed together along grim street frontages, and deteriorating, four-story commercial buildings with three vacant floors.

In fact, based on projects developed in recent decades, compact development is likely to offer,

for example, multiplex apartments that look like upscale homes; buildings attractively grouped around landscaped areas and courtyards; and well-designed, appealing multistory commercial buildings. By comparison, conventional parked-up commercial strips and residential subdivisions can look quite unkempt.

To not appear ugly, compact development must be well designed. Poorly designed compact development cannot hide behind landscaping like poorly designed single-family houses can. But when it is designed well, compact development is at least as appealing as and often more appealing than well-designed low-density development. The beautiful streets in famous old cities illustrate well the ability of compactness united with good architecture and urban design to create superior urban streetscapes.

Nevertheless, many Americans seem to crave low-density living. To some people, suggestions that alternatives to a low-density lifestyle would help solve growth and affordability problems are suspect. (Such suspicions are perhaps reinforced by too-frequent references by city planners to the beauty of foreign cities.) Smart growth and compact development appear to imperil many people's vision of the good life—a single-family house with plenty of land around it. That dream may be unaffordable just now, but any perceived threat to realizing it is viewed as wrongheaded and almost un-American.

But not all Americans desire a single-family house on a large lot. As noted in chapter 1, many cannot afford to live and work in low-density areas and many others actually prefer life in higher-density neighborhoods. One size does not fit all. Smart growth proposes to widen the choice of housing styles to reflect the diversity of demand.

Bad Neighborhoods

Many people associate high density with crime, disorderliness, and delinquency. Without question, plenty of high-density neighborhoods are last-resort places to live for many residents—places where drug dealers and youth gangs make life difficult and dangerous, and where vandalism and disturbances of the peace are common. Rarely, however, can density itself be blamed for these conditions, which are primarily the result of concentrated poverty and unemployment, racial and ethnic discrimination, and related societal short-comings. Also without question, plenty of middle-class and upscale high-density neighborhoods are good neighborhoods by any standard.

Higher densities do create neighborhoods that feel different from spread-out suburban neighborhoods, but the difference is something that many people value. Certain kinds of people are attracted to older neighborhoods in cities. Compact development offers its residents more convenient ways of life and provides more opportunities for lively, interesting social encounters. Older neighborhoods in cities tend to have a more active street life. Their residents talk about community spirit and community events, interesting neighbors, and the convenience of living near frequently used shops and services.

A Mix of Uses

Smart growth promotes the mixing of employment, commercial, and residential uses because mixing helps to create more interesting, functional, and environmentally sensitive built environments.

Zoning was invented to separate different types of activities, but the sterile urban landscapes wrought by almost a century of traditional zoning have stimulated city planners and public officials to find ways to remix uses. An early advocate was Jane Jacobs, who 40 years ago attacked planning approaches that removed diversity from neighborhoods; she stressed the importance of recognizing the reality of diversity in people, buildings, housing, and uses.[7]

A group of experts convened by the U.S. Department of Housing and Urban Development and ULI in the early 1980s identified a mix of uses as a key tenet of sensible community development. As stated in its report, *The Affordable Community:* "The mingling of work and commerce with residences makes for healthy and vibrant neighborhoods."[8]

The question of what constitutes a mix of uses has a history. Interest in mixed-use development was emerging in many communities in 1976 when ULI defined mixed-use projects specifically as having three or more significant uses, being functionally and physically integrated, and having been developed according to a coherent plan.[9] Midtown Plaza in Rochester, New York, and Water Tower Place in Chicago were cited as single-structure

models of mixed-use development and Rockefeller Center in New York City and Peachtree Center in Atlanta as multibuilding models.

In 1985, ULI conducted a survey of 240 mixed-use projects, out of an estimated 400 to 600 such projects in North America that met ULI's definition of a mixed-use development.[10] Of the 240 projects, 62 percent were located in the central city's CBD, 14 percent elsewhere in the central city, 12 percent in suburban downtowns, and 11 percent elsewhere in suburban communities. The data showed that mixed-use projects were increasingly likely to be located in suburban locations, a trend that has undoubtedly continued into the present.

Most of the 240 projects were overwhelmingly commercial in nature, but almost half of the projects begun in the 1980s included some housing, compared with only 19 percent for earlier projects. The ULI study credited the favorable climate for multifamily investment for the trend toward including housing in more mixed-use developments and it predicted that such projects in the future would be sited in suburban locations, which tend to be more suitable for housing than are central-city CBDs.

ULI's 1976 definition of mixed-use development excludes projects that combine only two uses, such as office/retail developments or residential/retail developments. And although the definition does not apply to master-planned communities, the mix in many of those communities comprises a number of extensive single-use areas—business parks, regional shopping centers, and residential neighborhoods—designed to function as quite separate areas of activity. ULI's 1987 *Mixed-Use Development Handbook* revised its definition of mixed use to include these sorts of projects as multiuse developments—a catch-all term that describes any project with more than one significant use. Multiuse development encompasses mixed-use developments as well as business and research parks, large-scale communities, and suburban activity centers.[11]

Today's mixed-use and multiuse projects are dramatically different those of the 1970s and 1980s. According to Dean Schwanke, who is updating ULI's 1987 mixed-use handbook, mixed-use projects now occur mostly in suburban areas, are more frequently horizontal than vertical in design, and

▲ The Easton shopping center on the edge of Columbus, Ohio, is designed as a traditional town center with a mix of uses oriented to the street.

▲ The vacant Belmont Dairy building in Portland, Oregon, was converted to residential lofts and retail and office uses. Additional apartments were constructed in a second phase.

feature connected buildings rather than megastructures. Many recent mixed-use projects, influenced by the principles of new urbanism, site buildings in rows along pedestrian-oriented streets reminiscent of older commercial areas and create pedestrian-friendly town centers.

To promote smart growth, however, the importance of a mix of uses is how they function in relation to each other—how people use them. A smart-growth mix of uses will perform the following beneficial functions:

▲ facilitate meetings and other interactions at various interesting centers of activity;

▲ encourage workers and shoppers to walk, bike, take transit, or share a ride;
▲ accommodate the variety of services required by a diverse population; and
▲ create distinctive places that establish an identity for the neighborhood or community.

To perform these functions, the mix of uses must keep some proportion of residents, shopping, employment, and civic activities within easy reach of each other. Ewing recommends that developers mix land uses "at the finest grain the market will bear and include civic uses in the mix."[12] This means that an assortment of different uses should be as close to one another as possible and that areas devoted to single uses should be as small as possible, thereby making it convenient for people to satisfy their daily needs. Essentially, a smart-growth mix brings together common travel origins and destinations to afford people opportunities for reducing travel distances and times.

A variety of techniques for accomplishing a fine-grain mix of uses is available, including the following:

▲ Mix uses within buildings. Apartments can be located over shops and offices. Offices can be located over shops. Limited businesses can be allowed on the first floor of live/work units and home occupations can be allowed in houses or apartments.
▲ Mix small retail shops, business and personal services, and civic and cultural uses within neighborhood centers.
▲ Add residential and retail uses to business parks, making sure that the design facilitates walking between uses.
▲ Develop one or more residential buildings on the site of a community shopping center or regional shopping center.
▲ When designing office and retail developments, provide attractive and convenient connections to adjoining neighborhoods.

Two different examples of the successful mixing of uses are Belmont Dairy in Portland, Oregon, and the redevelopment of the former Lowry Air Force base in Denver.

Belmont Dairy demonstrates an imaginative adaptation of an industrial building for a mix of uses. The abandoned dairy was an eyesore in its neighborhood until it was rehabilitated—partly retained and partly rebuilt—to house 19 market-rate residential lofts plus retail shops and offices. The Belmont Dairy project includes an addition containing 66 affordable apartments. The project design opened the structure to the street in an appealing way, and now the building is a neighborhood asset.

At Lowry, a fine-grained land use plan for a multiuse neighborhood is being implemented under the auspices of the Lowry Development Authority. The plan calls for a town center with retail, residential, educational, and commercial uses. Just as important, the plan also calls for a mix of other uses immediately outside the town center. These include housing for seniors south of the town center, a series of office buildings nearby, and more residential construction north-west of the town center. Combined with building- and tree-lined streets and unobtrusive parking lots, this mix of uses creates a walkable and convenient neighborhood.

Mixing uses provides choices not offered by conventional development patterns. Of course, not all residents of or employees at mixed-use communities will take full advantage of the convenience available. Many people who work at the offices and commercial establishments that locate at Lowry will choose to live elsewhere. Many people who live at Lowry will work elsewhere. Residents will drive to outside stores and shopping centers for at least some of their shopping.

Two new studies confirm that mixing uses reduces long-distance travel. A study of trips made by residents of 22 mixed-use, master-planned commu-

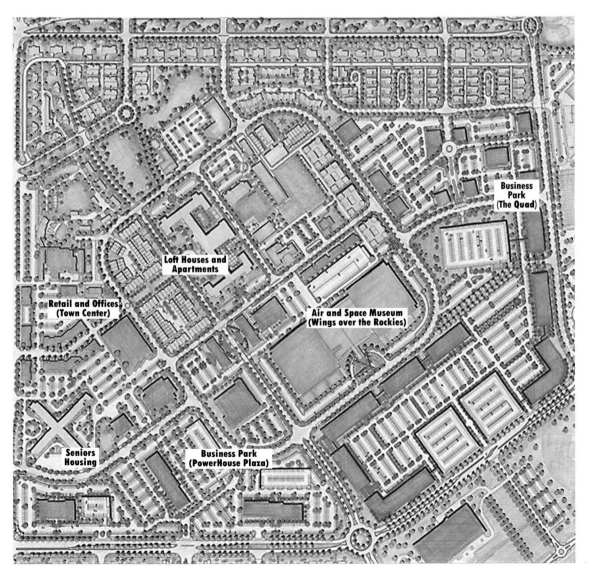

◄ The kind of fine-grained mix of uses that creates a walkable community is found in the town center of Lowry, a redeveloped former air base in metropolitan Denver. The town center includes an array of office, retail, and civic facilities, houses, and apartments.

Business Park (The Quad)

Loft Houses and Apartments

Retail and Offices (Town Center)

Air and Space Museum (Wings over the Rockies)

Seniors Housing

Business Park (PowerHouse Plaza)

nities in Florida indicates that at more than half the communities more than 25 percent of resident trips stayed within the communities. Several communities captured up to 50 percent of all trips.[13] A study of two mixed-use neighborhoods in Seattle finds that the residents of nearby neighborhoods traveled (by all modes) 42 percent more miles per day than residents of the mixed-use neighborhoods, and that residents of outer suburbs traveled 119 percent more miles per day.[14] In both studies, about 20 to 24 percent of the trips made by residents of the mixed-use developments remained within the developments. Therefore, close to 80 percent of trips made were beyond the developments.

Does the principle of mixing uses mean that the development of 500-acre business parks or large commercial complexes is not smart growth? Not necessarily, not if these complexes incorporate or are bordered by residential uses and provide convenient access from the housing to the business and commercial uses. Should every neighborhood include employment and retail uses? Not necessarily, not if such uses are located nearby or are accessible by transit.

Issues in Mixing Uses

The major question about the potential consequences of combining uses is the obvious one: How is it possible to mix uses without some uses harming others? The whole concept of zoning arose from the desire to separate uses to avoid possible conflicts and adverse impacts among uses. Advocates of mixing uses must ask themselves, for example: How can residential uses be protected from potential traffic, noise, and litter generated by shops located next door? How can townhouses be made good neighbors for single-family detached houses in the next block? How can office buildings function successfully next to grocery stores or gas stations?

The following sections discuss the major issues involved in mixing uses.

Feasible Mixes

Mixing uses is not an anything goes proposition. Certain uses—refineries, landfills, or abattoirs, for example—are not nice neighbors. Performance-based zoning criteria should be retained or enacted to keep such uses out of residential, office/commercial, and mixed-use areas.

That being said, certain other uses—namely offices, retail shops, restaurants, cinemas and other entertainment venues, hotels, and high-density housing —are quite commonly clustered in various ways. Developers and planners have gained considerable experience in creating mixes among such uses that echo many of the qualities of traditional downtowns. They have proved that mixed-use projects and multiuse complexes can be successful both in the marketplace and in building communities, although their implementation may raise some tricky design and development questions.

For many other uses, their suitability for mixed-use or multiuse development must still be determined. These uses include many types of housing, many kinds of retail shops and services, some industrial uses, and many kinds of public and quasi-public facilities.

When determining what mixes are likely to work, developers and planners must consider the scale and function of proposed uses and the quality of design, as discussed in the following sections.

Scale and Function

For any use, its packaging (that is, the size and type of building it occupies) and the activities it generates bear heavily on its compatibility with other uses. The size and shape of the building(s) planned for a particular use will significantly affect that use's compatibility with neighboring uses.

Residential uses packaged in one- and two-story buildings will affect their neighbors differently than residential uses in high rises. The same with office uses. Retail uses can take a variety of forms including small commercial strips, space within office or residential buildings, stand-alone buildings along highways, or malls of all sizes. Government services can be provided from huge complexes or from storefront offices.

A use's function (its purpose or the activity it generates) also affects its suitability for association with other uses. Adult entertainment businesses and halfway houses have drawn considerable attention as uses not generally welcomed in neighborhoods because of their function. Employers that draw employees from throughout the region, businesses that depend on a great deal of trucking, and businesses that generate substantial amounts of waste products all present obstacles to combining uses. The potential association of family housing full of small children with other uses may be limited. The same is true of assisted-living housing. Many uses—for example, takeout restaurants, car-sale lots, multiplex theaters, libraries, and sales offices—generate constant in-and-out traffic that can interfere with nearby uses.

The appropriate mix of uses in terms of scale and function depends ultimately on the desired character of the community or neighborhood in which the uses are to be located. The designers of new towns and, more recently, of new urbanist developments have helped planners understand opportunities for mixing uses at the neighborhood scale. Choose uses, they say, that primarily serve neighborhood needs rather than community needs, that will attract pedestrians (and thus pare down parking lots), and that will occupy buildings scaled to fit into traditional residential neighborhoods. New urbanists also have revived the idea of town centers in which a mix of community-serving uses would be grouped in an accessible and unthreatening manner.

Quality of Design

High-quality design is generally a necessity for the success of projects and districts with a mix of uses. Design solutions are needed to mitigate the potentially incompatible qualities of adjoining uses—by reducing, screening, or avoiding them. Solutions may be as simple as enclosing a store's outdoor storage space, providing trees and other landscaping to soften the appearance of parking lots, or ensuring that restaurant ventilators are not channeling cooking odors into apartments next door.

On the other hand, establishing an effective mix of uses may require thoughtful attention to building heights, massing, and facades in order to achieve a project scale compatible with adjoining uses and nearby development. Reasons for the success of the Belmont Dairy development (described earlier in this chapter) include its opening up to the neighborhood and its remaining in scale to other buildings in the neighborhood.

Systemic Obstacles to Compact, Multiuse Development

Although compact and mixed-use development are principles of smart growth and forms of development that respond to real needs and demand in the marketplace, they face many obstacles of a systemic nature, including nearly automatic resistance from neighbors, regulatory complexities, and industry conservatism. These obstacles, which are discussed in the following sections, can combine to produce inertia in public and private development processes, an inertia that favors conventional forms of development and resists more compact, multiuse forms.

NIMBYism

NIMBYists are so called after their response to development proposals—"not in my backyard"—and a favorite target of NIMBYism is proposals for compact and mixed-use or multiuse projects. Frequently the established residents of any neighborhood or community are prone to object to any development proposal, usually because they fear that it will adversely affect traffic, schools, property values, or other community qualities. If the proposal involves compact development or an unconventional mix of uses, its neighbors are apt to become twice as fearful.

The assumptions and attitudes of people reacting to development proposals in their neighborhoods and communities frequently exaggerate the potential impacts of projects beyond all reason. The developer faced with two battles, one to obtain approval for any development at all and one to obtain approval for innovative development, is likely to avoid the second by retreating to standard development practices.

Regulatory Complexities

It is difficult in conventional zoning and subdivision regulations to define precisely the site and design elements that go into the creation of successful, lively, workable, affordable neighborhoods and communities. Regulatory agencies seem to respond to proposals for unconventional higher-density or mixed-use development by adding requirements and procedural layers to the approval process.

Although some cities have created zoning districts to promote a mix of uses, few have simplified the process for project approval in those districts. Unable to define specific standards for mixed-use development, regulatory agencies frequently resort to special review processes. Special review processes, however, introduce opportunities for lengthy permitting delays and unpredictable decisions.

Added regulatory complexity is a disincentive for developers to engage in compact and mixed-use development. Communities inclined to support innovation are not immune from the problem. Some years ago, in the interest of conserving natural open space and serving a varied population, the town of Duxbury, Massachusetts, adopted special regulations to allow the clustering of certain types of housing. Although the regulations were well crafted, design and conservation boards were established to evaluate and approve projects. The boards, responding to design issues generated by initial projects, gradually tightened the requirements to the point that developers stopped using the optional provisions in favor of standard subdivision designs that required no special hearings. Clearly, regulations to stimulate innovative design will not work if they become too onerous or if they require too long an approval process.[15]

Industry Conservatism

Knowing a product well seems to make success more likely in real estate development. Many developers concentrate on the types of development with which they have experience. The real estate industry in general seems to reward producers of standard products.

Given the use-specific variations among development projects in terms of their siting requirements, design and engineering, construction methods, financing, regulatory approvals, and marketing, it is no wonder that developers tend to cultivate certain niches of activity. But repetition is the enemy of change. This conservative tendency in the development business means that a turn toward more compact development and a greater mixing of uses will take time and effort.

Real estate lenders and investors tend to be equally cautious. Once they have identified the types of projects that have proved effective over time, they focus on them and shy away from what they regard as risky ventures into the unknown or less known. (Public agencies have the same tendency.)

According to Christopher Leinberger, a real estate analyst, lenders quickly recognize 19 product types as "standard," products such as build-to-suit offices, neighborhood retail strips and centers, and low-density suburban apartments.[16] The Leinberger list is notable for including no mixed-use or multiuse products and no unconventionally

compact projects. Given the checkered history of success for the retail components of mixed-use developments, lenders also shy away from financing them. Caution among lenders and investors makes securing financing for new types of projects as they evolve a challenge.

Key Qualities of Compact, Multiuse Development

This chapter has suggested the key qualities of compact, multiuse development that can help make it a cornerstone of efforts to promote smart growth. These qualities are recapitulated in the sections that follow. Consideration of these key qualities can guide developers seeking to meet the growing market interest in more compact and varied forms of development and can guide communities seeking to make smart growth work.

Uses Land Wisely

The wise use of land is a fundamental quality of compact, multiuse development. It provides the same elements of the built environment as conventional development on fewer acres and affords opportunities for reducing dependence on automobiles, and thereby improves air and water quality and conserves important natural resources. The efficiency of compact, multiuse development is achieved by integrating related activities within relatively small, easily traveled areas and making connections between such areas to create more functional and sustainable communities.

Raises Average Densities

Smart growth needs to be appropriate growth. It calls not for high-density-only growth, but for more compactness and more mixing of uses. The degree of compactness and use integration that is appropriate in given situations depends on site-specific conditions and the community context. Smart growth takes into account market demand, the nature of nearby development, and community infrastructure. Smart growth does not necessarily foreclose some low-density development, but it does raise average densities in neighborhoods, communities, and the region.

Widens Travel Options

Responding to the increasing diversity of households and workplaces, compact, multiuse development creates activity centers, neighborhoods, and communities that not only satisfy a wide variety of needs, but also make walking, transit, carpooling, and other travel alternatives to single-occupancy cars convenient and attractive options. Walkability is an important aspect of smart growth.

Stresses Good Design

The widely held myths about the adverse consequences of compact, multiuse development stem largely from experience with poor design rather than from the inherent living qualities of such development. Smart growth insists that compact, multiuse development adheres to a high standard of design quality, with the basic goals being to create a convenient, safe, and livable environment; to assure the compatibility of buildings and uses with adjacent development; and to create an attractive, functional, and distinctive place.

In such development, the architecture, the landscaping, and the arrangement of common spaces and pathways must work together. Siting buildings close together requires paying attention to privacy needs as well as to the need for public spaces. Mixing uses requires care in establishing the relationships between them. Building near existing development calls for establishing workable physical connections and using compatible styles and building massing.

Reasons for Hope

Indications exist that compact, multiuse development can be successfully promoted despite the daunting obstacles it faces. Considerable experience has already been gained by developers in packaging unconventional projects that meet compact, multiuse criteria and by communities in permitting them. (Chapters 6 and 7 provide many examples.) Developers and public officials alike have learned to seize opportunities and have discovered ways to overcome obstacles.

One kind of recent experience has been in older urban neighborhoods around the country, where a resurgence of market interest has spurred many projects that provide on-the-ground examples of compact, multiuse development. Examples of new compact, multiuse development can be found in many suburban areas as well.

A recent study focusing on suburban areas of the Puget Sound region in Washington identified 85 small clusters of medium-density housing in unexpectedly close proximity to retail and office uses.[17] Although they exhibit no distinctive architecture or highly visible presence, these clusters form rather integrated (multiuse) living environments. These are low-level concentrations of activity, which cannot be characterized as edge cities or suburban activity centers. Their presence around the Puget Sound region—an area not unlike many others in the United States—indicates that clusters of activities occur naturally, if haphazardly, even in nondescript suburban neighborhoods.

Finally, as discussed in chapter 1, demographic changes point to the likelihood of increased interest in living and working in multiuse, medium- to high-density neighborhoods. A strengthening market for compact, multiuse development together with a growing familiarity with this form of development augur well for its future.

Notes

1. James E. Frank, *The Costs of Alternative Development Patterns* (Washington, D.C.: ULI–the Urban Land Institute, 1989), p. 40.

2. Robert Burchell, remarks at the annual American Planning Association conference, Orlando, Florida, April 1996. These findings are generalized from studies for states, regions, and localities. The results of fiscal impact analyses may be affected by typical payment methods (for example, developers build many roads and utilities are usually paid by user fees), the fact that capital costs are only a small part of municipal budgets, and the probability that very low density development located some distance from built-up areas will substitute on-site water and sewer systems and low-cost roadways for standard urban facilities. The latter caveat, however, must be evaluated in turn in terms of the likely long-term costs for replacing those facilities as urban growth overtakes the formerly remote areas and in terms of the potentially adverse environmental effects of septic systems and runoff from low-cost roadways.

3. Reid Ewing, *Best Development Practices: Doing the Right Thing and Making Money at the Same Time* (Chicago: APA Planners Press, 1996), p. 133.

4. Maryland Highway Administration, *U.S. 301 Corridor Task Force Study* (Baltimore: 1995).

5. Thomas L. Daniels, "Farm Follows Function," *Planning*, January 2000, p. 16.

6. Metro, *Recommended 2040 Alternative* (Portland, Oregon: fall 1994), pp. 10–11.

7. Jane Jacobs, *The Death and Life of Great American Cities* (New York: Random House, 1961).

8. Council on Development Choices for the 80s, *The Affordable Community* (Washington, D.C.: ULI– the Urban Land Institute, 1981), p. 46.

9. Robert E. Witherspoon, Jon P. Abbett, and Robert M. Gladstone, *Mixed-Use Development: New Ways of Land Use* (Washington, D.C.: ULI–the Urban Land Institute, 1976).

10. Dean Schwanke, Eric Smart, and Helen J. Kessler, "Looking at MXDs," *Urban Land*, December 1986, pp. 20–25.

11. Dean Schwanke, *Mixed-Use Development Handbook* (Washington, D.C.: ULI–the Urban Land Institute, 1987).

12. Ewing, p. 21.

13. Eric Dumbaugh, Reid Ewing, and Mike Brown, "A Study of Internal Capture Rates for Mixed-Use Developments in South Florida," *Transportation Research Record 1780* (Washington, D.C.: National Academy Press, 2001), pp.115–120.

14. Edward McCormack, G. Scott Rutherford, and Martina G. Wilkinson, "The Travel Impacts of Mixed Land Use Neighborhoods in Seattle, Washington," *Transportation Research Record 1780* (Washington, D.C.: National Academy Press, 2001), pp. 25–42.

15. See Douglas R. Porter, Patrick L. Phillips, and Terry J. Lassar, *Flexible Zoning: How It Works* (Washington, D.C.: ULI–the Urban Land Institute, 1988).

16. Christopher Leinberger, "The Connection between Sustainability and Economic Development," in *The Practice of Sustainable Development*, ed. Douglas R. Porter (Washington, D.C.: ULI–the Urban Land Institute, 2000), pp. 53–66.

17. Anne Vernez Moudon and Paul Mitchell Hess, "Suburban Clusters: The Nucleation of Multifamily Housing in Suburban Areas of the Central Puget Sound," *APA Journal*, summer 2000, pp. 243–264.

Principles of Smart Growth
Open-Space Conservation

3

More than 30 years ago, sociologist William Whyte asserted in his classic book, *The Last Landscape*, that the less of our landscape there is to save, the better our chances of saving it. He may have been right. As suburban development spreads ever outward into the countryside, converting farmland, filling wetlands, and paving over or hemming in wildlife habitat, communities are fighting to protect their remaining open spaces.

For example, in November 2000, voters in 22 states from California to New Jersey approved, often with large majorities, more than three-fourths of more than 100 ballot measures to protect, conserve, and improve parks, farmland, historic resources, watersheds, greenways, and other environmental enhancements. The approved measures triggered $3 billion in local spending for conservation, according to the Land Trust Alliance and the Trust for Public Land.[1] Two years earlier, voters approved 72 percent of 553 state and local ballot measures that would affect the pace, quality, and shape of growth. Nearly half of these measures dealt with the preservation of open space.[2]

At the federal level, on 29 November 1999, President Clinton signed the omnibus spending bill that appropriated $464 million in fiscal 2000 to fund 119 land purchases in 42 states.[3] Two months later, he created three new National Monuments —Grand Canyon-Parashant, the California Coastal National Monument, and Agua Fria—

thus protecting more than 1 million acres of pristine canyon lands, rugged coastline, and archeological treasures.[4]

Why the surge of interest in protecting open space? Apparently, residents of communities across the United States are increasingly worried about the rate that open space is being taken by development. In fast-growing communities, open space is rapidly disappearing as farms are converted to subdivisions, wetlands are drained for industrial parks, and scenic views are littered with strip malls.

Growing metropolitan areas are consuming more land than ever before. A recent analysis of metropolitan growth trends finds that most metropolitan areas in the United States are adding urbanized land at a much faster rate than they are adding population. Between 1982 and 1997, the amount of urbanized land increased by 47 percent while the nation's population grew by only 17 percent.[5] Over this 15-year period, Phoenix and its surrounding suburban jurisdictions became more densely populated according to this analysis, but still this region is developing land at about an acre per hour.[6] The urbanized area around New York City expanded by 65 percent between 1960 and 1985, while the population grew by only 8 percent in the same period. And between 1970 and 1990, Cleveland's urbanized area expanded by 33 percent while the regional population actually fell by 11 percent.[7]

From 1992 to 1997, urban and other uses converted nearly 16 million acres of forests, cropland, and other open space nationally, an annual rate more than twice the 1.4 million acres per year that were lost in the previous decade.[8] The nonprofit American Forests organization has documented the continuing loss of forest lands in many metropolitan areas. Urbanization caused natural tree cover in the Puget Sound region in Washington, for example, to decline by 37 percent between 1972 and 1996.[9]

While wetlands protection laws have dramatically slowed wetlands losses, 58,500 acres are still being lost annually, about 30 percent of the decline due to development.[10] The National Wildlife Federation reports that roughly one-third of the nation's animal and plant species are imperiled, in part by development of habitats.[11] Although many communities are recognizing the importance of protecting farmland, more than 13,000 farms and nearly 14 million acres of farmland were lost in the United States from 1992 to 1997, mostly on the urban fringe of metropolitan areas.[12] And while regulations in many communities steer development away from floodplains, a considerable amount of older development located in floodplains remains at risk from flooding.

These are the reasons that the conservation of open space to protect valued natural features and qualities is a major principle of smart growth. Smart growth values open space for its key role in sustaining the environment—local, regional, and global—and for the host of economic and social advantages it provides for urban and suburban residents.

Open space—a park, a ribbon of land along a lake or a railroad right-of-way (called a greenway), an expanse of farmland—is a part of a community's essential infrastructure. Green infrastructure is as fundamentally important for a community's economic well-being as its bridges or its sewage treatment plant. In scenic rural areas, open space draws tourists who contribute to the local economy. A region's outdoor recreation opportunities attract relocating companies, because their employees will be attracted to such areas. Increasingly, what draws people to move to a community is not just the prospect of a good job, but also the promise of a decent place to live. Communities with scenic, ecological, and recreational assets have a competitive edge over those without.

Preserving open space is not just about economics. It is also about sustainability. As communities become more cluttered, they become less attractive, less recognizable as distinctive communities, and ultimately less sustainable. Henry Diamond and Patrick Noonan, prominent environmentalists, conclude that many communities are rapidly approaching what they refer to as the "marginal disutility of suburban sprawl," which is the point at which "each new subdivision subtracts more from the quality of life than the new inhabitants will contribute to the economy."[13]

This chapter provides an overview of open-space conservation as a smart-growth principle. It describes types of open space, discusses the value of open space, summarizes the obstacles and issues involved in open-space conservation, and identifies the key qualities of open space that make it an instrument for achieving the aims of smart growth.

Open Space: What and Why

Open space means different things to different people. Some use open space—a field or a forest—as a place for quiet reflection or spiritual enrichment. Farmers or loggers may use the same field or forest to make a living. Still others use open space to play Frisbee, walk a dog, watch birds, or play a rousing game of touch football.

Generally, open space, in the minds of most people, includes undeveloped places that provide a respite from the hustle and bustle of everyday life: Golden Gate Park in San Francisco, for example; the Mall in Washington, D.C.; Forest Park in Portland, Oregon; the Chicago waterfront on Lake Michigan; or the Great Dismal Swamp along the Virginia–North Carolina border.

All kinds of open space provide benefits for both the natural and built environments. People need natural open spaces as well as designed open spaces—parks, playgrounds, pathways, and other facilities—for recreational enjoyment. In the fast-paced world of automobiles, wireless phones, and fax machines, people need a way to connect with nature—and particularly with natural environments that change only slowly over time. "It is, by common consent, a good thing for people to get back to nature," said Aldo Leopold in his classic book, *A Sand County Almanac.*[14] One of the challenges of smart growth is to make it possible for people to connect, in their own way and for whatever reasons, to the natural environment. At the same time, the wetlands, woodlands, floodplains, rivers, mountains, and valleys, and other natural elements that make up various ecosystems are needed to maintain a healthy and sustainable environment.

Among the types and uses of open space that are important to consider in a smart-growth context are the following:

▲ **Wetlands.** Wetlands are low-lying areas that tend to occur along streams, rivers, and coastlines. They include marshes, swamps, and bogs and are among the most biologically productive and diverse natural systems in the world. The salt marshes blanketing the New Jersey coast, the mangrove swamps clinging to Florida's water edges, the prairie potholes in North Dakota, and the small vernal pools found across southern California are all wetlands. So are the wetlands constructed by developers to treat stormwater. Among their vital natural functions are providing habitat for wildlife; reducing flooding; improving water quality by capturing, breaking down, and removing pollutants; providing shelter and spawning grounds for fish and shellfish; and protecting coastal and upland areas from erosion by absorbing and dissipating the energy of waves.

▲ **Floodplains.** Floodplains are the adjacent flat areas along rivers, streams, lakes, and other bodies of water onto which water spills during storms, thereby slowing and reducing downstream flows. They contain specialized plants and animals that have adapted to life in soggy and occasionally inundated conditions. The natural flood control provided by floodplains is gaining greater respect as a low-cost alternative to erecting massive levees to protect development in flood-prone areas. Floodplains also lend themselves to use as recreational open space with facilities, such as ballparks, that can tolerate occasional flooding.

▲ **Woodlands.** Forests, woods, and groves of trees shelter wildlife, manage stormwater flows, and cleanse and cool the air. They provide habitat for thousands of species. They intercept rainwater and calm its flows, which facilitates its infiltration to groundwater and reduces erosive surges of runoff into streams and ponds. Trees convert water and carbon dioxide to oxygen and capture and break down pollutants. Trees cleanse and cool the air around them, a contribution to livability long valued by urban residents. Trees, wherever they are found, add aesthetic and scenic value.

▲ **Farmland.** The nation's 375 million acres of cultivated land and pastures easily produce enough food for domestic needs and export as well. To be sure, farmland seldom conserves high-quality

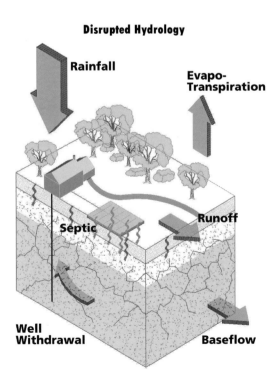

Natural Hydrologic Flow

Rainfall 45"

Evapo-Transpiration 24"

Infiltration

Aquifer

Runoff 8"

Baseflow 13" or 967 gpd/ac

Disrupted Hydrology

Rainfall

Evapo-Transpiration

Septic

Runoff

Well Withdrawal

Baseflow

◀ The infiltration of stormwater into the aquifer is part of the natural water cycle and retaining the soil's permeability reduces stormwater runoff and stream erosion. Wetlands facilitate the natural water cycle and also filter pollutants from stormwater.

wildlife habitats. Furthermore, the chemicals applied to crops often pollute surface water and groundwater. Nonetheless, to the residents of urban areas driving by, farms serve as open space that is pleasant to view. Also, farms close to urban centers frequently provide special products and services, such as organic fruits and vegetables, pick-your-own produce, horse riding, and stables for horses.

▲ **Urban open space.** Urban open space comes in a wide variety of sizes, shapes, and kinds. These include parks small and large intended for people's restful enjoyment of the outdoors, walking and biking trails, formal public squares and gardens, tree-lined streets, landscaped lots and yards, leftover or yet-to-be-developed lots, rivers and lakes, waterfronts, and sports facilities. These types of spaces have been set aside in cities from time immemorial for an equally wide variety of purposes—as venues for civic activities and settings for significant buildings and building complexes, to relieve urban congestion, and to provide a recreational infrastructure.

Many of the benefits of open space can be variously quantified, as the following items show:

▲ Trees use solar radiation to transpire water—depending on the type and size of the tree, up to 100 gallons per day, which provides the cooling equivalent of five window air conditioners running for 20 hours. Trees thus make neighborhoods more comfortable on hot days.[15]

▲ In 1996, the tree cover in the Atlanta metropolitan region removed 19 million tons of pollutants from the air, a function valued by American Forests at $47 million saved in potential externality costs (such as health costs). In addition, the shade offered by Atlanta's trees saves $2.8 million per year in energy costs.[16]

▲ A Minnesota study determined that the flood control function of 5,000 acres of wetlands is worth $1.5 million—the cost of replacing those wetlands with flood control facilities.[17]

▲ In Boulder, Colorado, property values have been shown to decline an average of $4.20 per square foot for each foot of distance from a greenbelt.[18]

The economic arguments for protecting open space are compelling. For achieving a variety of important community objectives—including reducing vulnerability to flooding, protecting streams from polluted runoff, and safeguarding drinking-water supplies—conserving open space is often the cheapest and most environmentally sound approach.

Developers have come to understand the value of open space, including its positive contribution to marketing. They have long been well aware that houses situated next to parks, golf courses, woodlands, or streams command higher prices than houses farther away. Many take great care to preserve the natural features that help sell projects. Clustered developments in which farmland and natural landscapes are integrated into the projects are increasingly being undertaken. Many developers recognize also the place-making value of attractive public spaces and streetscapes.

A Green Infrastructure

The value of open space as an element of smart growth can be greatly enhanced by making related open spaces into a whole open-space system and interweaving it with the built environment. In other words, smart growth advocates the development of a green infrastructure that, like the road infrastructure, the water infrastructure, or the sewer infrastructure, is considered a basic community-support system.

An American Planning Association publication provides one definition of green infrastructure: "an interconnected network of natural areas, conservation lands, and working landscapes that support native species, maintain natural ecologic processes, sustain air and water resources, and contribute to the health and quality of life for America's communities and people."[19]

Two principal ideas are embodied in the concept of green infrastructure. First, even in urbanizing areas some fundamental elements of natural ecosystems can and should be maintained. Second, elements of natural ecosystems function most effectively when linked into a system of multifunctional spaces.

Smart conservation attempts to preserve the connectivity of basic hydrologic, wildlife, vegetative, and even topographic systems to maintain their functions as much as feasible within the urban environment. Green infrastructure interconnects different types of open space—conserved natural areas and features such as wetlands, woodlands,

The Value of Open Space

Economists have developed a variety of techniques for valuing open space, including those discussed below.

Market Value

The most direct measure of the economic value of open space is its real estate market value, which is defined as the cash price that an informed and willing buyer will pay an informed and willing seller in an open and competitive market. In most metropolitan areas, the market value of open space is its value for development. The development value can be calculated separately from the land itself, as occurs in purchasing a conservation easement.[1]

Contingent Valuation

Contingent valuation of open space is an attempt to assess through surveys how much people would be willing to pay to preserve a scenic view, canal path, mountain trail, or the like. Surveys may indicate that residents would be willing to pay in taxes or fees a certain amount per year to preserve a particular forest or retain the privilege of fishing in a trout stream. Knowing the contingent value of the forest or stream can help in the design of bond initiatives to preserve them.

Production Value

The production value of open space is the value of goods produced from it—crops, animal products, timber—that would be erased by its conversion to urban uses.

Enhancement Value

The enhancement value of open space is the value it adds to adjacent or nearby properties. Property adjacent to such open-space amenities as a golf course or a waterfront traditionally sells for more than property several blocks away. And the higher value of properties enhanced by open space boosts property tax revenues. Analyses of enhancement value attempt to isolate the price effect of open space from the many other factors, such as building size and condition, that affect property values. In general, open space is likely to increase property values when it 1) is preserved in its natural state, 2) limits vehicle access, and 3) is secure and well maintained.

Fiscal Benefits

Another way to assess the value of open space is to compare how much it costs local government to provide services to open space on the one hand and developed land on the other. Compared with the cost of serving conventional subdivisions, the fiscal impact of most open space is a bargain. In most cases, farms and other types of open land actually subsidize local governments by generating more in property taxes than they demand in services.[2]

Natural System Value

Where open space performs functions that would need to be accomplished by constructed means were the open space to be developed—levees to control floods, drainage and detention systems to channel and treat runoff, treatment plants to render water drinkable—the cost of replacing the natural system with constructed systems can be considered a measure of the value of the natural system.

Intangible Value

Much of the value of open space is not readily quantifiable. Its intangible value may contribute more substantially to its overall value than do its quantifiable benefits. Among its intangible values are the respite it gives people from the noise and clutter of the modern world, the contribution it makes to forming the character of communities (imagine Boulder without its mountain vistas or Manhattan without Central Park), and its role in generally enhancing the quality of life.

Notes

1. Charles Fausold and Robert Lilieholm, *The Economic Value of Open Spaces: A Review and Synthesis* (Cambridge, Massachusetts: Lincoln Institute of Land Policy, 1996), p. 7.

2. Holly L. Thomas, "The Economic Benefits of Land Conservation" (Dutchess County, New York: Dutchess County Planning Department, technical memo, February 1991).

waterways, and wildlife habitats; public preserves such as parks, historic sites, and wilderness areas; and private lands of conservation value such as forests and farms.

These interconnections recognize that many of these types of open space perform several functions and serve both ecosystem and community needs. Floodplains, for example, can be used for recreation fields. Or stream valleys in which native vegetation and wildlife habitats are protected can be used to filter stormwater runoff and reduce erosion in developed areas.

Villa Rosa, a master-planned community being developed by Westfield Development Corporation on a 631-acre site near Tampa, Florida, exemplifies the concept of green infrastructure. The award-winning plan by David Jensen Associates (see illustration on next page) calls for a series of housing clusters within a connected open-space system encompassing recreation areas, freshwater ponds, existing wetlands and wildlife corridors, village gardens, and dense stands of cypress trees.

Often the best means of making connections among different types of open space is to establish a network of greenways, which are conserved strips of land along linear features of a community, such as rivers, streams, lakes, abandoned canals, roads, and railroad rights-of-way. These ribbons of greenery can serve as the connective tissue of commu-

LOT SUMMARY

189	50'X110'	21%
199	60'X110'	22%
267	70'X110'	30%
84	85'X125'	9%
54	100'X150'	6%
81	52'X96'	9%
27	1/2 ACRE	3%
901	TOTAL LOTS	100%

27 — ONE HALF ACRE

LUTZ — LAKE FERN ROAD

Westfield
Development Corporation

Site plan used by permission of David Jensen & Associates

▲ **The green infra-structure at Villa Rosa frames the developed areas of the master-planned community. It protects key environmental features of the site and provides valuable community amenities.**

nities, tying together series of open spaces, linking neighborhoods to one another, and connecting people to the natural world.

Greenways, like open space in general, come in a variety of types, including, for example, walkways along revitalized urban waterfronts, tree-shaded footpaths along streams, and corridors of undisturbed land through which different kinds of wildlife can make their seasonal migrations. Two varieties of greenway are shown in photos on the opposite page. Neighborhood walking and biking trails along abandoned rail lines, sometimes called rail trails, are a popular new type of greenway. More than 1,000 abandoned railroad corridors stretching over more than 10,000 miles have been converted to trails in the United States.[20] Pennsylvania alone boasts 105 rail trails totaling 900 miles, with an additional 1,100 miles under construction.[21]

Some of the best-known greenways include Boston's Emerald Necklace; Boise, Idaho's riverfront park system; and the Chesapeake and Ohio Canal towpath, which extends nearly 185 miles from Washington, D.C., to Cumberland, Maryland. The latter greenway follows the C&O canal, on which goods were transported from 1828 to 1924, and the scenic Potomac River, and it attracts more than 4 million hikers, runners, bikers, and strollers a year. The

trails in all these greenway systems link a variety of conserved open spaces, allowing a variety of recreational experiences.

Greenways are an opportune way of bringing nature into areas that are compactly developed. A network of connections to preserved and multiuse open spaces winding between and through neighborhoods helps retain substantial open-space qualities even in highly urbanized settings.[22]

When complete, Baltimore's Gwynns Falls Trail restoration project will bring beneficial open space into the city's neighborhoods. This project began in the early 1900s when the sons of Frederick Law Olmsted designed a 14-mile linear park along a stream in the Gwynns Falls Valley, to be anchored by an existing 1,400-acre park. But the vision was never realized and eventually the stream valley—scoured by floods and piled with trash—was all but abandoned by the residents of the neighborhoods through which it passed. Today an effort funded by local philanthropies, the city, the state, and the federal government has resurrected the idea of a linear park. The valley is being cleaned up, open space is being added, and the Gwynns Falls Trail soon will connect Baltimore's neighborhoods to the city's redeveloped harborfront.[23]

On the South Platte River just west of downtown Denver is an example of a great urban greenway. Once littered with dumped tires and junked cars and lined with abandoned and polluted industrial sites, this section of the river now boasts a continuous bike trail that connects 15 individual parks and water recreational areas, which feature 105 miles of kayaking and a permanent, constructed whitewater run.[24]

One of the largest greenways in the United States is the Marjorie Harris Carr Cross-Florida Greenway State Recreation and Conservation Area now under development. Like Baltimore's Gwynns Falls Trail, this project has its roots in an earlier effort. It began as the Cross-Florida Barge Canal, which was to run from the Gulf of Mexico at Yankeetown to the St. Johns River in Palatka. Construction of the canal, which was never completed, began in the 1930s and continued until the early 1970s, consuming more than $70 million in state and federal funds along the way. The investment was not a total loss, however, as the land set aside for the

canal is now in the process of becoming the 110-mile, 70,000-acre Cross-Florida Greenway.

Tools for Protecting Open Space

The effective conservation of open space within developing areas requires an understanding of regional ecosystems. It calls for the identification of important ecological features and qualities before development takes place and proactive planning to preserve key elements as urbanization takes place. The concept of open space as infrastructure implies that both public and private investment in protecting open space will be required.

Traditionally, the public sector bore the primary responsibility. Many older towns were laid out with parks designated as public spaces. As the towns grew, other parks and recreation areas were added, some by donation and some by public purchase. In more recent times, many communities began requiring developers to set aside natural areas to conserve environmental qualities and provide open space.

Acquisition

For many years, the conservation of open space depended on its acquisition and protection by local, state, and federal governments and special public agencies set up to acquire and manage public land. Spending by public agencies, however, has not kept up with growth in demand.

Property tax revolts in the 1970s curtailed municipal spending on open space. And until 1999 when President Clinton signed legislation funding significant new land purchases in states, federal grants to states for open-space acquisition through the Land and Water Conservation Fund had been declining for years. During this period of decline, several billion dollars of authorized land acquisition and maintenance projects in federal parks went unfunded.[25]

Despite the spate of recent ballot measures (described earlier) approving public investments in open space, state and local governments are still

Photo used by permission of David Jensen & Associates

struggling to keep pace with the demand for open space. Also, open-space standards and prices for land acquisition (or for development rights) have risen, further widening the gap between supply and demand.

Regulation

The usual alternative to acquisition is regulation, either by zoning to restrict development or by exactions of open space (or payment of open-space acquisition fees) from developers applying for project approvals. The regulatory tool is not all it could be hoped to be. Regulations that require open-space conservation increasingly have been challenged as a taking of private property without compensation.

Property owners and developers resist open-space regulations, characterizing them as a means of saddling owners/developers with the financial burden of what is a communitywide responsibility. The courts have sympathized with property owners when zoning is too strict or exactions and fees too large. Consequently, although developers may incorporate extensive open spaces in their projects to appeal to the market, in most instances regulatory approaches fall short of protecting enough open space to meet community needs.

Incentives and Partnerships

It is clear that traditional regulatory and public acquisition programs will not suffice to meet the demand for open space in and around growing communities. Public officials will need to work more in partnership with the private sector to protect open space. Some public incentives include programs that defer or reduce property taxes for conserved land, development density bonuses in return for open-space set-asides, and transfers of development rights to other properties.

Rather than trying merely to minimize the negative impacts of development, communities should take advantage of the opportunities development brings for open-space initiatives to restore and enhance the environment. Developers should be asked to pitch in, either with land or fees in lieu of land, but their contributions should occur within the context of an open-space protection plan or policy framework. For development to be sustainable—that is, for it to conserve and link key open spaces—communities must be proactive in defining what they want to protect. And then they

must establish incentives for the private sector's participation in the protection program.

The town of Lincoln, Massachusetts, shows how important the establishment of a policy framework to guide growth can be in open-space conservation. In the 1960s, farms started becoming subdivisions, and the town's leaders became concerned. The first comprehensive plan, which had been adopted in 1958, classified almost 40 percent of the land as vacant open space and called for doubling the number of homes. When growth began in earnest, Lincoln's residents resolved to retain the open, rural landscapes that gave the town its rural character.

Lincoln's town leaders and citizens forged a remarkable collaboration to promote clustered development and acquire key parcels to save open land. Yet the town came to understand that it needed to frame a more comprehensive strategy for conserving open space.

Based on analyses of carrying capacity, the town adopted an open-space plan in 1976 that designated 1,450 acres for conservation and issued a prioritized list of properties it hoped to acquire or preserve in some fashion. The plan has played a key role in linking many of the town's conserved lands into an open-space system. In turn, Lincoln's open space has became part of the region's network of trails, which is, in effect, a multifaceted greenway offering many recreational options and conserved natural features. Updated in 1983 and 1989, Lincoln's open-space plan remains a core working document for guiding town decisions on development and conservation.

Across the country, the city of Olympia, Washington, has made restoring the natural functions of urban open space a key part of its open-space planning. Recognizing the benefits of tree cover for stormwater management, city officials are taking steps to protect and enhance wooded areas. One of these steps is a pilot program to intensify the tree canopy along streams and streets in three watersheds.

Green Cove Basin, for example, is designated in the city's comprehensive plans as a unique area subject to enhanced environmental regulations. Development here is to be tailored to fit the preservation needs of the basin's creeks and wetlands. A new residential low-impact zoning district allows a variety of housing types on small lots, but limits impervious surface per lot to 2,500 square feet. Projects must include a minimum 200 trees per acre, which is about 55 percent tree cover. Driveways and sidewalks may be constructed of porous materials to improve water infiltration.

Issues and Obstacles

Across the United States, natural features are continuing to lose ground (in both senses) to forces of urban growth. Ways by which open-space resources can be conserved, restored, and enhanced are covered specifically in chapter 6. All these approaches raise important issues about smart conservation of open space. How can needs for open space be balanced with needs for development? How can needs for open space be reconciled with private property rights and market forces?

Conservation versus Development
Defining a feasible and workable balance between urban and natural functions is a pressing issue in smart growth. Environmentalists and land planners often use the approach described by Ian McHarg in *Design with Nature*, which calls for analyzing natural processes in metropolitan areas to determine appropriate locations for urban development.[26]

The concept of carrying capacity, built on McHarg's ideas, seeks to assess how much development can be sustained by the capacity of natural systems, such as soils, an area's geology, or water features. At the simplest level, mapping important natural features in advance of potential development can determine which areas within a region need to be conserved and which can be developed without adversely impacting natural qualities.

The use of such an approach would seem to put the first two principles of smart growth—compactness and open space—into conflict. It is not simple to weigh the importance of natural features against the importance of creating functional patterns of urban development.

Over time, the great cities of the world—Paris and London come to mind—evolved wonderfully functional urban centers atop wetlands and woodlands and up to the edge of channeled waterways. San Francisco developed its enchanting urban scene by disregarding topographic constraints and taking full advantage of waterfront access. Washington, D.C.'s grand Mall was developed largely on wetlands. To some extent such cities compensated for erasing some natural features by creating extensive parks—for example, Boston's Emerald Necklace, New York's Central Park, and San Francisco's Golden Gate Park.

◀ Regulations designed to reduce the runoff impacts of development protect the quality of streams and wetlands in Green Cove Basin (Olympia, Washington).

▶ Creek restoration at Coffee Creek Center, a conservation development near Chesterton, Indiana. The development plan calls for preserving and restoring the creek and bordering natural areas to maintain the natural functions of the site, treat wastewater, and provide open space.

As big cities grew, they had to switch from relatively natural life-support systems, such as wells and septic tanks, for example, to much more intensive systems involving pipes and central treatment facilities. On the other side of the coin, these infrastructure systems allowed living and working space to become more concentrated, which reduced the need to convert open space to urban uses.

But the general pattern of metropolitan growth in the United States in the second half of the 20th century has continued to be low density. Making urban-level services available in suburban areas has increased the cost of urbanization without slowing the demand to convert open space to suburban uses. In calling for more compact development, the smart-growth strategy is to trade off some losses in environmental value for securing the conservation of more open space within regions. Approaches to implementing such a regional strategy are discussed in chapter 8.

Some planners advocate balancing conservation and development demands at the project level through "conservation" or "limited" development. Conservation development proposes to reconfigure typical subdivisions by clustering buildings on a part of the site and leaving the remainder of the site in farmland or natural landscapes.

Prairie Crossing and Coffee Creek Center, both in the Chicago region, are two projects among a number of such projects that have received considerable media attention as constructive responses to the aims of smart growth. Both of these clustered developments incorporate protected and restored wetlands, streams, farmlands, and other open space, which perform important natural functions and also serve the residents as vistas, parks, and value enhancers. (See page 84 for a description of Coffee Creek Center.)

On a site-by-site basis, suburban conservation developments are more environmentally sound than conventional suburban developments. However, they do not offer a suitable regional pattern of development for smart metropolitan growth. Individual conservation developments aggregated add up to an overall pattern of low densities, which runs counter to smart-growth principles. Rarely are the individual patches of conserved land designed to connect to larger natural networks. Furthermore, they can be difficult to manage over the long term.

Insofar as the conserved land is preserved in perpetuity as open space, this militates against the evolution of more urban development as the community and market mature. Conservation subdivisions may be preferable to conventional subdivisions and even useful in meeting one kind of market need, but they hardly constitute a complete response to the aims of smart growth.

Property Rights and Market Forces

Public actions to acquire open space or to conserve privately owned open space often are opposed vigorously by the owners of the property. The owners and their supporters usually base their case on the private property right enshrined in the Constitution. The steady drumbeat of support for private property rights—combined with market forces that often make the rewards for converting open space to development extremely high—represents a real obstacle to conserving open space in developing areas.

The extent to which the right to own private property and the right to make potential profits from the development of property can be limited by public actions has always been controversial, both in the legal and political senses. Legally, although the nation has ultimate sovereignty over all land, governments must compensate private landowners for taking their land for public use, or for taking actions that erase or severely reduce the value of their property. Property rights are a political issue as well. Because private rights to property are popularly held to be so important, elected decision makers frequently are reluctant to limit those rights through zoning or other regulatory means.

Even clear public purposes affecting whole communities may be subordinated to private property rights. Some state transportation departments, for example, refrain from acquiring property for highways or highway-access management except from willing sellers.

In many cases, the wider public interests in sustaining open space give way to private property interests. The use of condemnation to acquire property for parks and other open space is generally only done as a last resort. Many elected officials are leery of adopting regulations that restrict the use of land to conserve open space. This is no doubt why many local governments continue to zone two- or three-acre lots in farming areas in the name of retaining open space, despite the experience of communities across the nation that only zoning that requires lot sizes of at least 20 to 25 acres can protect farmland from development.

Support for private property rights is motivated in large part by market opportunities to make plenty of money speculating in land for development. When the value of farmland in the path of development soars by multiples of ten, 20, or 30 over its production value as farmland, it is difficult to make a compelling argument for retaining farms or woodlands as open space.

In many developing areas, farmers are the first to fight any restrictions on future development. To them, their land is a birthright and its increasing value a just reward for years of farming. The argument that they are benefiting from regional economic forces more than their own investments falls on deaf ears. Also among the frontline opponents of restrictions on the use of farmland are the speculators who move five to ten years ahead of the wave of urbanization to lock up land at low prices for future sale at high prices—wily investors taking advantage of the system.

The differences in land values between urbanizing and rural areas that price farm uses out of the market are exacerbated by public policies that directly or indirectly stimulate and even subsidize development on open land, and by an economic system that assigns high value to land used for development and low value to land preserved for environmental and agricultural purposes.

Development Profits and Benefits

Long-time property owners and speculators who want to sell land for development strongly support respect for property rights and market forces. So do other major recipients of development profits—developers, builders, and others in the construction business. Local governments also can enjoy the fruits of growth (although some may reap fiscal shortages instead). And of course many people benefit from development, finding the housing they need as well as shopping and work opportunities. These winners in the development game can muster strong opposition to efforts to divert development from areas with open-space assets.

But the development game has losers as well. Residents in the region lose access to open space as it disappears. Long-time residents of older areas bypassed by growth face escalating property taxes and declining services. Residents of communities near booming growth areas must cope with increasing traffic and pressures on basic community facilities such as schools.

People who enjoy the presence of expanses of natural open space or farms near their homes are especially vulnerable as the development objectives of individual local governments collectively work to convert such spaces to other uses. Regional organizations frequently are powerless to implement large-scale acquisition and regulatory programs to protect open space. And the federal and state programs that might address open-space needs often conserve too little and too late.

Key Qualities of Smart Protection of Open Space

This chapter has suggested the key qualities of smart protection of open space. Smart growth calls for retaining the environmental sustainability value and the human use value of open space as cities and towns develop, keeping in mind the following key qualities that will ensure the greatest benefits from open-space conservation.

Takes Advantage of Existing Open-Space Assets

Smart protection conserves open space to protect specific characteristics. These characteristics should be defined in advance of preservation measures. Natural assets—such as significant features and rare or threatened qualities—represent values that not only will furnish a rationale for conservation but will suggest ways in which those assets should be protected.

Farmland preservation, for example, may require right-to-farm laws that allow farmers to spread manure on their land and operate tractors at dawn without harassment from the residents of new subdivisions in the area. Protecting habitats may necessitate fencing or other controls to minimize disturbance from human intrusion. By contrast, creating greenways will involve ensuring convenient access by humans and relating the use of the trails to the types of open spaces that will be linked by the trails.

Recognizes Sensitive Interrelationships

Smart protection programs determine areas to be conserved based on the interrelationships of natural qualities. They perpetuate and restore linkages and connections among open spaces and their natural qualities. Smart development that occurs within ecosystems attempts to maintain natural linkages whenever possible by preserving systems of multiuse open spaces rather than by creating fragmented bits and pieces of open space.

The natural qualities of open spaces function as interrelated elements of larger ecosystems. Sever-

ing or disrupting individual elements can alter the character and long-term viability of the ecosystem as a whole. Stormwater, for example, drains naturally into streams and into the water table through seepage aided by tree cover, wetlands, and floodplains. Declines in any of these functions—for example by the proliferation of pavements and hard surfaces that prevent seepage into the soil—can generate high stream flows that will erode watercourses and produce flooding.

Considers Open Space as Infrastructure

Smart protection programs recognize that open space is an essential element of development. It supports development in the same way as the system of roads supports development, in the same way that sewer and water lines support development, and in the same way that fire stations and other facilities support development. Like these other essential elements of development, open space is infrastructure—green infrastructure.

As infrastructure, open space demands as much public sector and private sector attention to its role and relations as is given to the provision of other facilities. Its planning should take a systems approach. Smart growth seeks to integrate open space within the framework of a community's or region's other infrastructure systems and constructed buildings to produce a satisfying living and working environment.

Looks beyond Acquisition

Restoration, enhancement, and management are important concerns of smart protection of open space. Creating a green infrastructure is not simply a matter of preserving or setting aside open space within projects or communities. Open spaces frequently require rebuilding or upgrading to function properly. Wetlands degraded by dumping and an invasion of exotic vegetation, for example, might need water quality upgrades and some reintroduction of native plant species. Greenways might need new plantings or the pruning of trees and shrubs. Woodlands might benefit from selective thinning or removal of undergrowth. In general, protected open space also requires long-term management to retain its natural values.

A Sustaining Role

As a smart-growth principle, the conservation of open space necessarily requires balancing open space and development, as well as integrating open spaces into development. Creative planning and design are needed to 1) retain the values of open space, 2) maintain open-space systems within the ecosystem, and 3) make best use of the specific assets of each type of open-space. Smart growth means much more than simply designating open space for protection. Open space must be planned and managed to give it a sustaining role in the human and natural environment.

Notes

1. "Open Space Wins across Country," *Common Ground* (Conservation Fund), November/December 2000, p. 1.

2. Phyllis Myers, "Livability at the Ballot Box: State and Local Referenda on Parks, Conservation, and Smarter Growth, Election Day 1998" (discussion paper prepared for the Brookings Institution, 1999), p. 4.

3. "Congress Boosts LWCF Spending," *Common Ground*, January/February 1999, p. 1.

4. See Defenders of Wildlife homepage at: www.defenders.org.

5. William Fulton et al., *Who Sprawls Most: How Growth Patterns Differ across the U.S.* (Washington, D.C.: Brookings Institution Center on Urban and Metropolitan Policy, July 2001).

6. Jeff Gersh, "Subdivide and Conquer: Concrete, Condos, and the Second Conquest of the American West," *Amicus Journal*, fall 1996, p. 15.

◀ Preserving and enhancing the area's natural, historical, and archaeological features were the guiding principles in developing Bonita Bay, Florida, a 2,400-acre community in which half of the land will remain as open space.

7. Dwight Young, *Alternatives to Sprawl* (Cambridge, Massachusetts: Lincoln Institute of Land Policy, 1995), p. 5.

8. U.S. Department of Agriculture, Natural Resources Conservation Service, *Natural Resources Inventory* (Washington, D.C.: 1997).

9. See American Forests homepage at: www.american forests.org.

10. Committee on Mitigating Wetland Losses, Board on Environmental Studies and Toxicology, Water Science and Technology Board, National Research Council, *Compensating for Wetland Losses under the Clean Water Act* (Washington, D.C.: National Academy Press, 2001), p. 17.

11. National Wildlife Federation, Smart Growth & Wildlife homepage at: www.nwf.org/smartgrowth.

12. U.S. Department of Agriculture, *Census of Agriculture* (Washington, D.C.: 1997).

13. Henry Diamond and Patrick Noonan, *Land Use in America* (Washington, D.C.: Island Press, 1996), p. 89.

14. Aldo Leopold, *A Sand Country Almanac* (New York: Oxford University Press, 1949), p. 165.

15. George B. Brewster, *The Ecology of Development: Integrating the Built and Natural Environments*, Working Paper no. 649 (Washington, D.C.: ULI–the Urban Land Institute, 1997), p. 29.

16. American Forests, *Urban Ecosystem Analysis, Atlanta Metro Area* (August 2001), available at: www.americanforests.org.

17. Reported by Environmental Law Institute at: www.eli.org/publications.

18. Charles Fausold and Robert Lilieholm, *The Economic Value of Open Spaces: A Review and Synthesis* (Cambridge, Massachusetts: Lincoln Institute of Land Policy, 1996), p. 2.

19. Mark A. Benedict, "Green Infrastructure: A Strategic Approach to Land Conservation," *PAS Memo*, October 2000, p. 1.

20. Rails-to-Trails Conservancy, Trails and Greenways Clearinghouse homepage at: www.trailsandgreen ways.org.

21. "Greenways," *Common Ground*, September/October 1999, p.7.

22. For more information on greenways, see Loring Schwarz, ed., *Greenways: A Guide to Planning, Design, and Development* (Washington, D.C.: Island Press, 1993).

23. See Martin J. Rosen, "Reviving Urban Parks," *Urban Land*, November 1997, pp. 54–57.

24. Neal R. Peirce, "Age of the 'Smart Park,'" 20 August 2000 (syndicated column posted on: www.citistates.com/np-columns.html).

25. John Tibbetts, *Open Space Conservation: Investing in Your Community's Economic Health* (Cambridge, Massachusetts: Lincoln Institute of Land Policy, 1998), p. 3.

26. Ian McHarg, *Design with Nature* (New York: John Wiley & Sons, 1992). McHarg's book was originally published in 1969 by the Natural History Press, New York.

Principles of Smart Growth
Expanded Mobility

4

The traffic congesting the streets in almost all growing communities is a potent force driving interest in smart growth. Traffic tends to be a top complaint in surveys pertaining to the quality of life in respondents' communities. In metropolitan regions, rarely a day goes by without media reports of backups extending for miles, incidents resulting from road rage, or other major traffic-related problems. And traffic congestion generates high costs in terms of time wasted sitting in traffic, deteriorated air quality, and delays in development. (The delays come from regulatory limits on development that would add traffic to already overloaded highway systems.)

Achieving smart growth requires smart transportation, the goals of which are to widen travel choices and improve the capacity of transportation systems to meet the mobility demands of a growing population and economy. In short, the goal is expanded mobility. Smart transportation, in turn, requires smart patterns of growth. David Winstead, former secretary of transportation for Maryland, puts it this way: "There is no transportation solution without a land use solution."

Smart transportation is not simply a matter of more high-occupancy-vehicle (HOV) lanes, improved public transit, or more biking and walking paths. People's choices of travel are highly dependent on development patterns that can make it easy or difficult to use various forms of transportation. The prevailing development patterns of the last

50 years—overall low densities and a penchant for stand-alone (single-use) projects—tend to preclude forms of travel other than automobile. Therefore, the principle of smart transportation goes hand in hand with the principle of compact, multiuse development that shortens trips and widens opportunities for a variety of travel modes. It goes hand in hand also with the principle of enhanced livability (see chapter 5), which includes among its goals the revival of streets as an integral part of the social and pedestrian network of communities and the provision of travel options for people unable to drive.

This chapter has as a constant theme the linkage between potential transportation improvements and changes in development patterns. The chapter explores the transportation problem, which is that increasing travel demands are overwhelming available capacity while a growing share of travelers have no other choice but to drive. As a result, investment requirements for capital and operating expenses are growing immense and air quality is deteriorating. The chapter examines prospects for expanding capacity and widening travel choices. And it identifies the key qualities of expanded mobility that make it a principle of smart growth.

The Current Situation

Metropolitan transportation systems comprise a wide assortment of travel possibilities provided and managed by various federal, state, and local

Figure 4-1 Factors Increasing Traffic Congestion

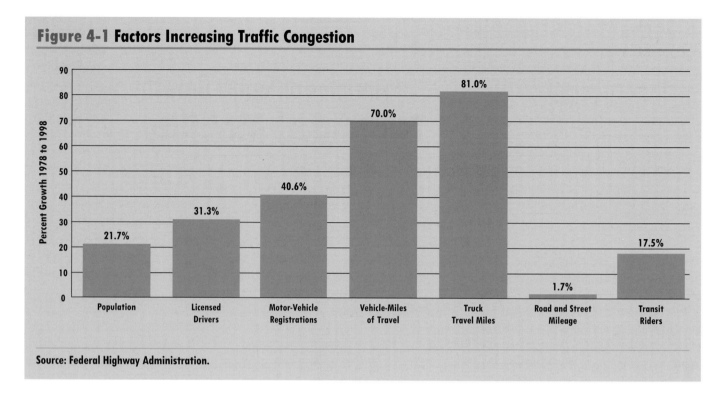

Source: Federal Highway Administration.

agencies and by private developers. Travel facilities are being expanded constantly and becoming more complex. But these improvements somehow are not satisfying the mobility demands of many residents of urban regions. Getting around is becoming more frustrating every day, it seems.

Road Congestion

People's still growing proclivity to drive coupled with the robust population growth affecting many urban regions is exacerbating congestion, which is possibly reaching a crisis stage in some communities. U.S. Department of Transportation data show that from 1987 to 1997 traffic on urban interstate highways grew by 2 percent annually per lane-mile and by 1.4 percent annually on other main roads.[1]

In city after city, growth in vehicle-miles of travel has exceeded the rate of population growth, frequently by two or three times. The Atlanta urbanized area, for example, saw a 53 percent increase in population growth from 1982 to 1996 and a 199 percent increase in vehicle-miles traveled (VMT). The population of the Salt Lake City urbanized area grew by 32 percent during the same years, and VMT increased by 129 percent.[2]

A study by the Texas Transportation Institute (TTI) of congestion in 68 urban areas shows that the

share of total travel occurring in congested conditions increased from 32 percent (about five hours a day) in 1982 to 45 percent (about seven hours a day) in 1997.[3] The study calculates that in 1999 peak-hour trips required 29 percent more time than non-peak-hour trips.

The TTI study estimates that in 1999 the cost of congestion in terms of wasted fuel and time stuck in traffic came to $78 billion, which is more than triple the 1982 level. Most of this cost is borne by the ten most congested regions.

Pogo's famous observation that "the enemy is us" rings true for the traffic mess. A combination of demographics and affluence has led to unprecedented levels of vehicle ownership and use. The maturing of the baby boom generation has played out in travel demand as it has in many other elements of the social order. The cohort in the peak driving age—between 35 and 45 years—has increased disproportionately. The rising number of women in the workforce has further increased travel demands.

From 1978 to 1998, as shown in figure 4-1, ownership of private vehicles sharply outpaced population growth. Truck trips grew even faster, a consequence of increases in orders from dot.com retailers and increases in deliveries to just-in-time manufacturers. Even transit ridership grew, producing levels not seen since the 1960s.

While travel demand climbed sharply during this period, roadway capacity in the form of new construction grew by about 2 percent, making all but inevitable the increase in congestion quantified by TTI. While congestion has worsened, average peak-hour commuting times remained virtually unchanged from 1978 to 1998. The principal reason for this is that commuting destinations have changed. Suburban employment has grown in relation to downtown employment, and driving to suburban jobs takes less time on average than driving or riding transit to downtown jobs.

Elements of Metropolitan Transportation

The transportation system in metropolitan areas combines a wide variety of modes and physical facilities that offer many choices for travel. Among these are the following (not included on this list are airports, seaports, and railroads, which constitute important elements of metropolitan transportation systems but are oriented primarily to intercity and long-distance travel):

▲ **Highways.** The interstate and state highway network carries 86 percent of urban traffic but accounts for only 20 percent of urban road mileage. Originally, federal and state highways were built to provide access to one urban center within a metropolitan area. New highways are increasingly designed to intercept suburb-to-city traffic (ring roads and beltways) or serve suburb-to-suburb travel. To increase their efficiency of use, many major highways are being modified to include, for example, HOV lanes and high-tech surveillance and traffic-control systems (known as intelligent information devices).

▲ **Local roads.** Local-road systems provide access from major roads into and through neighborhoods and commercial centers. Once laid out as rather uniform grids, most local streets now are designed with curves and culs-de-sac to discourage through traffic and accommodate rolling topography. A return to the grid pattern of neighborhood streets—but mitigated by traffic-calming devices such as narrower streets—is advocated today by new urbanists and practitioners of traditional neighborhood design.

▲ **Parking.** Parking is usually accessed from local streets, although park-and-ride lots serving pub-

lic transit and carpooling often are accessed from major streets. Parking for individual projects usually requires more space than the buildings it serves, so that parking facilities become a major element in any development plan.

▲ **Public transit.** Bus routes, light-rail lines, heavy-rail systems serving a wide metropolitan area, and commuter trains offering service along corridors that stretch far from the central core are the main elements that can go into a metropolitan area's transit mix. Most transit systems provide radial service to and from the central-city core. Bus and rail routes serving suburbs only are increasingly common. People's use of transit depends largely on destinations, that is, on the existence of business and residential areas to which many people are attracted and within which walking is a good travel choice.

▲ **Private transit.** Alternatives to mass transit for short-distance or unscheduled trips such as taxicabs, jitney cabs, and shuttle buses have become an essential component of many metropolitan transportation systems.

▲ **Pedestrian and bicycle pathways.** Pathways can serve a variety of travel needs if they are designed to provide convenient and attractive access to important destinations. In older urban areas they

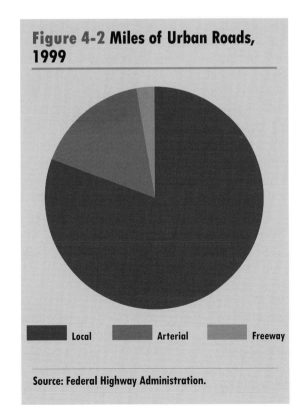

Figure 4-2 Miles of Urban Roads, 1999

Local Arterial Freeway

Source: Federal Highway Administration.

may be provided as part of the street system. In many suburban areas they may be entirely lacking. Many recently developed pathway systems focus on recreational use.

Metropolitan transportation systems are expected to connect the dots in the spreading mosaic of regional development and interlocking activities, to let people travel anywhere at any time. Mobility has come to be seen as a right. People assume that they can choose to live a far distance from their jobs and still make it to work on time. Circles of relatives and friends who interact on a daily basis are scattered all over the metropolitan area, some 15 and more miles apart. The closest grocery store may be miles away from home, the closest regional shopping center five to ten miles away. Delivery trucks supply that store and that mall from distant distribution centers—and even the UPS truck that makes e-shopping convenient travels miles from its distribution center to deliver the goods.

Transportation capacity helps determine the locations for the multiple activity nodes and centers that function as destinations for much metropolitan travel. Prime locations benefit from their transportation capacity and they also stimulate travel demand. The central business districts of older cities were centrally located and centrally accessible: all roads and transit lines led downtown.

Transportation facilities have been the critical element in defining desirable development locations for the large suburban business districts that often are called edge cities and that every region has at least one of, even Tyler, Texas. Because transportation access is critical to their desirability as centers of development, many edge cities have been established along interstate highways. The booming development at Tysons Corner, Virginia, on the Capital Beltway is one example and the South Coast Metro complex along I-405 in Orange County, California, is another. In some cases, the highway has even given edge cities their name, such as metropolitan Boston's Route 128 high-tech corridor.

Households, on the other hand, appear to make their locational choices without much thought to transportation or traffic. In a nationwide survey conducted in 2000 by Public Opinion Strategies for the National Association of Realtors, among community attributes deemed "important" or "somewhat important" in making a decision to purchase a new home, little or no traffic ranks ninth and a shorter commute to work ranks 11th.[4] Higher-ranking concerns include: safety, access to doctors and hospitals, green space, good schools, neighborhood feeling, access to shopping, and lower property taxes. But once people have settled into a neighborhood, traffic concerns seem to become more important as highway congestion grows.

Fragmented Decision Process

The task of providing transportation services to support metropolitan development is complicated by the involvement of many different providers. Responsibility for planning, financing, and constructing transportation improvements is shared among developers, local officials, metropolitan planning organizations, state transportation agencies, and the federal government. More than 35,000 governments manage the road system nationwide and almost 2,000 agencies manage general-purpose transit systems.

Responsibility is usually divided along the following lines. Highways are built mostly by state agencies using mostly federal funding. New local streets are planned and constructed by the developers of subdivisions and commercial complexes and usually turned over to the county or municipality. Most new parking is provided by private owners, although local governments or special taxing districts may construct parking lots and garages to support business centers. Most public transit services are provided by regional transportation agencies, again, with infusions of federal money, although suburban jurisdictions may provide local-bus services. New sidewalks and other pedestrian and bicycle pathways are generally provided by the developers of subdivisions and commercial complexes as part of local street or trail systems or by local or regional agencies as part of park and greenway systems.

Coordination among travel modes is a key to cost-effective mobility within metropolitan regions. Having a variety of public and private entities and state, regional, and local authorities responsible for providing different parts of the transportation system means that the various modes function almost independently of each other. This lack of overall coordination renders assessments of transportation needs difficult and decision making on improvements confusing.

As the major coordination point for large-scale transportation improvements, the federal government requires the establishment of a metropolitan planning organization (MPO) in each urban region to be responsible for coordinating federal transportation investments. MPO boards usually are made up of local officials representing the local governments in the region, and about half of MPOs are associated with regional planning councils or regional councils of governments whose boards also consist largely of local officials.

This involvement of local officials helps to coordinate regional planning for transportation, but it also tends to limit the ability of MPOs to adopt strategic regional programs that might focus investments in some jurisdictions at the expense of others. Furthermore, these locally oriented regional organizations are not well suited to make or promote the land use decisions that are critical in supporting regional transportation plans. They tend to go to pains to avoid consideration of land use issues because they can be so controversial.

Thus, internecine funding fights and the reluctance of local governments to share decision-making powers at a regional level hobble the coordination of transportation systems and improvements in many urban regions and divorce transportation decisions from development decisions. The usual result is that more attention gets paid to programs to build the highways that serve developing greenfield areas, and less attention gets paid to mobility needs in older cities and suburbs, even though the latter are likely to require less dramatic investments in maintenance (road repair, for example) and replacement (new buses, for example).

Much of the travel within metropolitan areas is regionally oriented while virtually all development approvals are local in nature. But pigeonholing transportation as a regional matter and land use as a local matter seriously disconnects related local and regional concerns. The approval for the development of a regional shopping center demonstrates this disconnect. The new center may bring important tax benefits to the jurisdiction in which it is located. It will also bring traffic that is likely to increase congestion in adjacent jurisdictions. Some state planning and smart-growth programs hope to introduce more regional accountability for local development approvals, but the politics of accomplishing this are perilous.

In a few regions, MPOs have been able to overcome the jealously guarded local power over development approvals and have crafted effective regional visions that make carrying out a consistent transportation policy a more achievable, if still difficult, effort. One of the more effective agencies in this regard has been the San Diego Association of Governments (SANDAG), which originates and administers regional growth management strategies and transportation investment programs. SANDAG administers a regional sales tax that was adopted to fund highway and transit projects. It is one of only a few MPOs with purse-strings control over transportation funding.

Transportation/Travel Spending

Transportation facilities are expensive. So is travel. The combined spending on transportation facilities at all levels of government in 1997 was $125 billion—$101 billion for highways and $25 billion for transit. The nation's total transportation bill in 1997, including the cost of personal travel as well as the cost of shipping goods to consumers and intermediate points, amounted to $905 billion, or 11 percent of the gross domestic product.[5]

Highway and Transit Spending

As shown in figure 4-3, transportation funding over the years has grown steadily larger. This has occurred in response to increasing demand. Total spending for highways in 1999 came to $117.4 billion, or 88 percent of all transportation expenditures. The U.S. Department of Transportation predicts that just maintaining the nation's highway system in the future will require an increasing share of the federal budget. Transportation Efficiency Act (TEA-21) funds are expected to halt further deterioration in the road system, but they will not add sufficient capacity to significantly reduce existing or anticipated travel congestion.

Transit spending from all sources (federal, state, local) came to $27.9 billion in 1999, of which $8.4 billion was spent on capital projects. With this level of spending, it is certain that many transit system improvements and extensions proposed for federal funding will go unfunded.

Figure 4-3 Transit and Highway Capital and Operating Expenditures, Selected Years

	Transit Expenditures (millions of dollars)			Highway Expenditures (millions of dollars)			Transit Share Of Total Capital Expenditures
	Capital	Operating	Total	Capital	Operating	Total	
1961	120	568	688	6,795	4,692	11,487	1.7%
1971	446	1,446	1,892	12,299	10,174	22,473	3.5%
1980	2,095	6,084	8,179	20,305	21,478	41,783	9.4%
1990	4,535	14,711	19,246	35,151	40,257	75,408	11.4%
1999	8,443	19,460	27,903	59,499	57,935	117,434	12.4%

Sources: Federal Highway Administration; and Federal Transit Administration.

Personal Travel

On average, households spent about $7,000 on personal travel in 1999, almost three-fifths of what they spent on housing.[6] Almost 95 percent of household transportation spending, or $6,400, was for owning and operating automobiles.

Residents of outlying neighborhoods tend to spend more on all forms of transportation, according to studies of transportation expenditures in the Chicago, San Francisco, and Los Angeles urban regions.[7] For example, the average family living in Chicago's close-in Edgewater neighborhood spends $4,000 yearly on automobiles, while the average family in suburban Schaumburg spends $6,800. This finding probably reflects variance in household incomes and in access to other modes of travel.

Personal travel costs, in fact, far exceed government spending on transportation. A study of transportation costs in the Twin Cities region by the University of Minnesota's Center for Transportation Studies finds that all private costs for transportation (including travel time and costs resulting from accidents) are almost ten times government transportation expenditures (see figure 4-4).[8]

The Primacy of the Suburban Model

Critics chide Americans for their love affair with the automobile, hoping perhaps that after a fling we will return to more responsible means of travel. However, a more realistic metaphor for the relationship Americans have with the automobile might be a marriage of convenience. The growing use of cars has been reinforced by a lifestyle in which the car is king. Development patterns have adapted to accommodate this lifestyle.

The lower an area's development density, the more people drive. Suburban densities generate a lot of driving; higher urban densities generate less. Urban areas are more likely to be served by transit and trip origins and destinations are likely to be closer together—some within walking distance. At the top of the list of urban areas with high per capita rates of driving is Houston where residents log an average of 37 miles of driving per day, followed closely by Atlanta, Indianapolis, and Dallas/Fort Worth—all cities that grew rapidly in the postwar era when cars became the travel mode of choice for most Americans.[9]

The lowest levels of driving occur mostly in older cities that experienced most of their growing when transit was the best way to get around, and where it is generally easy to use transit and to walk and generally harder to drive. New Orleans residents drive the least (14.5 miles per person per day), followed by New York City, Philadelphia, and, surprisingly, Las Vegas—a city of relatively high density.

According to a survey of 150 of the nation's leading experts on urban development, the most important factors that influenced the development of U.S. metropolitan areas in the 20th century are the creation of the interstate highway system starting in the 1950s and the subsequent dominance of the automobile among travel modes.[10] (These experts also identify a number of other important factors that helped make traditional urban lifestyles less desirable and create an entirely new suburban pattern suited to raising the postwar baby boom generation. Among these factors are the mortgage programs and subdivision regulations of the Federal Housing Administration, the deindustrialization of central cities, urban renewal, the introduction of mass-produced suburban tract houses, and the invention of shopping malls.)

The undoubted success of the suburban model, according to economist Anthony Downs, has created a common vision of unlimited low-density development that has dominated American growth strategies for the last four decades.[11] Americans affected by this vision dream of

▲ living in detached homes on spacious lots;
▲ traveling by means of their own vehicles;
▲ working in attractive low-density settings with free parking; and
▲ influencing their environment through strong local governments.

Even though this vision is flawed, says Downs, in that it generates excessive travel, lowers the supply of affordable housing, and creates difficulties in siting undesirable land uses, for many people it represents the American dream come true.

Traffic and Public Expenditure Issues

Suburban style development on the fringes of metropolitan areas is proliferating, creating transportation needs that public agencies must strive to satisfy. A main attraction of fringe locations is their relatively low housing costs (and, for employers, their low office rents). People are willing to trade off time and money spent commuting by car or train for significantly lower housing costs.

According to a recent ULI study of new-home sales in the Sunset Corridor outside Portland, Oregon —the center of Oregon's high-tech industry—the price of a same-size house drops $5,000 for each mile from downtown that it is located.[12] This savings translates into an annual mortgage payment reduction of $444 per mile—or about $2 per mile per commuting day. The mortgage savings on a house 15 miles from downtown, for example, can pay for a lot of household travel.

But accommodating this travel may require considerable public spending. Homeowners in fringe and rural areas are optimizing their choices on the backs of transportation providers, creating transportation needs that public agencies must strive to satisfy. Transportation agencies stand to gain from smart-growth strategies that can reduce travel demand and thus the need to enlarge transportation capacities.

While raising travel demand, suburban style development also often hampers traffic movements. Strip commercial development along major highways not only generates trips, but also diminishes road capacity by adding turning movements. The familiar pattern of franchise restaurants, service stations, and small strip centers one after another, each with its own access to the road and its own parking, produces maximum interference with traffic along the road. Once such a pattern is established, fixing the traffic problem by highway improvements or by smarter development becomes extremely difficult.

Suburban style residential developments also create traffic problems—both internal and external.

Figure 4-4 Annual Transportation Costs, Twin Cities Region
(millions of dollars)

Government Spending	**$2,560**
Streets and Highways	1,535
Transit	260
Other	765
User Spending	**$22,875**
Vehicles	9,100
Transit	220
Parking	2,040
Travel Time	10,150
Crashes	1,365
External Costs[1]	**$1,890**
Full Cost of Transportation	**$27,325**

1. Includes pollution and other external costs.

Source : University of Minnesota Center for Transportation Studies.

They do this typically by channeling all traffic in and out through one or two access points, by not connecting to the road systems of surrounding subdivisions and thus limiting route choices, by impeding opportunities to walk or bike to nearby destinations, and by making no provision for current or future service by public transit.

Air Quality Issues

Vehicle emissions have long been a target of environmental policy and there have been some considerable successes. The ban on lead in gasoline has virtually eliminated lead from vehicle emissions. Emissions of volatile organic compounds (VOCs) and carbon monoxide (CO) have declined since the mid-1970s, despite considerable growth in vehicle travel. Emissions of nitrogen oxide (NO_x) have increased, however. NO_x and VOCs are contributory factors to smog, which causes breathing problems.[13]

It is clear that anything that can be done to reduce driving will have environmental benefits as well. Air quality has been a major consideration in transportation plans since the Clean Air Act Amendments of 1977, which required metropolitan transportation plans to aim for conformity to a state implementation plan (SIP) for attainment of air quality goals.

Transportation Solutions

Smart growth goes hand in hand with two related transportation goals: the balancing of traffic solutions with other goals and the provision of a wider choice of modes for travelers. Both goals require a closer integration of transportation systems with land use and development policies. Smart transportation must be pursued on a broad front that affirms some fundamental truths about metropolitan transportation systems:

▲ Automobiles driven on highways and major arterials will continue to be the dominant travel mode.
▲ Transit's share of travel cannot be expected to increase rapidly, but it will serve an important role in selected markets, even in small regions.
▲ Travel demand will continue to grow, making traffic congestion an ongoing problem.

Car-oriented development patterns make up a sizable and growing proportion of existing metropolitan regions. For the most part, driving is more convenient than any alternative. And public policies and private development processes still tend to favor conventional, auto-dependent forms of development. For these reasons, most people will continue to prefer long-distance driving for getting to work, stores, and other daily destinations.

Public transit attracts a relatively small share of travel in most communities—most frequently from 3 to 5 percent of total trips. A substantial increase in transit's share awaits the evolution of more transit-friendly development patterns, which will be, no doubt, a slow process given the current extent of low-density, use-segregated development.

Even if massive investment expands access to transit systems, transit use will be limited because it is often not competitive with automobiles in terms of speed—and Americans perceive it as a low-prestige means of travel. Adapting and redesigning already developed areas to make transit (and walking) a more feasible travel option will certainly take time. Remaking some areas into transit-friendly communities will require radical redevelopment. Meanwhile, transit-unfriendly patterns of development continue to be the dominant form of development in fringe areas.

As transit service and transit-supportive development patterns evolve, travel demand and thus traffic congestion will continue to grow. A few walkable, transit-oriented projects dropped into a sea of conventional projects will do little to reduce overall traffic congestion, although they may accommodate growth without adding to congestion.

Because driving is by necessity—now and for a long time into the future—the travel mode of choice for most people, smart transportation cannot be anticar. Advocates of transit-only solutions to traffic congestion—who argue that adding highway capacity only promotes auto-dependent, low-density sprawl and undercuts motivations for greater use of transit—ignore this reality. It will take decades of transit-oriented development to generate substantial increases in transit use.

The observation that widening roads to reduce traffic congestion is like letting one's belt out to solve a weight problem is simplistic. More apt is the view that doing nothing to alleviate congestion in order to discourage driving is like trying to control a child's foot size by refusing to buy her bigger shoes. It is important to realize that even development that fits smart-growth precepts generally will add more cars to the roads than riders to transit lines, except for development occurring in large, high-density areas.

Living for the most part in areas where noncar travel possibilities are scarce, inconvenient, or nonexistent, Americans have become too fond of jumping into their cars for every trip. But while, as many transportation experts believe, it is unrealistic to expect that traffic congestion can be substantially reduced in most metropolitan areas, the huge increases in congestion projected over the next 20 years or so by many regional travel demand models may be alleviated or averted by measures that improve the efficiency and capacity of highways, that decrease driving distances, and that begin to shift a significant number of trips to other travel modes.

Being There

Being there—locating in close-in neighborhoods that provide good housing, essential services, and easy access to jobs—is the smartest transportation solution. Locating housing close to major employment and retail centers, even those with poor transit service, is the most effective means of shortening driving trips, promoting transit improvements, and encouraging transit use and walking. Compared with the cost of constructing the road capacity needed to serve development in exurban locations, the public sector costs for development in built-up areas are minimal unless public parking facilities are needed. Locating new development in urbanized areas or in places where a broad mix of uses is evolving obviates the need for new roads simply by shortening many auto trips.

Buckhead Lofts, a 104-unit condominium apartment project that opened in 1998 in a close-in Atlanta neighborhood, exemplifies being there.[14] Built on land left over from a highway project, the development has attracted a young, hip crowd that enjoys walking to local shops and restaurants. Since its residents do not require cars for every trip, Buckhead Lofts adds less to area traffic and parking needs than would a more isolated development.

Another example is Orenco Station, a project currently under development in Hillsboro, a suburb of Portland, Oregon. Planned to take advantage of a new station on the Tri-Met MAX light-rail line, the development is designed as a walkable, mixed-use suburban neighborhood providing convenient, attractive access to the transit line into downtown Portland and other employment districts.[15]

People living in neighborhoods that qualify as being there may drive less because driving distances tend to be shorter (rather than because they take more trips on transit). Most of the residents of a sample of neighborhoods in downtown Orlando, Florida, that are new urbanist in character —containing a grid street network, a mix of uses, and a variety of housing types—drive to work in nearby Orlando.[16] (Driving even short distances to work is encouraged by employer-provided free parking.) Only one in four residents walks to neighborhood destinations as many as ten times a year, mostly to convenience stores and parks. But their driving trips to work and to other destinations are less than one mile on average, which is considerably shorter than other auto trips in this car-oriented region.

Being there is a transportation solution that both developers and public agencies can work to promote. Developers can help by selecting sites that have good connections to nearby services and to regional concentrations of development and by designing their projects to provide as convenient as possible access to those services and concentrations. Public agencies can help by making development in urban and urbanizing areas—where regulatory disincentives abound—easier and by increasing access to a variety of travel modes in these areas.

Protecting and Improving Highway Capacity

The highway network in every metropolitan area is a critical economic and social asset. This network should be preserved and enhanced through programs to reduce congestion and increase the efficiency and safety of highway travel.

Access Management

By and large, highways should be designed to accommodate relatively long-distance trips rather than incidental trips. The number of intersections and entrances to highways should be limited to avoid the traffic-flow disruptions of turns onto or off of the road. This is called access management.

Public agencies can control access to a new highway by restrictions put in place during land acquisition and planning. Limiting access to an existing highway may be tougher—especially if highway-oriented uses such as strip shopping centers have already sprung up along significant stretches of it. Even in these situations, however, the number of entrances to adjoining uses can still be limited by, for example, constructing service roads or by the adoption of minimum requirements for the spacing of entrances.

Safety-Oriented Improvements

Many arterial roads and highways that were built for lower traffic volumes and speeds than they now experience stand in need of safety upgrades. Growing congestion and complex traffic movements, especially at intersections, raise the risk of accidents. Making highways safer also increases capacity by reducing the number of accidents that tie up traffic.

Many safety upgrades represent a relatively inexpensive means of improving highway capacity. Among the possibilities are improving signage and signalization, correcting certain design hazards such as discontinuous lanes, and adding acceleration and deceleration lanes at intersections.

Capacity-Oriented Programs

Transportation experts have paid a great deal of attention in recent years to reducing congestion by encouraging the more efficient use of existing highways. This fix-it-first approach is faster, cheaper, and usually less disruptive to traffic flows than major road construction or reconstruction projects.

Many capacity-oriented approaches have been proved effective in providing relief for congested highways—although, over time, they may fail to keep up with increased demand from continued development in the highway's trafficshed. Improving traffic signalization can help get traffic moving better, as can quickly clearing disabled vehicles from the roadway. High-tech surveillance and traffic-control systems known as intelligent information devices, which can incorporate real-time communications with travelers (showing, for example, the best routes), can help keep traffic moving.

Dedicated high-occupancy-vehicle (HOV) lanes for buses and carpools have proved successful in many highway corridors, allowing speeds twice that of rail transit. Carpool or vanpool programs operated in conjunction with HOV facilities can offer commuters a highly effective alternative to solo driving. On some toll highways, charging a higher peak-hour toll has worked to limit peak-hour traffic.

Transportation Demand Management

Transportation demand management (TDM) programs involve measures, including information clearinghouses and financial incentives, to increase travel choices and people's awareness of them in order to reduce solo driving. They are more effective if they are a collaborative effort among a number of sizable individual developments or among an area's property owners and developers. Collaborative TDM can be managed though a transportation management association (TMA), which can include developers, major businesses, and public agencies. A TMA spreads the burden and costs of TDM and gives more parties than the directly affected commuters a stake in commute alternatives.

Ride-matching—matching up commuters who are interested in carpooling, based on a variety of criteria, including location of home and workplace and personal compatibility—is a basic TDM service. So is determining the best transit route for individual commuters. Other TDM services, which may be provided by employers and public agencies, include organizing and providing financial support for vanpools, which typically carry seven to 15 people traveling long distances, and financial incentives to encourage people to use transit.

Voluntary programs to reduce solo driving can be effective when employers are solidly committed to them. Otherwise, the results of such programs tend to be lackluster, even when they involve financial and other incentives. When traffic reduction is made a condition of development approvals, the developer has a greater stake in implementing an effective program. But this developer's burden still does not constitute a stick compelling the participation of businesses and their workers.

It may be more effective to place the requirement for reducing traffic on the landowner rather than the developer, especially in business parks where the property is sold to companies. Or, at the extreme, all businesses—or at least large businesses—could be required to participate in TDM and penalties could be assessed for noncompliance. The South Coast Air Quality District serving the Los Angeles basin tried this approach, but switched to a voluntary program because of political pressures. Not surprisingly, when the program became voluntary, participation dropped.

The focus of most of the early TDM programs and TMAs was on sprawling suburban business parks designed to depend almost exclusively on car access. Such after-the-fact attempts to open up opportunities for other travel modes can have some good results, but designing alternative travel options as part of a project from the beginning of the development process is likely to have much better results in terms of traffic reduction.

New Construction

Adding highway capacity encourages people to live in low-density areas far from their work and other destinations, according to many die-hard opponents of proposed new highway construction or highway enlargements. More highways make possible longer commutes, in this view, a contention that is borne out by the data on growth in vehicle-miles traveled (VMT) reported earlier in this chapter. Commuters are traveling longer distances to work but average commuting times remain unchanged.

In one highway corridor after another across the nation, the result of capacity expansions has been sprawl. This is because efforts to manage growth concurrently with highway construction are rare. Development along a corridor generates traffic that after a while threatens to reach gridlock (although it rarely actually reaches that point). This creates demand for more or larger highways. New capacity expansions allow a new round of development even farther out, restarting the cycle. Eventually, employers and retailers shift their locations outward to be nearer their employees and customers, adding to the need for more highway expansions.

Can roads be built to meet the real and rising needs for traffic improvements in both the built-up and developing areas of growing communities without unduly encouraging sprawl development? The simple answer is that roads must be built to serve new development and new travel needs. The more complex answer is that any highway construction that is undertaken should be in the context of an integrated approach to transportation needs, as discussed in the next section.

Serving Real Needs

The problem of serving real and rising needs for mobility in inner and outer parts of growing communities while controlling the spread of urban sprawl is a knotty one that resists an easy answer. Solutions will no doubt be easier to find if communities adopt an integrated approach that seeks a workable balance of transportation modes. There are perhaps five key elements of such an integrated approach:

▲ an interconnected network of high-speed highways and associated arterial roads that provides a basic framework for mobility within and between metropolitan areas;
▲ a collateral network of local and regional transit services designed to function interactively with highway travel;
▲ webs of local streets, transit service, and walking/biking pathways that provide multiple opportunities for satisfying local travel demand and thus reduce demand on long-distance road and transit capacities;
▲ town centers and regional business districts that are multiuse and pedestrian friendly, so one trip—whether by car or transit—can serve multiple purposes; and
▲ development regulation in support of a workable balance of transportation modes.

This last element, supportive development regulation, includes restrictions on sprawling development that lives only by the road as well as policy and planning commitments to the emergence of concentrated development that is transit-oriented and walkable in both urbanizing and greenfield areas.

Moving in the direction of a workable balance of transportation modes clearly will call for much greater regional coordination of various transportation modes and for paying more attention to the relationship between transportation systems and land use patterns, a subject that is revisited in chapter 8.

Investing in Transit

The relatively small role transit plays in urban travel in the United States is often referred to as evidence of its irrelevance for solving traffic problems. However, transit use is growing and transit serves some important purposes. In 2001, transit ridership grew by 1 to 2 percent, marking the sixth year in a row in which transit use grew faster than highway use, according to the American Public Transportation Association.

Today's market for transit has three major components, according to the U.S. Department of Transportation.[17] These may be characterized as transit dependents, transit diehards (patrons by choice), and traffic evaders, as follows:

▲ **Transit dependents.** For some people, transit provides basic mobility. It is the fallback mode of travel for people without cars because of income or other limitations. Transit dependents represent the core constituency of most transit agencies, accounting for 40 percent of transit trips in 1995.

▲ **Transit diehards.** Transit diehards are transit patrons who can afford to own cars but are carless by choice. They typically live in areas with good access to transit and with many services within walking distance. Such individuals account for 25 percent of transit riders (data from 1995).

▲ **Traffic evaders.** Traffic evaders, or people who choose transit as an alternative to driving, account for 35 percent of transit trips. Traffic evaders choose transit—mostly rail transit—especially for work commutes over long distances or through crowded transportation corridors.

Transit diehards tend to live or work in transit-friendly areas. For example, half the increase in

transit ridership in the United States during the 1990s occurred in New York City. Smart growth in its desire to take people out of their cars and seas of parking out of activity centers aims primarily at this market, people who can be convinced to use transit to get to destinations and to walk between uses within destinations if the opportunities to do so are attractive. Traffic evaders tend to live in areas less well served by transit. They require high-speed, high-amenity services that may entail driving to transit stops.

Types of Transit Systems

This section describes the variety of transit systems that can serve transit markets and patterns of land use that can support transit.

Average speeds and the spacing of stops are key elements in transit systems, along with capital and operating costs. The principal types of transit systems are listed here in a generally increasing order of cost.

▲ **Local-bus service.** Local buses operating on fixed routes are the workhorses of public transit. They carry two-thirds of the transit trips in the United States. Frequent stops make local service slow but convenient, offering riders short walks to and from bus stops. Bus service is very flexible in its ability to change routes and add buses to meet demand.

▲ **Express-bus service.** Express buses typically operate with limited or no-stop service on part of the route, thus offering faster trips than local buses. Most express-bus service is on routes between downtown and outlying areas. Some regions are experimenting with express-bus service between suburban business complexes. Express buses can pick up passengers in park-and-ride lots near freeway exits and then travel on the freeway to downtown, sometimes on express lanes. Riders have only a short drive to the pickup point and the convenience of nonstop freeway service to downtown. Bus rapid transit, a transit option being offered on a demonstration basis in a handful of metropolitan areas, operates on its own guideway much like a rail system and achieves high average speeds.

▲ **Light rail.** Previously known as trolleys, light-rail trains travel at moderate speeds in mixed traffic on existing streets or on exclusive rights-of-way with at grade crossings for cross traffic. Sharing the street avoids the cost of securing a

Figure 4-5 Comparative Statistics for Transit Modes

	Average Speed (mph)	Miles Between Stops	Operating Expenses	
			Per Trip	Per Passenger-Mile
Local Bus	13	0.125	$2.04	$0.54
Express Bus	30[1]	1–5	—	—
Light Rail	16	0.25–0.5	$1.81	$0.44
Heavy Rail	20	0.75	$1.48	$0.29
Commuter Rail	33	3	$6.19	$0.27

1. Average speed for bus rapid transit in demonstration projects in Denver, Pittsburgh, San Diego, and San Jose.

Source: Federal Transit Administration.

Transit Tales

Transit has become a significant element in the transportation mix of a number of spread-out Sunbelt cities, even though it carries a small share of trips outside downtown. In Atlanta in 1990, for example, 7 percent of trips in the region and 17 percent of trips in the city were by public transit. These cities have made great strides in transit even while continuing to expand their highway systems. Four of the more successful Sunbelt transit programs are described here.

Atlanta

Atlanta voted in 1971 to fund a heavy-rail system under the Metropolitan Atlanta Rapid Transit Authority (MARTA). MARTA rail is highly ranked nationally and is clearly the best such system in the South. Even though rail service is limited to only two counties—Fulton and DeKalb—and the system has less than half the rail mileage of San Francisco's Bay Area Rapid Transit (BART) system,

MARTA rail carries trips equal to 90 percent of trips carried by BART. Bus ridership on the MARTA system is also strong, totaling about the same number of trips as rail trips.

Houston

Houston embarked on a major mobility initiative in the 1980s, and transit is an important part of the package. A regional sales tax was adopted in 1978 to fund a 95-mile system of express-bus and HOV lanes, allowing bus speeds above 50 miles per hour. Bus ridership doubled between 1980 and 1990. (Since 1990, the growth in bus ridership has slowed.)

San Diego

In 1975, the Metropolitan Transit Development Board (MTDB) was created to coordinate six transit operators in the San Diego region. MTDB initiated light-rail service in 1981. It has become the most

successful new light-rail system in the United States in terms of growth in ridership, with a combined bus and rail ridership gain of 159 percent from 1980 to 2000 and 53 percent from 1990 to 2000.

Phoenix

Bus ridership in Phoenix doubled during the 1980s. However, two efforts to enact a countywide sales tax to fund an expansion of transit service to meet demand failed. Finally, the city of Tempe enacted such a sales tax in 1996, and Phoenix did so in 1997. With this funding in hand, the region is now constructing a 20-mile, $1.2 billion rail system. The transit plan includes expanded conventional bus service as well as high-speed bus service.

---

separate right-of-way, but also makes light rail subject to traffic delays and thus lowers speeds.
▲ Heavy rail. Heavy-rail service operates on exclusive rights-of-way without grade crossings and often is placed in underground subways. Heavy-rail stations are spaced generally farther apart than are light-rail stops, especially on the outer segments of lines.
▲ Commuter rail. Commuter-rail lines provide high-speed service to downtowns over long distances. The Long Island Railroad and Chicago's METRA are examples of traditional commuter-rail operations. A number of communities, such as Dallas and Seattle, recently have established commuter-rail service. Commuter rail with station parking often draws riders who drive in from a wide area around each station.

Supportive Development Strategies

To be effective, investment in transit needs to be reinforced with development strategies aimed at building a compelling market for transit. The best markets for transit (in terms of market share) are to be found, ironically, in basically stagnant development markets, specifically in the large Snowbelt cities of New York, Boston, Philadelphia, and Chicago. On the other hand, transit has a low

market share in many large Sunbelt communities—places like Atlanta, Charlotte, Orlando, Houston, Dallas, Phoenix, and Los Angeles—where rapid development is occurring but at low densities.

These fast-growth communities need to find an appropriate transit paradigm. Seminal research on the transit friendliness of various forms of development was conducted under the auspices of the New York Regional Plan Association.[18] It determined that the likelihood of people using public transportation will increase:

▲ the higher the density and larger the size of the downtown;
▲ the closer people live to downtown; and
▲ the better the transit service.

Transit use in U.S. metropolitan areas illustrates these factors. Classic downtowns like New York, Philadelphia, and San Francisco constitute important destinations for commuters, are well served by radial transit lines, are densely built, and contain a mix of uses and pedestrian pathways—all of which make transit desirable and successful in these cities. Furthermore, parking is expensive and transit service is relatively cheap.

Figure 4-6 Minimum Densities for Supporting Transit[1]

	Intermediate Service Local Bus[2]	Frequent Local Bus[3]	Light Rail[4]	Rapid Transit[5]
Dwelling Units per Acre	7	15	9	12
Residents per Acre	18	38	23	30
Employees per Acre	20	75	125+	—

1. Employment (destination) density is more important in influencing trips than residential (origin) densities.
2. Average density; varies as a function of downtown size and distance to downtown.
3. Average density over a two-square-mile tributary area.
4. Average density for a corridor of 25 to 100 square miles; transit to downtowns with 20 million to 30 million square feet of nonresidential space.
5. Average density for a corridor of 100 to 150 square miles; transit to downtowns with more than 50 million square feet of nonresidential space.
Sources: For residential densities: Boris Pushkarev and Jeffrey Zupan, *Public Transportation and Land Use Policy* (1997). For employment densities: Reid Ewing, "Transit-Oriented Development in the Sunbelt," *Transportation Research Record 1552* (1996); and Lawrence Frank and Gary Pivo, *Relationship between Land Use and Travel Behavior in the Puget Sound Region* (1994).

The downtowns of newer cities and edge cities and other suburban activity centers are usually less densely built and usually poorly served by transit —making them much less attractive to transit users. And driving is easy and parking free. The job centers that are scattered around the fringes of metropolitan areas are even more difficult—almost impossible—to serve economically by transit.

Transit service is feasible at minimum levels of density, depending on the type of service and the acceptable cost per passenger-mile. The average density of development most supportive of transit travel at accepted levels of cost has been the subject of several studies. (See figure 4-6.) Transit could serve lower densities than those indicated in figure 4-6 only with sharp increases in costs per passenger-mile.

The development densities that typify suburban areas generally are not conducive to transit service. Even an intermediate level of local-bus service (buses every half hour) requires seven or more dwelling units per acre and 20 employees per acre on average. Light-rail transit requires nine or more dwelling units per acre along an extended rail corridor leading to a downtown containing at least 23 million to 30 million square feet of non-residential space.

Transit trips increase sharply in cities with population densities above 10,000 people per square mile, according to a 1990 survey, from under 0.1 daily trips per capita at densities of 7,500 to 10,000 people per square mile (roughly five housing units per acre) to 0.5 trips per capita at densities of 10,000 to 50,000 persons per square mile.[19] However, only 7 percent of U.S. households in 1990 lived in such high-density areas.

A strong correlation exists among transit use for commuting, residential density, employment density, and the mix of uses, according to a study in Seattle.[20] Employment density becomes especially significant above the threshold of 75 employees per acre. Research shows that the most important variable affecting transit use is not density itself, but what goes along with density—that is, the type of use, the mix of uses, and the emergence of major traffic congestion.

The density requirements of transit service mean that the successful extension of transit service to urbanizing and suburbanizing areas depends on creating compact, mixed-use nodes of development. Such nodes can emerge over time, as experience demonstrates in places such as Bethesda, Maryland; Arlington, Virginia; and San Diego. But their development requires a supportive public policy context that promotes and supports higher-density growth along transit routes.

People make choices among travel modes based on trip frequencies, trip distances, and the number of mode changes required per trip. People will drive a car to work every day, for example, if the alternative is taking three buses or biking 30 miles. Many studies have demonstrated that how these factors affect choices is closely linked to socioeconomic characteristics.

According to an analysis by transportation researchers Reid Ewing and Robert Cervero of more than 50 recent studies of travel and the built environment, how frequently people make trips is primarily related to their socioeconomic characteristics and secondarily dependent on the characteristics of development where they are going or whence they are coming.[21] For example, people who can afford to drive (socioeconomic characteristic) and who can park inexpensively at their destinations (characteristic of development) usually choose to use cars quite often.

On the other hand, how far people travel on trips is related most closely to the characteristics of the built environment and secondarily to socioeconomic characteristics. People who live in communities that are close-in and intensively developed typically make shorter trips than those who live in rural areas far from their workplaces. What travel mode people choose depends on both socioeconomic and place characteristics, though probably more on socioeconomic factors.

Some evidence that the form of development affects auto travel behavior comes from the Institute of Transportation Engineers' handbook on traffic impacts titled *Trip Generation*. According to this handbook, the average single-family house, for example, generates about ten trips in or out daily, while a typical high-rise apartment building generates about four daily trips per housing unit. (Demographics are of course responsible for some of this difference to the extent that single-family houses tend to contain larger households with higher incomes.) More evidence comes from the Ewing and Cervero analysis of recent travel studies, which concludes that compared with typical suburban style development, communities developed with greater density, a greater diversity of uses, and connective design generate up to 13 percent fewer auto trips.[22]

A Natural Resources Defense Council study compares the driving behavior of residents of relatively high density neighborhoods with the driving habits of residents of neighborhoods half as dense. People in the higher-density neighborhoods drive an average of 20 to 30 percent less.[23] This study refers to nationwide data for 1990 that indicate a similar density/driving relationship.

There is little question that neighborhoods and communities rich in transportation options (including walking and biking) and local destinations take cars off the road and shorten car trips. The challenges faced in smart growth are to advertise the advantages of less suburban lifestyles to strengthen the market for living in such neighborhoods, to expand development opportunities in transportation-rich communities, and to keep on improving transportation services to meet the needs of expanding populations in these areas.

However, shifting mode choices away from driving, transportation experts warn, may not significantly reduce overall driving. Demand expands to fit capacity. Substantial improvements to transit service could result in both greater transit use and the quick absorption of the highway capacity thus gained by people driving as much or more than before. Similarly, making walking easier might increase pedestrian activity, especially for recreational purposes, but have little effect on total car use.

In the final analysis, the travel decisions of individuals depend on a variety of factors—such as housing location, work location, and opinions on what is an acceptable level of congestion—that change over time. Smart growth hopes to achieve its transportation goals by expanding opportunities for people to make different travel choices that fit their needs and their pocketbooks.

Promoting Nonmotorized Travel

Walking and biking, sometimes grouped as nonmotorized travel, have received much less attention from transportation planners than has transit. Traditional travel forecasting models project highway and transit trips and ignore foot or bicycle trips or treat them as leftover trips.

Walking is probably the biggest victim of auto-dependent development patterns in which uses are spaced too far apart for people to walk between them and sidewalks and other pedestrian pathways are either nonexistent or unconnected to popular destinations. Suburban commercial strips rarely are designed to entice pedestrians. Many of the arterial streets that serve strip shopping centers seem to be designed to thwart walking. Even walking to school is a risky venture in many suburbs. With the decline in walking has come widespread obesity, leading the Centers for Disease Control to say that suburban design patterns may be affecting public health.

Short trip opportunities that are suitable for walking are what makes walking a travel alternative. These are provided by compact development that includes attractive sidewalks and pathways. The average walking trip is about two-thirds of a mile (compared with two miles for bicycle trips and ten miles for car trips).[24] Therefore, walking origins and destinations are best placed no more than one-quarter mile apart, and the pathways between them must be attractive for walkers.

A 1997 ULI panel recommended promoting walking in downtown Bellevue, Washington, as part of a revitalization strategy for the central business district. The panel's strategy called for pedestrian-friendly, green streets—with landscaping, lower speed limits, and on-street parking—as opposed to urban streets focused mainly on automobile access and traffic movement.[25]

Metro, the regional agency for Portland, Oregon, measures walkability (and bikability) in neighborhoods by reference to four attributes of effective pedestrian environments.[26] These attributes include:

▲ easy street crossings;
▲ sidewalk continuity;
▲ local-street connectivity; and
▲ relatively flat topography.

Portland neighborhoods exhibit sharp differences in walkability (and bikability) based on these measures. Almost one in five trips within downtown are by walking or biking. Walking and biking make up only 7 to 8 percent of trips within the rest of the city of Portland and under 2 percent of trips within suburban jurisdictions. In Metro's view, putting a pedestrian-oriented development (or a new urbanist community) on an isolated site in a car-dominated suburb will not lead to the kinds of beneficial mode choices found in traditional neighborhoods.

Among U.S. transportation experts, biking gets even less respect than walking as a means of travel. Political pressure from cyclists has resulted in an

increase in bike paths, and bicycle facilities are becoming common at transit stations and workplaces. But biking is treated primarily as a recreational pursuit needing only pathways through parks. Bike paths that can serve commuting and other travel purposes remain a rarity on principal metropolitan traffic routes.

This disrespect of biking as a travel choice is not so much the case in Europe. In Munich, a reduction in speed limits for motor vehicles combined with an expansion of the bike-path network and bicycle parking facilities tripled the number of bicycle trips.[27] Attitudes have much to do with the potential for bicycle travel. According to a European Union study of the potential for substituting walking and cycling for short car trips, residents of Barcelona are reluctant to travel by bike because of safety concerns, while committed cyclists living in Amsterdam and Copenhagen, cities in countries with more of a cycling tradition, would travel by bike under almost any circumstance.[28]

Connecting Transportation Systems

Major highways and transit links generally do a good job of connecting primary destinations. It is the connections from primary destinations to networks of local streets and bus routes that can be maddeningly inconvenient.

Transportation agencies operating at the regional level and metropolitan planning organizations responsible for long-range planning have an important role to play in improving transportation connectivity.

At the community level, local governments must stop erecting walls and instead build connections to surrounding communities and encourage connections within the community. They should establish development policies that promote connectivity. Among these may be incentives for development to locate near transit lines and stations, design guidelines for projects aimed at improving their access to transit, and planning for a network of arterial roads to link local destinations (such as shops and schools) without requiring the use of main roads.

At the project level, developers and site designers need to establish good connectivity to adjacent properties as well as within their developments.

The design of most recently developed suburban projects does just the opposite, forcing all trips—even those from one development to a neighboring one—onto adjacent arterial streets. Suburban design also creates pressure to locate all commercial development along arterial streets or highways. A well-connected development creates multiple points for access to outside destinations; it provides direct road and pedestrian routes to nearby destinations and transit stops.

Rio Vista West, one of the first transit-oriented developments in San Diego, exemplifies better connectivity in project design. It was developed under guidelines adopted by the city in 1992. Sited adjacent to a station on the San Diego Trolley line, Rio Vista West comprises 1,000 units of moderate-density housing, a mixed-use village adjacent to the station, and a highway-oriented shopping center along the main road.

Including a big-box shopping center as part of a transit-oriented development was controversial. It is, however, located in the part of the property farthest from the trolley station and, more important, when Rio Vista West's development began in the mid 1990s, it was the only one of the components that had strong market appeal. With the turnaround in California's economy in recent years, the transit-oriented housing and commercial components have become more marketable.

When road systems are connected, taking steps to tame traffic within and through neighborhoods is critical. Slowing down the speed of traffic helps create a good walking neighborhood, and also makes bicycling more attractive.

Making sure that residential streets are properly designed for their function is the key to traffic calming.[29] The paramount function of streets in residential developments is to provide access to residences; the smooth movement of through traffic is only a secondary function. Long, wide, and straight streets built to accommodate through traffic encourage speeding—and they have been the cause of many neighborhood battles over traffic.

"Yield flow" is the name given by the American Association of State Highway and Transportation Officials (AASHTO) to the condition of one unobstructed moving lane on a road, requiring opposing traffic to yield and pause on the parking lane until there is sufficient room to pass. Yield flow is the condition under which the vast majority of streets in the United States operate, and AASHTO endorses such traffic operations.

Supportive Parking Strategies

Parking is the Rodney Dangerfield of transportation. It gets no respect from planners. This is unfortunate because the design of parking is a critical factor in introducing the potential for walkability and vibrant street life in projects.

"Parking drives development," says developer Christopher Leinberger, "because you need far more space to park cars than to house people."[30] A 1 million-square-foot mall (equivalent to 23 acres), for example, would require 44 acres for parking based on a parking ratio of six spaces per 1,000 square feet of floor space. The 1999 edition of ULI's Shopping Center Development Handbook reports that some recently developed shopping centers use 2.5 to 3.5 times as much land for parking as for the retail structure. Chicago developer Jeffrey Gelman agrees that the first consideration in building a new project is not architecture, but parking. "I start with parking, then I go back into the number of units, then I back into the financials," he says.[31]

Zoning ordinances generally require developers to provide parking on site. The amount of parking required is often excessive. Public officials often want to give themselves a comfortable margin of error to make sure that no neighbor is ever inconvenienced by parking generated by a project they approve.

With conventional suburban parking ratios of five spaces per 1,000 square feet of building space, at least 50 percent more square footage will be devoted to parking than to space under roof. According to city estimates, parking covers 54 percent of the site of a typical commercial development in Olympia, Washington—while the building covers half that much of the site. Parking lots for apartment and townhouse complexes usually occupy a smaller but still considerable portion of residential sites.

The seas of parking around most of the commercial and apartment and townhouse projects in suburbs make them virtually inaccessible except by car, even from neighboring development. In denser developments, such as business parks and regional shopping malls located in established urban areas, structured parking becomes economic, enabling buildings to be developed within walking distance of each other. In some cities and mature suburbs, public parking garages are provided to support town centers and other business concentrations.

Parking should be thoughtfully planned and designed so that it can both serve the demand for parking and contribute to the attractiveness of the destination. A variety of parking strategies are available to further the goals of smart growth, as described in the following sections.

Downsized Parking

The amount of space devoted to parking can be most effectively and least painfully reduced within projects by not supplying more parking spaces than demand warrants and by providing less space per vehicle. More fundamentally, parking demand can be managed—primarily by offering meaningful alternatives to driving—to reduce parking needs. But the demand that remains should be served; not to serve it would impair the marketability of the development's uses and encourage spillover parking in adjoining areas.

How much parking is enough? Most developers say that local codes, not traffic studies, determine their parking levels. The parking requirements in local codes are typically based on the parking ratios promulgated by the Institute of Transportation Engineers or on what other cities require. In jurisdictions without the resources for localized parking studies, which means most jurisdictions, traffic engineers often take a fairly simplistic approach to estimating parking needs, based almost exclusively on a single variable: floor space.

According to a 1998 survey by ULI and the International Council of Shopping Centers of 169 shopping centers, parking demand peaks at 4.5 spaces per 1,000 square feet of gross leasable area.[32] (Surveys taken in the 1980s indicate that demand peaked then at a higher five spaces per 1,000 square feet of GLA.) Centers with a significant amount of space used most heavily at nighttime— such as restaurants or cinemas—have even lower peak-parking requirements. Detailed studies like this one can help make the case for downsizing local parking requirements.

Local governments are not the only players in the parking ratio game. The standard site plans of many national retailers and other businesses often include a high level of parking. Good data can persuade corporate planners to reduce those levels. For example, Wal-Mart has gone into an outdated regional mall in Englewood, Colorado, that was redeveloped with a transit orientation. Although Wal-Mart usually requires six spaces per 1,000 square feet of GLA, the company was persuaded to accept a city standard of five spaces per 1,000 square feet on the basis that a sizable share of shoppers would use transit.

On-Street Parking

For transportation engineers, the idea of parking on streets is close to heresy. Their standard approach is to eliminate on-street parking in order to preserve the traffic capacity of roads. But among community designers a different approach is gaining ground, namely to reinstate on-street parking as a means of slowing traffic, providing more convenient access to buildings along the streets, and adding pedestrian activity. In this view, streets are considered more as significant public places and less as trafficways.

Mizner Park, a former mall redeveloped as a mixed-use, neotraditional downtown for Boca Raton, Florida, uses on-street parking to enliven its concept of being a village in the city. Two parallel streets, each lined on one side with retail and residential buildings, face a linear central park. These streets are designed with special pavers, plaza details, and parking on both sides. The on-street parking is an attractive alternative to the structured parking behind the stores and restaurants.[33]

Behind-the-Store Parking

Placing parking behind rather than in front of buildings helps to preserve an attractive streetscape and improve pedestrian access to bordering activities, and it provides an urban border for the street. Behind-the-store parking is not a novel idea —it is commonplace in many small-town downtowns—but it flies in the face of standard designs for commercial strip centers, which strive to showcase available parking as their chief attraction to consumers. Nevertheless, town centers that feature parking lots or parking structures behind buildings that line the streets are being developed in many suburban communities.

Shared Parking

The concept of shared parking, which ULI developed in the 1980s as an element of mixed-use development, is simple. If different uses generate parking demand that peaks at different times and if the parking spaces are available for all the uses, one parking space can do double (or triple) duty. Parking for office uses, for example, peaks in the morning while parking for restaurants peaks during meal times. Providing exclusive parking for each of these uses would require a combined total of five to six spaces per 1,000 square feet of GLA and each parking area would be empty much of the time. Providing shared parking for these uses would require only 2.5 to three spaces per 1,000 square feet of GLA, and these spaces would be more fully occupied throughout the day.

Albina Place, a mixed residential and retail project in Portland, Oregon, used a shared-parking model. Lenders were convinced that sharing parking was feasible when they saw that parking lots in the project's neighborhood were virtually empty during the day. A total of 42 off-street spaces provides parking for 48 apartment units on nights and weekends and for 12,000 square feet of retail on weekdays.

Shared parking can be located off site if it is a convenient walking distance from the uses it serves. Well-located parking facilities—private and public—in downtowns often serve multiple uses. However, if regulations require on-site parking, which is frequently the case, developers cannot take advantage of such nearby facilities.

The adaptive use of the American Can Company complex in Baltimore for a mixed-use office and retail project received a parking variance from the city on the basis of shared parking. The infill site presented a parking challenge. The developer adapted two floors of one building for a parking garage dedicated to office use during the day and retail use during the evening and provided a surface lot as well. But parking still fell short of meeting total demand, so the developer arranged to use 45 spaces in a nearby municipal lot. Because of the shared demand, the city allowed a variance from its normal parking requirements.

Coming full circle from requiring on-site parking for every development, many communities have been willing to provide parking for redevelopment projects. Typically this parking is in public facilities that are shared among several user groups. For example, in old town Pasadena, the city pledged provision of parking as part of development approvals. In Bethesda, Maryland, the county's parking authority constructed a 1,000-car garage in the center of a redeveloped retail block, a critical element of the success of the highly acclaimed Bethesda Row (see page 129).

Structured Parking

Structured parking's smaller footprint makes parking a less obtrusive use and helps produce a more urban environment. Whether placed underground where it can serve as the foundation for buildings or above ground, parking structures can be designed to minimize the impact of parking on the appearance of projects and on pedestrian access—often by linking the structure directly to adjoining offices and retail uses or by providing such uses on the ground floor of the parking garage.

Although much more costly than surface parking, structured parking is a viable option in areas with high-priced land or with inadequate space for surface parking. Once land reaches $30 per square foot, structured parking saves enough in land costs to compensate for the additional construction costs.[34]

Pacific Place in downtown Seattle (see page 126) and Bethesda Row in Bethesda, Maryland, illustrate design possibilities for structured parking in areas where land values are escalating. In both projects, the parking structures were integrated unobtrusively into retail clusters. The Pacific Place garage serves adjoining stores and three levels of retail and entertainment uses above it. The Bethesda Row garage is built in the center of a block to provide parking for the retail uses that line the streets around the block.

The Safeco Insurance Company headquarters in Redmond, Washington, illustrates some of the virtues of structured parking. The headquarters expansion in 1999 included three underground parking garages built at a cost of $18,000 per space. Placing the parking underground preserves green space and avoids impediments to walking around the campus. Safeco has a transportation demand management plan similar to the TDM programs described earlier in this chapter. Because the company intends to reduce solo driving to work by its employees, it was allowed to limit parking for the space added in the headquarters expansion to 2.1 spaces per 1,000 square feet, instead of providing the normal three spaces per 1,000 square feet.[35]

Structured parking also opens up the option to charge for parking, a strategy beloved by economists and environmentalists alike as a means of recouping otherwise hidden subsidies for providing parking.

Smarter Financing for Transportation

Economists assert that current transportation systems and growth patterns represent rational decisions by people optimizing their economic choices relating to how they travel and where they live. People choose housing (and business space) in suburban rather than urban locations because of lower costs, which compensate for the higher transportation costs of a distant location. People choose cars over transit because of lower costs (calculated as direct capital and operating costs) and more convenience (better service). People choose to drive in peak hours because their calculations of the cost of doing so does not include the public cost of providing peak-hour capacity on the highway system.

The manner in which transportation facilities are financed and priced to users will therefore affect travel modes. Subsidizing driving or hiding some of its costs will encourage driving. Subsidizing public transportation will attract riders. Free parking, a treasured perk of corporate life, will encourage driving to wherever it is offered—work, shopping center, or transit station.

The actual costs of travel for individuals and for society as a whole are not often apparent. Economists argue that revealing the full costs of various modes of travel will allow people to make smarter choices about where they live, where they work, and how they travel. Transportation solutions for smart growth therefore will require making transportation costs visible, or making known the extent to which various travel modes are subsidized. Furthermore, such solutions may depend on adopting financing mechanisms that directly affect mode choices by better relating people's payment for transportation with their use of transportation.

The Subsidy Argument

Much of the debate over transportation solutions concerns the calculation of the so-called "real" costs of various travel modes. Real costs account not only for direct capital and operating costs, but also for unrecognized or indirect costs.

That cars pay their own way by covering the costs of highway improvements is a myth according to many transit proponents. They argue that although the federal Highway Trust Fund, which is financed by gasoline taxes, covers most of the capital expenses for improving and maintaining certain categories of highways, auto use is still subsidized in numerous ways. Among major auto use subsidies are free parking (subsidized by employers or other providers), tax exemptions for the business use of cars, spending on highway police services, and spending on highway emergency response services. Furthermore, say these transit proponents, driving imposes costs on people who do not drive and on society as a whole, but drivers are not charged for such costs.

In 1991, Mark DeLucchi of the University of California at Davis developed estimates of the hidden costs of car travel. According to this analysis, motorists receive a hidden subsidy of more than $1 trillion annually. Among the costs they give rise to but are not asked to pay are the costs of air pollution, the time (delay) cost of congestion, and the cost of parking provided by retailers and employers. Applied to the number of miles driven in 1991, the car travel subsidy amounts to $.38 per mile.[36]

Transit too involves high costs and subsidies, counter proponents of investment in highway improvements. They cite the high capital and operating costs of transit per rider and per mile. The overall subsidy for transit is said to be about $.38 per passenger mile (the same as DeLucchi's estimate of the subsidy for car travel). Highway proponents also point to transit's declining share in total trips (even while transit ridership is rising), despite major investment in transit improvements in many cities.

Whatever the relative merits of different transportation systems in terms of their subsidy requirements, the substantial reduction of subsidies or their removal is quite difficult. Except for a few isolated cases, says a recent report prepared for

Transport Canada, governments at every level have taken little action to make transportation costs more visible.[37] And, as has been argued in this chapter, smart growth proposes that rising travel demand in U.S. metropolitan areas puts all transportation systems, whatever their subsidy requirements, in need of greater investment and more effective integration.

Matching Payment to Use

Transportation facilities are funded in a variety of ways, from direct fees, fares, and tolls to taxes on gasoline, retail sales, and development. Some of these funding sources are direct user charges, while others collect money from users and non-users alike. Many transportation experts think that better relating the incidence (or timing) of payments to use would be a workable way to enhance people's understanding of the real user costs of various travel modes.

A growing range of technology-driven mechanisms for collecting fares makes matching payments to use faster, more convenient, and cashless. Among the various transportation funding mechanisms that are available are the following, some of which are more direct than others in the incidence of payment and therefore smarter in terms of bringing home real costs for various transportation modes.

▲ **Paying at the pump.** Fuel taxes are the conventional means of financing highway improvements. Fuel cost is a use price that is regularly visible to drivers. (The greater cost of the car, insurance, and depreciation is, by contrast, divorced in time from the use of the vehicle.) Unfortunately for highway revenues, most fuel taxes are assessed on a fixed fee per gallon, so that improvements in fuel efficiency lower revenues. Raising gas taxes is politically unpopular.

▲ **Paying by the trip.** Requiring travelers to pay by the trip makes them consider costs in making travel decisions. Paying by the trip is the traditional method of charging for public transportation. The fare requirement can penalize transit in the minds of potential users. Highway tolls are a trip fare for drivers. Toll collection is a historical means of financing roads, and it is making a return in some high-growth areas.

Toll collection is smart transportation because it forces drivers to consider whether the trip is worth the cost each time it is made. A refinement on the concept of highway tolls offers drivers access to less congested roadways for a higher toll. Dubbed "Lexus lanes" by critics, the few such projects in operation suggest that lower-income drivers as well may choose to pay more to save time.

▲ **Paying periodically.** Some highway toll facilities offer monthly payment arrangements similar to access fees by Internet service providers. (Some transit systems offer weekly or other periodic passes, sparing commuters the twice-daily fumbling for the right coins and bills and significantly reducing fare collection costs for transit agencies.) Drivers on a budget can benefit from the predictability of a monthly charge. Although monthly payments move the incidence of payment away from the actual travel, periodic toll bills may be high enough in combination with periodic credit-card gasoline payments and car insurance payments to affect driving behavior.

▲ **Local sales taxes.** The use of sales taxes to finance transportation improvements is increasing in some states. When sales taxes are used for building roads, the argument can be made that such improvements benefit not just drivers but society broadly—and since the majority of the population drives anyway, it matters little whether transportation funding comes from fuel buyers or bread buyers. But this is not smart transportation finance, because it can have no effect on driving behavior.

▲ **Development fees.** Fees imposed on the development of housing and commercial space are a means of financing local transportation. They link development to its transportation impacts, but they do nothing to affect the individual driving decisions of people living in or working in new developments. Paying for roads through higher housing prices or commercial rents is too separate from the travel decision. This method of paying for roads provides no incentive for drivers to conserve on trips.

Key Qualities of Expanded Mobility

This chapter has suggested the key qualities of expanded mobility as a smart-growth principle. Expanded mobility is a cornerstone of efforts to promote smart growth. Staying mindful of the following key qualities will ensure the greatest benefits from efforts to expand mobility.

Balances Car Travel and Transit Strategies

The transportation strategy most supportive of expanded mobility and smart growth in general focuses on multiple needs: 1) adding car travel capacity through roadbuilding and road-use programs, 2) reducing car travel demand through more compact and mixed-use development, and 3) making nonauto forms of travel more feasible through additional transit facilities and supportive development.

Driving is a fact of life for most Americans. Most people live in circumstances that demand car travel. Development that fits the smart-growth model will still add more cars to the road than riders to transit lines.

Expanded mobility is not anti-road. It proposes to find a better way to accommodate car travel within a smart-growth environment and at the same time it proposes to improve opportunities for alternatives to car travel, including transit, walking and bicycling, and even telecommuting.

The principle of expanded mobility conditions transportation improvements on supportive development, promoting forms of development that reduce driving needs and make the use of transportation facilities—highways and transit—more efficient.

Connects Transportation Systems

Expanded mobility focuses on connections among related transportation systems. Good connections increase travel options. Highway and transit systems should function as an integrated travel network that makes the most efficient use of travel capacities and offers choices of routes and modes. Communities should build connections to surrounding communities and within the community. Local land use plans and policies should channel development to locations with access to various modes of travel. Individual projects should establish multiple links to adjacent roads, transit, and trails.

Recognizes the Transportation/ Land Use Connection

Transportation systems should relate closely to supportive forms of development. Therefore, regions and communities should predicate the planning and funding of transportation improvements on land use conditions. For example, compact and multiuse development warrants invest-

ment in various types of transportation and transportation-related improvements, including transit, trails and pathways, and attractive pedestrian environments. Transit service is most feasible at densities of seven housing units per acre or 125 employees per acre.

Reduces Parking Impacts

Current parking standards and practices—especially large surface-parking lots—are incompatible with the smart-growth goals of compactness, connectivity, and pedestrian-orientation within communities. Expanded mobility involves the adoption of more realistic parking standards, the promotion of shared parking, and the use of streets for parking. The adverse impacts of parking on urban activity and connectivity can be reduced by placing parking behind buildings, by using structured parking, and by designing parking structures to incorporate or connect to the uses they serve.

Balances Costs and Benefits in Investment Decisions

Expanded mobility seeks to clarify all the major costs involved in proposed transportation improvements and to weigh these against all the major benefits to be gained from such improvements—and to reach an equitable balance between costs and benefits in making investment decisions. Cost and benefit determinations can be exceedingly difficult to make.

For example, costs may include direct construction and long-term maintenance costs, the costs of providing ancillary services, and the difficult-to-estimate costs of external impacts (such as quality-of-life impacts or environmental impacts). Costs may be public or personal. They may take the form of direct investments or indirect subsidies. Benefits may be equally difficult to quantify. Among the benefits of potential transportation investments that are of interest in making smart-growth decisions would be user convenience, the expansion of travel options, reduced travel distances, reduced travel times, and reductions in adverse environmental impacts (less air pollution, for example, or less use of nonrenewable resources).

Investment Priorities

Expanded mobility, a central principle of smart growth, requires good transportation. Metropolitan economies without adequate transportation capacity will suffer. Traffic got so bad in Houston in the 1980s and in Atlanta in the 1990s that the business communities of those cities stepped in to help plan more effectively for multimodal mobility.

If consensus can be reached on investment priorities, the rich mix of local, state, federal, and private sources of transportation financing promises adequate funding for future mobility needs. A great deal of collaboration among government, civic, and business interests is needed, as well as broad recognition that only a truly multimodal transportation system in combination with more supportive built environments can provide adequate travel capacity at the metropolitan level.

Notes

1. U.S. Department of Transportation, *1999 Status of the Nation's Highways, Bridges, and Transit: Conditions and Performance* (Washington, D.C.: 2000), pp. 6, 4-7, and 4-10.

2. David Schrank and Tim Lomax, *2001 Urban Mobility Report* (College Station, Texas: Texas Transportation Institute, 2001), p. 17.

3. Ibid.

4. "Survey: The All American Community," *On Common Ground* (National Association of Realtors), winter 2001.

5. Bureau of Transportation Statistics, *Transportation Statistics, Annual Report 1999* (Washington, D.C.: U.S. Department of Transportation, 1999), p. 35.

6. U.S. Department of Labor, Bureau of Labor Statistics, *Consumer Expenditures in 1999* (Washington, D.C.: 2000), p. 3.

7. Barbara McCann, *Driven to Spend: Sprawl and Household Transportation Expenses* (Washington, D.C.: Surface Transportation Planning Project, February 2001).

8. David Anderson and Gerard McCullough, *The Full Cost of Transportation in the Twin Cities, 2000* (Minneapolis: University of Minnesota Center for Transportation Studies, 2000).

9. Texas Transportation Institute, *Highway Statistics 2000* (Washington, D.C.: Federal Highway Administration, 2000).

10. Robert Fishman, "The American City in the 21st Century," in ULI–the Urban Land Institute, *ULI on the Future: Cities in the 21st Century* (Washington, D.C.: 2000), p. 6.

11. Anthony Downs, *New Visions for Metropolitan America* (Washington, D.C.: Brookings Institution, 1994), pp. 5–6.

12. Robert T. Dunphy, *The Cost of Being Close: Land Values and Housing Prices in Portland's High-Tech Corridor*, Working Paper no. 660 (Washington, D.C.: ULI–the Urban Land Institute, 1998).

13. Bureau of Transportation Statistics, *The Changing Face of Transportation*, BTS-00-007 (Washington, D.C.: U.S. Department of Transportation, 2000).

14. "Buckhead Lofts," *Development Case Study*, no. CO30016 (Washington, D.C.: ULI–the Urban Land Institute, 2000).

15. For more details on the Orenco Station project, see David O'Neill, *The Smart Growth Tool Kit* (Washington, D.C.: ULI–the Urban Land Institute, 2000), pp. 106–110.

16. Ruth Steiner, "Travel in Traditional Neighborhoods in Downtown Orlando" (paper presented at a conference of the Transportation Research Board, Washington, D.C., January 2001).

17. U.S. Department of Transportation, *1999 Status* (see note 1), pp. 2-12–2-13.

18. Boris Pushkarev and Jeffrey Zupan, *Public Transportation and Land Use Policy* (Bloomington, Indiana: Indiana University Press, 1997).

19. Robert T. Dunphy and Kimberly Fisher, "Transportation, Congestion, and Density: New Insights," *Transportation Research Record 1552* (Washington, D.C.: National Academy Press, 1996), pp. 89–96.

20. Lawrence Frank and Gary Pivo, "Impacts of Mixed Use and Density on Utilization of Three Modes of Travel: Single Occupant Vehicle, Transit, and Walking," *Transportation Research Record 1466* (Washington, D.C.: National Academy Press, 1994), pp. 44–52.

21. Reid Ewing and Robert Cervero, "Travel and the Built Environment: Synthesis" (paper presented at a conference of the Transportation Research Board, Washington, D.C., January 2001)

22. Ibid.

23. J. Holtzclaw, "Explaining Urban Density and Transit Impacts on Auto Use," in *California Energy Commission Docket no. 89-CR-90* (San Francisco: Natural Resources Defense Council, January 1991).

24. Patricia Hu and Jennifer Young, *1990 NPTS Databook*, Nationwide Personal Transportation Survey (Washington, D.C.: Federal Highway Administration, 1993), p. 4-46.

25. *Downtown Bellevue, Washington: An Examination of Development Potential and Recommendations for Strategies to Shape a Vibrant Central Business District* (Washington, D.C.: ULI–the Urban Land Institute, 1997), p. 42.

26. Parsons Brinkerhoff Quade and Douglas, with Cambridge Systematics and Calthorpe Associates, *The Pedestrian Environment*, v. 4A (Portland, Oregon: 1000 Friends of Oregon, December 1993), pp. 18–21.

27. ICF Consulting, *Our Built Environment: A Technical Review of the Interaction between Land Use, Trans-*

portation, and Environmental Quality (Washington, D.C.: U.S. Environmental Protection Agency, 2001), p. 74.

28. "Analysis and Development of New Insight into Substitution of Short Car Trips by Cycling and Walking," *ITE Journal*, March 2000, pp. 12–14.

29. For more information on the design of residential streets, see ULI–the Urban Land Institute et al., *Residential Streets*, 3rd edition (Washington, D.C.: ULI, 2001).

30. Christopher Leinberger, interviewed on program on urban sprawl, *Morning Edition*, National Public Radio, 26 July 2000.

31. Jeffrey Gelman, quoted in John Slania, "Car Wars: Why Developers Are Seeking More Parking," *Crain's Chicago Business*, 19 June 2000.

32. ULI–the Urban Land Institute, *Parking Requirements of Shopping Centers* (Washington, D.C.: 1999).

33. "Mizner Park," *Project Reference File*, v. 22, no. 8 (Washington, D.C.: ULI–the Urban Land Institute, April–June 1992).

34. Mary Smith et al., *Parking Structures*, 3rd edition (Nowell, Massachusetts: Kluwer Academic Publishers, 2001), p. 24.

35. U.S. Environmental Protection Agency, *Parking Alternatives: Making Way for Urban Infill and Brownfield Development* (Washington, D.C.: 1999), p. 30.

36. Robert Cervero, *The Transit Metropolis: A Global Inquiry* (Washington, D.C.: Island Press, 1998), p. 61.

37. Gordon English et al., *Internalizing the Costs of the Transportation Sector* (Toronto: Research and Traffic Group, 2000), p. xiii.

Principles of Smart Growth
Enhanced Livability

5

As discussed in chapters 2 through 4, three major building blocks of smart growth—compact, multiuse development, open-space conservation, and expanded mobility—are concerned largely with the physical patterns of development that shape the built environment. A fourth major building block—enhanced livability—is concerned with how the built environment affects, relates to, and meets the needs of the people who live and work within it.

"Livability" rivals "smart growth" as a term that suggests a hopeful but very loosely defined concept of community development. Livability implies a community quality of life that is comfortable, convenient, hospitable, and sustaining. Livable communities are often described as "a nice place to live" or "a hometown kind of place."

Livability can be broadly defined by reference to the primary characteristics most people want for their neighborhoods—such as a good school system, a low crime rate, and affordable housing. But it is a very subjective term. What one person considers livable—a low-density, all-residential neighborhood, for example, or being surrounded by extended family and friends—might not appeal to someone who prefers a more active and diverse neighborhood, or who prefers privacy and independence. Whatever people's specific requirements for livability, livability always means a comfortable environment with essential support for everyday life.

In all metropolitan areas there are plenty of communities in which the living environment is less than nurturing—at least for less well off people. The reasons—including those on the following list—are well known and seemingly intractable:

▲ Competition among local jurisdictions for tax revenues motivates communities to seek high-value housing and commercial and industrial uses, to the exclusion of more affordable housing.
▲ Decisions on the character and location of proposed developments sometimes are strongly influenced by discriminatory, unjust attitudes concerning the class and race of the people who might live or work in them.
▲ Community residents fear that allowing more diversity in residential and employment uses might compromise neighborhood safety, depress property values, and otherwise result in the decline of the neighborhood.
▲ Fiscal disparities among jurisdictions, which tend to reflect the wealth of neighborhoods, reinforce the differences between rich and poor communities.

The economic status of communities affects their ability to become livable. Middle- and high-income communities have a head start in the race toward livability. They enjoy fiscal and leadership resources that allow them to set high standards for development and for community facilities and services. Poor neighborhoods, on the other hand, lack the resources to rise above the social and environmental injustices that go with poverty and to lessen their isolation in the regional economy and society. Often the only hope of neighborhood betterment is through gentrification, which achieves livability largely through displacement of the poor residents.

The list of community objectives related to social and economic conditions compiled by the Georgia Quality Growth Partnership (see box) is a good list of livability objectives, to which could be added two others, as follows:

▲ Appropriate public facilities and services (other than transportation), including water, sewage treatment, stormwater management, police and fire protection, and health services.
▲ Appropriate cultural and recreational facilities, including museums, concert halls, and stadiums.

This chapter focuses on the following aspects of livability and on the role of smart growth as a tool for making their attainment within neighborhoods, communities, and metropolitan areas possible:

▲ housing choices, including affordable housing;
▲ educational opportunities;
▲ employment opportunities;
▲ essential facilities and services; and
▲ a sense of place and community identity.

Housing Choices

The diversity of American society is reflected in a diversity of households. The detached, single-family subdivisions that have dominated suburban housing markets for the last half century were designed for a typical household of mom, pop, and two kids. This design household is not so typical any more, now amounting to only one-quarter of the market. Other types of households—including single persons, dual-income adults without kids, single parents with children, and groups of unrelated adults—have emerged as important segments of metropolitan housing markets.

Different kinds of households gravitate toward different types of housing and different locations. For example, many young adults without children and many empty nesters seek out housing in cities

Quality Community Objectives

The Georgia Quality Growth Partnership, a partnership of 30 state and Atlanta regional organizations, has developed a series of objectives called "quality community objectives" that are intended to guide growth in the state's communities. The objectives included here under the rubric "Community Development Patterns and Characteristics" reflect many of the smart-growth goals addressed in this book's chapters 2 through 4. The kinds of objectives listed under "Decision-Making Processes" are discussed in chapter 8. The objectives under "Social and Economic Conditions" focus on the livability quality of communities, and are therefore discussed in this chapter.

Community Development Patterns and Characteristics

▲ Traditional neighborhoods with a mix of uses and a walkable scale.
▲ Infill development to recycle existing buildings and sites.

▲ Transportation alternatives to allow a greater range of travel choices.
▲ Open-space preservation to protect environmental resources and provide parks and recreation areas.
▲ Heritage preservation to enhance historic areas and buildings.
▲ Building a sense of place and community identity by maintaining traditional downtowns and other central places.

Social and Economic Conditions

▲ Appropriate businesses matched to residents' job skills, related to regional economic prospects, and generating higher-skilled job opportunities.
▲ Employment options to provide a range of job opportunities.
▲ Housing choices to provide a range of housing size, cost, and density options for existing and future residents.

▲ Educational and training opportunities for community residents.
▲ Regional identity based on shared experience and common linkages.

Decision-Making Processes

▲ Preparedness for growth through established leadership and guidance mechanisms for expected development.
▲ Local self-determination to work toward achieving community visions.
▲ Regional cooperation in identifying shared needs and setting priorities for solutions.
▲ Shared solutions for achieving multijurisdictional collaboration.

Source: Paraphrased from a list of community objectives prepared by the Georgia Quality Growth Partnership.

and town centers because they prefer to be near their workplaces and urban amenities. As residents of townhouses and apartments, they are excused from the toils of lawn care and from exterior home maintenance chores, giving them time for other endeavors.

Households made up of young people and unrelated people are tending more to want to settle in central cities and to not seek suburban locations.[1] Townhouses and apartments, located either in cities or in suburbs, serve other types of households as well, including old people and single adults with children, who do not need or wish to maintain a large house. This is not to say that demand has disappeared for suburban or rural locations with lots of green grass and elbow room. Plenty of households still prefer that style of living.

Variety in Housing

Smart-growth communities should be expanding their universe of available housing forms. Serving the market for single-family houses alone calls for a variety of forms, including detached and attached and large-lot and small-lot houses. (Smart growth, of course, favors smaller rather than larger lots.)

Townhouses and apartments also come in many varieties and combinations. Townhouses and apartments may be combined. Rental and owned units may be combined. The form of ownership can vary from condominium, to cooperative, to co-housing. Market-rate and affordable units may be combined. Mother-in-law units may be attached to single-family houses. Apartments may be developed in four-plex or eight-plex (or any other plex) formats. Or they may be provided in high-rise or mid-rise buildings. Apartments may be developed above retail space. Projects may be designed and operated to serve special needs, such as retirement housing or assisted-living housing. The neighborhood design of townhouses and apartments may vary from conventional to neotraditional in response to different lifestyles.

Townhouses and apartments may be located in a variety of places as well. They may be in downtowns, town centers, suburban activity centers, suburban residential neighborhoods, and exurbs. They may be highway-oriented or transit-oriented. They may be developed in multiuse business parks and on university campuses. Historic buildings, former institutional buildings such as schools and

hospitals, and industrial buildings may be converted to apartments.

Many developers and builders specialize in a single type of housing, producing it in assembly-line style. This single-mindedness is encouraged by the prevalence of similarly minded zoning and subdivision laws. However, there are housing producers who are well experienced in siting and constructing a variety of housing types. Among these are developers of large-scale communities, who are adept in the design of a mix of housing that appeals to many market segments, and the growing number of developers of mixed-use town centers.

AvalonBay Communities, for example, is completing a 943-unit development on a 22-acre site in Arlington, Virginia, that is notable for its varied mix of housing. In recognition that the area's renter demographics include families with children, retirees, baby boomers tired of living in outlying subdivisions, and young singles, AvalonBay followed

▲ **Avalon at Arlington Square, a 943-unit development in Arlington, Virginia, provides a range of housing types, including these apartments above retail shops.**

new urbanist principles in the design of this apartment community, which mixes standard apartment buildings, townhouses, stacked townhouse units, and live/work units with first-level storefronts.

Affordability

The supply of housing priced to match the incomes of American households—that is, affordable housing—has not kept up with needs. In many metropolitan areas around the country, the construction of new housing has not kept pace with job growth and household formation. The pace of multifamily construction is far below that of single-family construction. Therefore, renters face a more serious shortfall in affordable housing than do homeowners.

Renters constitute one-third of American households, but rental units constitute only 21 percent of housing units built in the last six years. Since 1997, rents have been rising faster than the consumer price index. The U.S. Department of Housing and Urban Development (HUD) estimates that the number of housing units affordable by very low-income renters dropped by 7 percent—1.14 million units—in just two years (1997 to 1999).[2]

The Joint Center for Housing Studies of Harvard University reports that 10.1 million very low-income households spend over half their incomes for shelter—which leaves little for spending on other basic needs.[3] Housing consumes between 30 and 50 percent of income for another 6.3 million poor households, a growing number of which fall into the category of the working poor because they contain at least one person employed full time.[4] In 1999, more than 3 million working households had critical housing needs—meaning they spent more than half their household income on housing or lived in a severely inadequate unit— and during the three years from 1997 to 1999 the number of working families with critical housing needs rose by 23 percent.[5]

The homeownership rate is above 67 percent—a record high level. But the proportion of households that cannot afford the classic single-family house on a large lot in the suburbs is growing. In fact, many homeowners with relatively low incomes face significant and growing housing problems.

One way lower-income owners manage to stay in their homes is to defer maintenance.[6] Over time,

houses deteriorate and need costly repairs. (And as their owners age, expensive modifications such as adding ramps and widening door openings may become necessary.) When people fail to maintain their houses well, neighborhoods decline and housing values drop. Poor neighborhoods become poorer and less livable.

Not only is little housing that is affordable to low-income people being built, but also existing affordable housing is being removed from the inventory by price inflation, demolition, and conversion. For many poor households, urban revitalization means being displaced from where they live and being offered few opportunities for bettering their housing choices. HUD's energetic efforts to demolish dilapidated high-rise housing projects in many inner cities and replace them with mixed-income housing promise not only to improve distressed neighborhoods, but also to further diminish housing opportunities for poor people to the extent that the lost units are not replaced one for one. The supply of subsidized Section 8 housing is also in decline, largely because of the conversion of buildings to market-rate housing.

Housing affordability is an issue that reaches deep into nonpoor segments of the society as well. It affects young adults just entering the job market and paying off college loans. It affects professionals with limited incomes, among them teachers, firefighters, nurses, and social workers. And it affects many older people who are dependent on Social Security and small pensions. The livability principle of smart growth requires that communities and metropolitan regions recognize that their housing markets do not meet the needs of many of their residents, and that they take steps to remedy this problem.

Exclusion and Inclusion

Housing markets and public policy throughout metropolitan America tend to erect serious obstacles to satisfying the increasing diversity of housing needs. The propensity of housing markets to pick winners and losers has deleterious consequences for both.

The winners in housing markets are locations (communities or neighborhoods) that come to be considered as desirable. As they attract increasing interest as residential locations they become hot spots in which demand exceeds the supply of housing or the supply of land available for residential development. Prices therefore escalate, and eventually these locations become enclaves for comparatively wealthy households—and unaffordable for any other types of households.

The losers in housing markets are areas that come to be considered as undesirable. Housing in these locations loses value. Local governments begin to experience fiscal difficulties that cause them to cut back on investment in facilities and services. Thus begins a vicious cycle of decline, and eventually these locations become enclaves for the poor—and unattractive for any households that can afford to live elsewhere.

Obviously many communities and neighborhoods are more stable and diverse as local housing markets than the winners and losers at the extremes. But the tendency of the market to reserve desirable areas for only the well-to-do and to relegate the poor to waning neighborhoods works against the fine-grained diversity of housing and uses that smart growth advocates.

Public planning and zoning policies, for their part, militate against increased diversity by favoring the development of types of housing considered most desirable by current residents and deemed most likely to increase the value of existing property in the community. Frequently, the housing that is favored will have sale prices or rents that are high enough to exclude low- and perhaps moderate-income households. The people who espouse the exclusion of affordable housing justify this by saying that it threatens the value of existing housing. However, the perception that affordable housing poses a threat to housing values does not withstand evidence to the contrary from many studies.

In many, if not most, communities, neighbors always fight proposals for residential development that differs in character from existing housing. To keep the peace, some communities, especially suburban jurisdictions, adopt zoning codes that permit only one or two types of housing, which typically serve a relatively high-income segment of the housing market. This leaves the responsibility for serving low- and moderate-income households to other jurisdictions even though those jurisdictions may be far away from the job markets and other daily destinations of these households.

Local exclusionary planning and zoning practices over the years have been subject to court challenges and state legislative corrections, based on the theories that decent housing is a fundamental social need and affordable housing an essential component of community growth and development. Perhaps the best known anti-exclusionary program is in New Jersey, the result of a series of state supreme court decisions, known as the Mount Laurel rulings, declaring a constitutional requirement for every municipality to provide opportunity (generally through zoning and other land use regulation) for its fair share of regional affordable housing needs. In 1985, the state legislature established the Council on Affordable Housing to oversee municipal fair share housing plans.

Courts in New York, Pennsylvania, and New Hampshire also have invalidated exclusionary zoning practices by local governments. In 1979, Massachusetts enacted what is known as an anti-snob law, which requires local governments to adopt zoning that allows the production of affordable housing and which also provides for extraordinary regulatory relief for affordable projects. Connecticut and Rhode Island have adopted and adapted the Massachusetts approach. California's state legislature has enacted laws urging communities to grant density bonuses for the inclusion of affordable units in residential developments.

Many local governments have taken steps on their own to further the cause of affordable housing, usually through the adoption of inclusionary zoning ordinances or through programs that promote the production of affordable housing.

Mixed-Income Housing

Mixed-income housing is a smart-growth solution that addresses not only affordability issues, but also more general suburban livability issues. Residential suburbs are conventionally developed with housing segregated according to its size, type, and price. Devoting hundreds of acres to only one use—say, moderate-price three- and four-bedroom houses, or high-price four-bedroom houses—is common. More modestly priced townhouses clump together in dozens of six- or eight-unit clusters. Apartments zero in on one location several hundred units at a time.

All-of-a-kind housing enclaves attract people of a certain age, income, and family status. Life in income- and status-segregated precincts is not conducive to the mingling and interactions that create community. Furthermore, residents' grown children needing entry-level housing may be priced out of the neighborhood and even the community.

A finer-grain mix of housing styles and prices, community by community, can create more successful, sustainable communities as well as accommodate a fuller range of community and regional housing needs. Smart growth supports and encour-

ages development that mixes a variety of housing, from multiplexes of all kinds, clustered zero-lot-line houses, small-lot houses, large-lot houses, and houses with granny flats to group homes, co-housing projects, seniors housing, and assisted-living residences.

This kind of variety in housing represents life-cycle housing for communities. By making room for appealing choices for people at different stages of their lives, it allows neighborhoods to grow old gracefully. Both the concept of mixed-income hous-

▶ Bailey's Grove, a 364-acre development near Grand Rapids, Michigan, contains 1,075 housing units in a mix of single-family dwellings, townhouses, and apartments. The residential areas are framed by a relaxing greenway system.

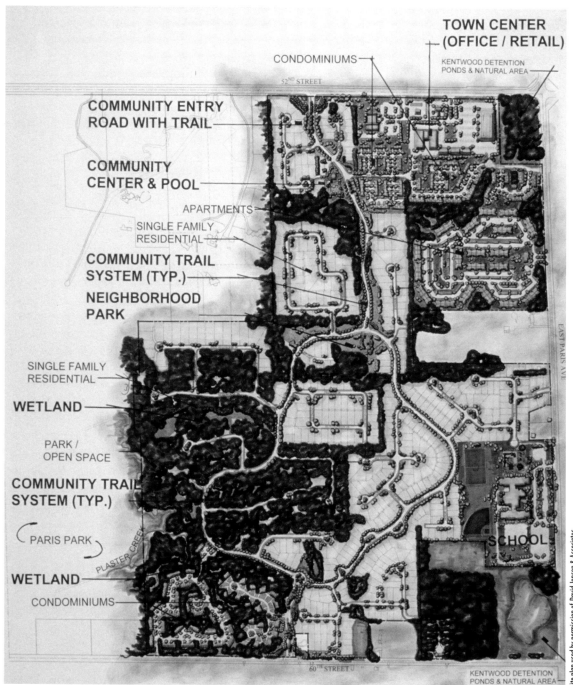

ing and the concept of life-cycle housing embrace a mix of housing opportunities—rental and ownership, suitable for entry-level households and also for upwardly mobile households, and suitable for families as well as individuals and for group living. The entry-level housing market is served by rental units. First-time and move-up homebuyers have a variety of choices within the neighborhood. Empty nesters and elderly residents can stay in the community even if they wish to move to a condominium, townhouse, or retirement or assisted-living residence.

Mixed-income housing is the concept animating the HOPE VI program of the U.S. Department of Housing and Urban Development, which is replacing inner-city public housing projects with garden apartments and townhouses incorporating public housing units as well as market-rate units. Scores of mixed-income HOPE VI projects have been started or completed in cities across the nation, aided by the back-to-the-city trend that is attracting many middle- and upper-income households to downtown neighborhoods.

In Baltimore, for example, a 303-unit development called The Terraces has replaced the Lexington Terrace high-rise public housing project. Built for the city's public housing authority by a private developer, The Terraces opened early in 2000. It includes 100 for sale townhouses, 203 rental townhouses, 88 mixed-income rental units for the elderly in a mid-rise building, and a building for community activities. (See page 126.)

A complex of five public housing projects known as ABLA totaling 3,600 units on Chicago's near West Side is being replaced or renovated as mixed-income housing as follows: 1,467 low-income rental units (some located off site), 845 moderate-price rental and ownership units, and 966 market-rate units. The Chicago housing authority's HOPE VI revitalization plan for ABLA was approved in late 2001. In 2000, the authority completed a $45 million reconstruction of 329 rowhouses for existing residents, and it is proceeding to select developers for the rest of the site. The city will provide a community center with an indoor swimming pool, gymnasium, and daycare; expand a park; and build a new fire station and a new police station nearby. A new neighborhood shopping center is scheduled to open in the spring of 2002.

Educational Opportunities

In livable neighborhoods, schools usually play a key role. They are where neighborhood meetings take place, people go to vote, local music and theater groups perform, and sports events are held. For families with children, schools function as centers of social interaction.

The central role of schools in community life helps to explain why urban planners in the early part of the 20th century tended to organize neighborhoods around elementary schools and to cluster groups of neighborhoods—communities—around middle and high schools. The designers of the prototypical garden city of Radburn, New Jersey, and the New Deal greenbelt towns focused building patterns and green spaces to provide natural pedestrian pathways to schools and associated playgrounds and sports facilities.

Designs for newer new towns and large-scale communities anticipate the use of schools for various community activities and events and frequently cluster parks and recreational facilities around them. Schools play such an important role in neighborhood and community life that the developers of large-scale communities make every effort to include a school in the first phases of construction. For three such communities—Anthem in the Phoenix area, Weston near Fort Lauderdale, and Hidden Springs, Idaho—the developers went so far as to build the first school with private funds.

The educational quality of schools is without doubt a primary force in residential markets. Neighbor-

▲ The Brooks Homes reconstruction represents the first phase in the conversion of Chicago's ABLA public housing complex to mixed-income housing. Its 329 rowhouse units were increased in size by 40 percent (and overall development density was halved).

hoods are known by the quality of their schools, and over time desirable schools go hand in hand with desirable neighborhoods. Good schools make good neighbors.

But good schools are not so easy to establish and maintain. Furthermore, schools may be an important factor in people's choices of where to live, but they are only one factor. Therefore, smart growth cannot simply recommend creating high-quality school systems to attract and support high-quality development, which in turn will maintain the high quality of the schools. In a multifarious society, the relationship between schools and neighborhoods is far more complex.

Neighborhoods and their schools serve people with a wide variety of capabilities and qualities, from their cultural heritage to their income and social status to their intellectual bent and perspective on what makes the good life. The place of schools in neighborhood life means different things to different people.

▲ Some people value good schools as important for their children's prospects. If able, they are willing to incur relatively high housing costs to locate in neighborhoods with good schools. Of course, many people who value good schools for their children may not be able to afford to live in such neighborhoods.

▲ Some people put little faith in the idea that school can improve their children's opportunities. (In many cases, this attitude may derive from the poor quality of the schools in the neighborhoods in which they can afford to live.)

▲ People without children or with grown children have few concerns about schools as part of their life. The quality of the schools may not be much of a factor in where they choose to live.

▲ Some people expect to educate their children in private schools for some or all of their school years. For them also, the quality of the schools may not be much of a factor in where they choose to live, though they may be able to afford and want to live in the kinds of neighborhoods that are associated with good schools.

However much people's perception of the value of education for their own situations varies, an educated society plays a vital role in building desirable communities. People must be educated in order to participate effectively in the evolving society, culture, and economy. Education is essential for developing the job skills that support economic growth. As part of its livability goal, smart growth favors expanding opportunities for high-quality education, which should be considered the foundation of livable communities and regions— as well as of the nation's future productivity.

Based on the role school buildings themselves play or potentially play in community life, they should be proactively located, designed, and programmed to promote smart patterns of development. Even many communities that make good use of school properties for civic, recreational, and cultural activities often could do more to integrate school facilities into the community's open-space systems—and the community's open-space resources into the school curriculum. Connected open space could serve, for example, as a living classroom for environmental education.

In many communities, school design and operating standards contribute to sprawl rather than counteracting it. A recent report from the National Trust for Historic Preservation contends that excessive site requirements, state funding formulas oriented to new construction, and the exemption of schools from zoning codes are promoting school sprawl on outlying undeveloped land at the expense of small, community-centered schools in older neighborhoods, schools to which children may walk.[7]

School boards often decide to build new schools rather than to rehabilitate existing buildings. Decisions on where to locate new facilities and on the size and design of new schools often favor large sites, deep setbacks from the street, and single-story structures. Some communities are building elementary schools for up to 800 or more students. Such large schools draw from a wide area, which means that many children cannot walk to school. They also have large staffs that generate a correspondingly large number of trips and significant parking requirements. School-bus and other traffic generated by large schools adversely affects nearby residents.

Middle schools and high schools may be even larger and more disruptive of the neighborhood scale. Many are two or three stories tall and surrounded by acres of sports fields. Often they are designed to be almost unapproachable by foot from nearby neighborhoods. Large buildings on large lots may bring educational benefits, but within low-density neighborhoods they make difficult the introduction of compact land use patterns and walkability.

Schools are important community resources and symbols of community aspirations. As such, they should be designed in accordance with the smart-growth goals of compact development, multiuse development, open-space conservation, and pedestrian and transit accessibility. They should be designed to enhance pedestrian and transit access from the surrounding area. They should use no more land than is necessary. And they should be contiguous to or within urbanizing areas. Schools and their grounds should be integrated into the community's system of conserved open spaces. Thought should be given to the multiple use of school facilities and land.

Smart growth suggests also that the design of existing schools and their sites should be reevaluated to determine ways to retrofit them to meet smart growth goals. It might even be possible, although improbable in this NIMBYist age, to use the excess land on school sites for building affordable housing.

Employment Opportunities

Livable communities need jobs as well as housing. Livable communities encourage the establishment and expansion of businesses and industries that will strengthen the regional economy and provide convenient and suitable employment opportunities for residents. They also promote job training to raise the skills (and incomes) of residents.

The relationship of job locations and housing locations is important for smart growth and for livability. Communities from which employment opportunities are conveniently accessible are by definition more livable because they fulfill (some of) the work needs of their residents. Making available various travel options—such as highways (including HOV lanes) and other roads, buses, rail transit, vanpool programs, and walking and biking pathways—can provide convenient access to jobs. Shortening distances between home and work also can make commuting convenient.

Development patterns featuring a compact mix of uses including employment uses offer employees who wish to live near their work many choices and the possibility of short travel distances to work. Housing and neighborhood designs that incorporate home offices from which workers can telecommute, live/work spaces from which people can operate small businesses, or above-the-store living spaces housing the storekeepers or professionals who run the "store" are the ultimate providers of convenient access.

In many cases, relocating employers try to select locations that will maximize opportunities for convenient travel to work. This is a way of letting employees know that the company or organization recognizes that their time is valuable. In some cases, employers choose to (or are required to) contribute funds for the construction of housing that their employees can afford and that is relatively near their workplace—a form of employee housing. Aspen, Colorado, is one of a number of isolated resort towns that require new employers to invest in the production of affordable housing. Some Silicon Valley employers have taken steps to make housing available to employees who otherwise might have to commute hours each day. (See pages 111–112 for a discussion of programs requiring developers or employers to provide affordable housing.)

As noted, the presence of economy-sustaining and employment-providing businesses is one indicator of community livability. Business activity also provides tax revenues and services for residents. Luring new enterprises that promise jobs and tax revenues is a traditional preoccupation of local governments. Many local governments have ambitious economic development programs, which tend to target certain types of industry. Most fervently wooed are high-tech industries because they are considered clean and they will occupy attractive buildings and pay high salaries. Unfortunately, local governments often find themselves competing head-to-head for the same industries.

Economic development programs take many different forms. Building on existing assets to strengthen local economies is generally a good strategy. The renovation of the Lee-Harvard shopping center in Cleveland's inner city provides an example. Through the joint effort of the city, neighborhood development organizations, and other local groups, the center was revitalized, local businesses that had been foundering were rescued, and some essential neighborhood services were restored to nearby residents. (See pages 130 and 135–136 for a profile of this project.)

Examples of other economic development tools that communities have enlisted in the effort to expand employment opportunities within a convenient distance of their residents include the following:

▲ training programs to improve the job skills of residents;
▲ development site assembly and financing;
▲ provision of low-rent incubator space for startup businesses; and
▲ welfare-to-work and other programs aimed at augmenting the pool of labor available for local businesses.

Community Services And Amenities

The quality of fundamental community services —drinking water, sewage treatment and stormwater management, police and fire protection, and health care—can (along with the quality of transportation, schools, and open space) spell the difference between a hospitable or a hostile living environment. Livability may be further enhanced by public amenities, which may include museums, performance venues, sports facilities, and public art.

Rapid unsmart growth in metropolitan America has had the effect of diminishing the quality of such community services in many older areas. Too often, local governments that are hard-pressed to meet the demand for service extensions to developing areas compensate by investing less on the maintenance of facilities serving established neighborhoods and business centers. Eventually, the failure to improve existing facilities diminishes the livability of older neighborhoods. People leave for greener pastures, real estate values and tax revenues sag, and government resources for needed repairs and replacements shrink even more. This cycle of neglect and decline in public services and facilities is all too evident in many older parts of cities and towns throughout America.

The establishment of a proper balance between funding for service extensions to developing areas and funding for the admittedly less glamorous task of repairing and replacing existing facilities

is important for smart growth. Balancing investment in public facilities between new and existing areas not only supports infill and redevelopment in urbanized areas, but also disposes the residents of these areas to support infill project proposals. City councils in more than one community have faced opposition to infill projects from residents who see attractive facilities and amenities provided in newly developing areas but few in their neighborhoods.

In anticipating needs for facility improvements, local governments—and state governments too—should do a better job of assessing the needs of built-up areas. For example, Dayton, Ohio's successful effort to revitalize the inner-city Wright-Dunbar neighborhood (see page 142) revolved to some extent around the provision of new community facilities. The revitalization sprang from the enlargement and improvement of a historic park and was furthered by investment by the city in new water and sewer, gas, and electric power lines. In Maryland, the state's Smart Growth program favors existing infrastructure in its decision to make improving existing schools a priority over the construction of new schools in the state's school construction budget.

In many communities, developers bear the brunt of providing basic facilities for new development. Their responsibility is spelled out in subdivision requirements, impact fee programs, and exactions negotiated as a condition of project approval. In built-up areas with basic facilities in place, local governments are reluctant to pay for replacing or upgrading infrastructure to support new development.

In circumstances where developers must provide the infrastructure, they can request the designation of special taxing districts in which assessments on newly developed properties will be used to repay city or developer outlays for infrastructure. The cities of Chicago, Houston, and Jacksonville, for example, have established tax-increment financing districts in which increases in property tax revenues derived from new development are earmarked to repay the city or the developer for infrastructure investments required for development.

Enhanced wiring has emerged as a new element of community infrastructure. As the California Association for Local Economic Development points out: "Telecommunications technology is changing dramatically the way business and government will be conducted. The need for telecommunications infrastructure such as rights-of-way, fiber-optic lines, and communications equipment will be as important as traditional locational factors such as roads, sewer and water systems, etc."[8]

It is not just wiring, but also computing and communications technology that offers communities opportunities in the area of community services and amenities. Many communities have launched public/private initiatives aimed at using new technologies to improve their economic competitiveness and make access to information easier.

For example, communities have computerized their recordkeeping to make the submission and tracking of applications for development permits easier and more accessible—a minor change yet a significant contribution to the development process. More broadly, most local governments host Web sites that provide basic information about public programs and services, and announce important meetings and hearings.

The city of Cincinnati's Web site provides descriptions of the key characteristics of its 51 neighborhoods, which are intended to attract interest in the development of infill housing. The city of Santa Monica has established a public access computer network, Public Electronic Network (PEN), that provides information about city services and events, makes it easy to e-mail city departments, and enables public electronic discussions on city issues (and other topics). It is free to residents and accessible 24 hours a day through any computer, including terminals in public libraries, schools, and community centers.

A growing number of master-planned communities offer residents and commercial tenants the latest in communication technologies. The Playa Vista development in Los Angeles is being wired for high-speed data transmission. Playa Vista residents will be able to establish home links with their employers, which can promote telecommuting. At Del Webb's Anthem community near Phoenix, fiber-optic cabling is provided to the curb in front of each residence. Access to such technologies will become increasingly significant in defining livability.

Place Making

Place making means establishing a sense of place or an identity for a locality—for a neighborhood, a community, a city, a region. A sense of place is an important element of livability. Place shapes people's lives and can remind them of where they came from. Place making is accomplished through the sharing of experiences, the invention and celebration of rituals and traditions, and the design of the built environment to nurture sharing and celebration.

The civic realm—its open spaces and streetscapes and monuments and public art—has much to do with place making. As does distinctive architecture. Place making seeks to incorporate into the built environment elements that people both enjoy and remember, elements that are pleasant as well as interesting. It seeks also to invite people in, to encourage collective activities.

The establishment of a special community identity has real value for residents and visitors alike. Developers recognize this value. In their subdivisions, even those located on the edge of cities, they are likely to retain the old farmhouse on the hill as a community center and open space. They invest in the provision of ample green spaces and impressive civic space because these are eminently marketable and place-making amenities.

Opportunities for establishing place makers—civic complexes, commercial complexes, and village greens—that will be centers of activity within the development are a particular concern of new urbanism and traditional neighborhood development (TND), two popular schools of community design. (Unfortunately, proponents of new urbanism and TND appear to be wedded to a single period of architecture—the 1890s to 1920s craftsman period—as the way to express community character in their projects.)

The evident and growing interest in the concept of place making has spurred developers to invest in adaptive use, infill, and redevelopment to revive once-distinctive places. Town centers with attractively designed buildings clustered around public open spaces are springing up across America. Examples of efforts to infuse development with lasting identity abound, among them Phillips Place in Charlotte, North Carolina (see page 129),

David Schwarz/Architectural Services Inc.

▲ Rows of shops and a government center frame an inviting central park in the new town center at Southlake, a growing community in the Dallas/Fort Worth suburbs. The town center has helped create a distinctive identity for Southlake.

and Southlake town center in Southlake, a suburb of Dallas (see pages 87–88).

Key Qualities of Smart Livability

This chapter has suggested the key qualities of livability as a smart-growth issue. Livability is a subjective but very real concept that is perhaps what smart growth is all about. It involves housing choice, educational opportunity, jobs and the balance of jobs and housing, essential facilities and services, and community identity. Keeping in mind the following key qualities of smart livability will ensure the greatest benefits from livability initiatives.

Recognizes Social and Economic Diversity

America's society and economy are increasingly diverse, but the choices of living and working environments offered by conventional suburban development are not. Smart livability aims at widening living and working choices.

All-of-one-kind neighborhoods are socially divisive in that they provide few opportunities for people of different backgrounds, incomes, and demographic status—and even sometimes age—to interact. Many communities have become so economically exclusive that not even the children of current residents can afford to live in them

after leaving the nest. Smart growth encourages an evolution within all communities toward mixed-income housing that accommodates the full range of community and regional housing needs and that makes room for people at different stages of their lives.

Architects, developers, and lenders have become more daring in their responses to the need for diverse housing, especially in seeking out niche markets attracted to specific types of locations and types of housing. Smart growth means modernizing zoning and subdivision codes to encourage providers of housing to use their expertise to design and market housing that meets today's real needs for livability.

Invests in Infrastructure in Both Developing And Existing Areas

Smart growth is not just about ensuring that new development is served by high-quality infrastructure. It is also about attending to the need for maintaining, replacing, and upgrading existing facilities, especially facilities in urbanized areas. Local governments and regional authorities that provide facilities and services must establish an equitable balance between the extension of services to developing areas and the repair and improvement of existing facilities. The livability of older residential neighborhoods and commercial centers depends in large part on the condition of their infrastructure.

Smart growth pays close attention to the contributions of schools to the social and economic lives of their communities. The quality of the education provided plays an essential role in livability and in developing the job skills that support economic growth. The physical design of schools is also important. Schools that are well located and well designed can become significant centers of community life and broadly useful to all residents.

Connects to Employment

Livability means economic activity and opportunities for jobs. Smart livability means optimizing the ratio of jobs to housing within communities to 1) strengthen local economies and 2) reduce long-distance commutes. Promoting a mix of uses within communities contributes to nearby employment for community residents. Incorporating work-at-home spaces in housing or locating residential units over shops and offices offers local employment opportunities (with short commutes). The development of employment concentrations near existing residential areas can shorten work trips and help to stabilize neighborhoods.

Makes Distinctive Places

Smart growth is distinctive growth, because community identity is a key aspect of livability. Sense of place signifies the special character of a neighborhood or a community. Place making involves paying attention to how civic spaces are shaped and how buildings are designed; it adaptively uses historic buildings and other structures that embody community identity; it seeks compatible mixes of the new and the old; it designs streets and public spaces to nurture community life; and it appreciates land uses for the interest they add to the scene as well as for their intrinsic economic and use values.

Creating Livable Regions

Many of the issues involved in livability and most of the problems associated with growth are regional in nature and ultimately require regional planning and regional solutions. Among the issues and problems that are essentially regional in nature are traffic congestion, air pollution, water pollution, affordable housing, the jobs/housing balance, economic development, and sustainable open space.

As the Georgia Quality Growth Partnership suggests in its definition of quality communities (see page 68), livability is not just a local issue. To achieve sustainable livability, communities must forge a regional identity based on shared experiences and common linkages.

The typical metropolitan area comprises dozens up to hundreds of local jurisdictions, each a self-governing entity. This multiplicity of jurisdictions fails to reflect the reality that many of the fundamental functions of urban areas—from transportation to environmental systems, and from economic activities to social relationships—consist of networks that cross jurisdictional boundaries.

Residents of urban regions cross these boundaries many times a day for work, for shopping, for visiting, for entertainment. They tend to like to sample the wares, as it were, of a variety of places—here a regional shopping center, there a business park, downtown a museum, across town friends. The region is an extended community that offers access to amenities—universities and colleges, theaters and concert halls, religious institutions and health centers, zoos and sports stadiums, and others—that single jurisdictions ordinarily cannot support. The accessibility of regional facilities, services, and amenities networks enhances the livability of all communities within a region.

As benefiting members of the community of communities that make up a region, individual jurisdictions should reach out to acknowledge and intensify regional connections, maximize their participation in regional networks, and work cooperatively with other jurisdictions on issues of regional importance.

Individual communities can take steps to enhance the livability of the region. They can improve their linkages to regional networks and facilities—to open-space systems, sports venues, cultural centers, transportation corridors, and transportation centers. In making development decisions, they can consider the legitimate concerns of neighboring communities. Jurisdictions that are well off can work cooperatively with less well off neighbors to lessen social and fiscal disparities, and thus improve conditions for all. Jurisdictions can work together to strengthen ties among the region's various centers of economic activity in order to energize the metropolitan economy and improve its competitiveness within the global economy.

Recognizing the essential interdependence of jurisdictions within urban regions—and basing investment priorities and development decisions on that recognition—is an essential element of smart growth. How regions might move in the direction of collaboration and cooperation is discussed in chapter 8, the last chapter.

Notes

1. See, for example, John D. Kasarda et al., "Central-City and Suburban Migration Patterns: Is a Turnaround on the Horizon?" *Housing Policy Debate*, v. 8, no. 2 (1997), pp. 307–359.

2. Leanne Lachman and Deborah L. Brett, "Our Elusive Dream: Housing Affordability," *Commentary* (Lend Lease Real Estate Investments), v. 4, 2001, p. 6.

3. Joint Center for Housing Studies, *The State of the Nation's Housing: 2001* (Cambridge, Massachusetts: Harvard University, 2001, available at: www.gsd.harvard. edu/jcenter).

4. Ibid.

5. Barbara J. Lipman, "Paycheck to Paycheck: Working Families and the Cost of Housing in America," *New Century Housing* (Center for Housing Policy), June 2001, pp. 6, 9.

6. Nicholas P. Retsinas, "Lower-Income Homeowners: Struggling to Keep the Dream Alive," *Housing Facts & Findings* (Fannie Mae Foundation), fall 1999, p. 4.

7. Constance Beaumont, *Why Johnny Can't Walk to School* (Washington, D.C.: National Trust for Historic Preservation, 2000).

8. Quoted in Rick Cole, Trish Kelly, and Judy Corbett, *The Ahwahnee Principles for Smart Economic Development: An Implementation Guidebook* (Sacramento, California: Local Government Commission, Center for Livable Communities, 1998), p. 32.

Growing Smart in Suburban Greenfields

"Greenfield development is 95 percent of what has been and will continue to be built in this country—unless we elect a kind of Stalin," said Andres Duany, a doyen of neotraditional design, at a Congress for New Urbanism conference in 2000.[1] The target of this remark was people who advocate infill and redevelopment as the principal answer to sprawl.

Duany may have exaggerated to emphasize his point, but many experts agree that future growth —perhaps as much as 80 to 90 percent—will continue to locate mostly in urbanizing and rural areas at the edge of towns and cities. If they are right, taking the main road to smart growth in metropolitan areas means growing smart in suburban greenfields.

But smart-growth principles find greenfields to be tough going. Newly developing areas need time to evolve the conditions that support smart growth. The rooftops that can support clustered retail and office uses are still under construction. Transit lines have not been extended. People in the market for greenfield housing want roomy living environments and affordable bargains—and their dreams will not be ignored by builders.

Immediate, wholesale change in development products and processes is not a feasible aim for smart growth, particularly in developing areas. It is feasible to seek to alter the form of urban development in an evolutionary rather than revolutionary fashion—to work toward a vision of

smart growth. Working toward this vision will demand collaboration among private, civic, governmental, and special-interest groups concerned with growth and development. This chapter is concerned with tools and techniques for gradually altering the form of development in urbanizing areas, tools that provide a starting point for the collaborative efforts that smart growth demands.

This chapter describes various ways by which developers, communities, and allied organizations can alter current patterns of greenfield development to reflect the aims of smart growth described in chapters 2 through 5. The tools and techniques discussed are grouped into market-based practices, incentive programs and policies, and regulatory actions. This chapter offers successful examples from around the nation of practices, policies, and actions that promote smart growth in suburban greenfield settings.

The Greenfield Challenge to Smart Growth

Growing suburban areas typically accommodate much of their growth on the edges—on land occupied by farms, ranches, and natural open space. By the time growth begins in earnest, some developers and builders have already begun to establish the emerging character of development. Although the details of the process vary from one metropolitan region to another, developers generally purchase options on rural properties of 50 to 200 acres and larger. These properties are located in accessible areas, thought to be readily developable, and able to accommodate substantial developments.

In newly developing areas, some infrastructure systems begin to take shape and land prices begin to rise in anticipation of imminent development. Still, many sites are available at low prices, and growth is expected and promoted by public planning and zoning policies.

In the rural areas just beyond currently developing tracts, some scattered development may have occurred along roadways, and speculative land acquisition gets underway in expectation of future development. Property is available in relatively large pieces and land prices are relatively low. Except for a highway or county road, almost no infrastructure is in place. The few residents depend on private wells and septic systems, volunteer fire departments, the county sheriff's department, distant schools requiring long bus rides, and isolated strip or crossroads commercial centers.

Developing and rural greenfields may be located within an incorporated municipality or its annexable area or in an unincorporated area of the county. The land is probably zoned for low-density development, in the expectation that developers will request rezoning for more intensive development. It is likely that planning and zoning has paid little attention to environmentally sensitive lands such as wetlands and wildlife habitat. Few residents oppose the prospect of growth.

All in all, raw but ready greenfield land awaits quick and easy development. The relatively low cost of the land and of infrastructure often not built to urban standards and the quickness of development approvals make it possible to build housing that is affordable, at least to the first wave of occupants. The development process generally operates freely with little hindrance from antigrowth groups, angry neighbors, or restrictive regulations.

Conventional, suburban style development is certainly the path of least resistance in this milieu. It is favored by financing sources as well as by permitting. Developers find it easy to supply the large lots and single-family houses that are most in demand, or to build clusters of townhouses and apartments which, though relatively isolated, can be priced well below in-town units. Developers find public officials ready to accept their propos-

als for revenue-creating strip malls, shopping centers, and business parks. Barring incentives for doing otherwise, conventional development seems smart for the time and place. Many communities have grown up that way and nurtured millions of families through the years. For many people, conventional subdivisions continue to offer a safe, rewarding living environment.

Therefore, to persuade communities and developers and homebuyers to adapt run-of-the-mill greenfield developments to satisfy smart-growth principles seems to be an uphill struggle. Smart growth asks developers to build compactly. Why would they in greenfields, where land is inexpensive, where housing market preferences seem to be for spacious living, and where markets for high-density commercial and business uses have yet to emerge? Smart growth calls for a mix of uses. The zoning regulations of greenfield jurisdictions rarely allow for mixing uses. Smart growth proposes multimodal transportation choices. Most greenfield locations are yet unserved by public transit. Smart growth promotes the conservation of open space. In greenfield areas, open space is still abundant and property owners are eager to sell land for development. Smart growth calls for high-quality design, facilities, and amenities to enhance community livability. This goal may raise development costs, which is not a welcome option for the many greenfield developers who seek to cut costs to the bone to produce inexpensive, affordable housing and business space.

Making smart growth workable in greenfield areas is a challenge for smart-growth advocates. They must try to create opportunities for altering ingrained habits of development and public regulation. They must be able to persuade developers and public officials that smart-growth concepts—and smart-growth locations—make economic sense in the marketplace. They must show developers reasons for rearranging their priorities to satisfy smart-growth principles. Smart-growth advocates must convince local elected officials to embrace policies that offer incentives for (and remove obstacles to) smart forms of development, to establish a level playing field for development that meets smart-growth objectives.

Development projects that exemplify smart forms of greenfields development can be found in every metropolitan area, although few of these represent an ideal application of smart-growth principles. They were developed, after all, in imperfect market and regulatory environments and they reflect political and market perceptions of desirable development. Nevertheless, some types of in-place greenfield projects point the way to smarter growth in developing suburbs, as follows:

▲ residential developments that follow design precepts for compactness, multiuse, and walkability such as those advocated by new urbanists and other planners;
▲ residential subdivisions within or near urbanizing areas that cluster housing to conserve farmland and other open space (frequently termed "conservation developments");
▲ clusters of higher-density housing or a mix of housing types near town centers, suburban activity centers, shopping centers, job centers, and transit lines and stations (including commuter-rail lines);
▲ town centers and mixed-use projects located within developing suburban neighborhoods; and
▲ master-planned, compactly designed communities sited at or near the urbanizing edges of cities and metropolitan areas.

Developing any of these specific types of projects requires collaboration among developers, builders, community officials, and interest groups. Most smarter greenfield projects that have been successful involved shared public and private commitment to the creation of an imaginative, attractive, and marketable form of development. Encouraging these types of projects on greenfield sites is possible through the use of numerous design, marketing, and regulatory tools and techniques that have evolved through practice. In the following sections, these tools and techniques are described in three categories: 1) market-based practices adopted by developers and builders; 2) incentives offered by public agencies; and 3) regulations adopted and enforced by public agencies.

Market-Based Practices

Developers and other private sector participants in the development process can promote smart growth in greenfield areas by locating projects well, by building for diversity and change, by designing communities for long-term value, and by making changes in financing practices.

Location Decisions

Location has much to do with a development's ability to support smart growth. At locations near or within developed or developing areas, local market forces frequently favor higher densities and a mix of uses. The generally higher land costs for close-in sites help to motivate and justify higher development densities. Adding to existing development helps create a critical mass of development that opens up opportunities for serving a wider market, opportunities for developing retail uses in a residential development, for example, or providing a broader mix of housing types. Conversely, locating residential development on rural sites virtually precludes support for a mix of uses—unless the development is dense enough or large enough by itself to support other land uses.

For close-in sites, the higher land costs may be offset by lower infrastructure costs. Roads and utility lines are generally available in close-in locations and can be easily and relatively inexpensively extended to a new development. In isolated rural locations, infrastructure has to be built from scratch and this can require significant investment.

But sometimes the higher land costs of close-in sites may be aggravated by higher infrastructure and related costs, depending on local governmental policies and practices. Stiff standards and impact fees may be imposed on development in jurisdictions where considerable development is occurring, while adjoining rural jurisdictions impose no such standards and fees. Also, rural jurisdictions may allow developers to provide low-cost infrastructure—septic tanks rather than sewer systems, for example. (See discussions on infrastructure development and financing on pages 94–96 and 107–110.)

Locations near transit—existing or planned—also furnish a rationale for higher-density development, and they provide mobility options as well.

Locations with environmentally sensitive areas such as wetlands and wildlife habitat provide opportunities for smarter development—although they also present development problems. Having to preserve wetlands or habitat land, for example, may complicate the design of projects and make approvals more difficult, but such areas within developments are appealing features that enhance project marketability.

The two projects discussed next—Coffee Creek Center near Chesterton, Indiana, and Hidden Springs north of Boise, Idaho—are well located within their greenfield locations and they use smart-growth design principles to offset the negative aspects of their locations outside a city. Both projects stand in sharp contrast to the character of nearby conventional development. And both have proven highly attractive in the marketplace.

Coffee Creek Center, a development of 1,200 houses, is situated in the Indiana dunes country almost 50 miles southeast of downtown Chicago. On its face, the greenfield location seems remote and unconnected to either city or suburban growth patterns. But the project site has redeeming features: it is only few miles from a commuter-rail line serving suburban employment areas and downtown Chicago and it adjoins—and the project design complements—a historic village. Furthermore, the housing is developed in pedestrian-friendly clusters to conserve a 240-acre park along a creek. This design is much superior to the conventional large-lot subdivisions spreading through the area. Coffee Creek Center is a greenfield development, for sure, but one that functions within regional and community growth patterns and establishes a sustaining living environment.

Hidden Springs, although tucked away in a foothills valley north of Boise, is located only a mile or so from the edge of the city's urbanizing area. The development is considerably closer to the Boise city center than are the towns of Eagle and Nampa, which are attracting many of the region's new residents. Even so, the developer of Hidden Springs included a general store (initially subsidized by the developer) and a school in the project's initial construction phase. The store and school reduce the need for residents to travel off site, and they constitute a nascent town center that can grow along with the development.

Building for Diversity and Change

Building to meet real needs is an essential component of several of the key principles of smart growth. Community developers in greenfield areas can promote smart growth by including a variety of housing types and a variety of uses that recognize the diversity (and changing nature) of regional demographics, and by designing for adaptability over time.

The developers of large-scale communities have long recognized that building to appeal to multiple market segments tends to strengthen both initial and long-term marketability and to increase project value over time. Incorporating flexibility into the design of neighborhoods and buildings so that they can accommodate changing needs, maturing markets, and successive uses (the use of space in different ways over time) helps developments to avoid eventual obsolescence. Many older city neighborhoods—with their rows of attached multistory buildings that can be converted easily to ground-floor retail uses and second- and third-story office or residential uses and with their well-built industrial and commercial buildings that can be adapted successfully for residential and mixed uses—offer the lesson that flexibility means sustainability.

Like the original builders of the older city neighborhoods that are still going strong, today's greenfield developers can design (and market) their developments for long-term value and adaptability to changing markets. They can, for example, set aside sites for future community facilities such as fire stations, libraries, and schools; design a variety of housing types; and plan for the development of special features and uses in later phases as the development matures.

Developers who choose to focus on a particular niche market also can contribute to diversity by relating their developments to surrounding development, which means fighting the urge to create walled-off, gated communities. Developments that establish connections to their larger community by pathways, streets, and green spaces can benefit from the mix of housing types and community amenities and services available nearby.

The two projects described next—Fairview Village located 15 miles east of downtown Portland, Oregon, and the revitalization of the Hunter's Woods village center in Reston, Virginia, in the Washington, D.C. suburbs—illustrate planning and designing for diversity and change in greenfield projects.

The 95-acre Fairview Village is located in the small city of Fairview. It integrates a mix of housing with existing commercial and civic buildings. Designed as a classic neighborhood anchored by a commercial and civic center, scaled to people rather than to cars, and designed to be compatible with existing housing in the town, Fairview Village was planned through a collaborative process that included city officials and residents.

The project's mix of housing ranges from midmarket to upscale and includes 138 small-lot

The availability of some basic services on site, such as this general store, reduces travel needs for residents of Hidden Springs, a residential development near Boise.

houses, rowhouses, and duplexes, and more than 420 multifamily units, including units above retail uses. A post office, Gold's Gym, and daycare center are included as the first phase of the commercial and civic center, which will grow with the town. Fifty acres of wetlands are integrated into the project as an attractive water feature. Nine parks and

A mix of housing types that fit a range of household incomes characterizes Fairview Village, a residential development on the urbanizing edge of the Portland, Oregon, region.

numerous pathways knit Fairview Village together and connect it to the adjoining town and to an adjacent 40-acre park. Fairview Village is well ensconced into its surroundings.[2]

The reconfiguration of the Hunter's Woods neighborhood shopping center exemplifies the kind of adaptation to changing circumstances that is needed as many (once-)greenfield developments mature over time. Seven years after the development of the new town of Reston, Virginia, began in the early 1960s, the Hunter's Woods village center opened with a supermarket, pharmacy, public library, restaurants, a hardware store, and other service retail establishments, all clustered around a covered plaza. Subsequently, a community center, an assisted-living facility, and a Lutheran church were added.

In the late 1980s, however, the center began losing customers and retailers, investment in maintenance became inadequate, and by 1996 retail occupancy was down to 20 percent. A year later, a new owner, Atlantic Realty, broke ground for a $14 million redevelopment. The center was substantially reconfigured and retenanted. The grocery store and pharmacy were enlarged and a mix of stores responsive to changed consumer needs was established. The entrances to community facilities were altered in order to integrate these facilities into the commercial center. The pedestrian plaza was redesigned to offer more convenient pedestrian movement among the buildings. Whereas the original center was designed as a self-contained destination oriented to leisurely shopping, the redeveloped center emphasizes shopping convenience. Parking has been significantly expanded and a bus shelter has been strategically located. Forty-eight condominiums converted from professional offices will occupy two acres fronting on the new plaza at the edge of the center.[3]

Building for Long-Term Value

Building for long-term value is an essential component of the livability/sustainability principle of smart growth. As has been noted, the kinds of design qualities that create long-term value include compactness, green infrastructure woven through developed areas, lively civic spaces, a mix of uses and community facilities that meets diverse community needs and creates distinctive places, and connectivity with surrounding neighborhoods and regional open-space networks.

Applying these design qualities in greenfield developments can be challenging. It requires great sensitivity to architectural detail, public and civic spaces, natural site features, and community identity—often in the face of stiff competition from other developers and builders, some of whom cut corners to reduce costs, and usually in defiance of obsolete regulations that discourage such design sensitivity.

The incentive for developers to build long-term value into their projects can be weak, especially for companies that develop relatively small projects one after another rather than large-scale projects that take many years to complete. Their customers seem often disinclined to put a high value on durability and sustainability, and political leaders are mostly concerned with winning the next election. The benefits of incorporating long-term concerns into development projects need to be quantified and communicated to both homebuyers and public officials. It is in the civic interest for city councils and planning commissions to establish policies and design requirements that will avoid neighborhood obsolescence and thus maintain community stability over time.

For smart growth to take hold in greenfield locations, the real estate financing industry, most of which tends to object to designs that differ from off-the-shelf concepts, must begin to look at the potential long-term value of projects that incorporate features that make for more sustainable development. The short-term bias of lenders, says real estate consultant Christopher Leinberger, frequently forecloses their consideration of projects that will deliver long-term benefits. Leinberger urges investors to seek projects with mid-term and long-term returns based on the improved performance of smart projects.[4] The real estate financing industry also has trouble dealing with proposed projects that mix uses, because each component requires a different investment approach. Cooperation from the lending community in facilitating mixed-use financing could make the development of smart projects much easier.

Project developers—and especially the developers of relatively small, single-use projects—can add value to their projects (and value to nearby development) by fitting them better into their surroundings. This is not easy in greenfield areas in which some development has already taken place, other

development is underway, and still more is yet to come. The possibility of extending protected open space through multiple developments to protect the integrity of habitat areas, wetlands, wooded areas, or ridgelines should be investigated. As should the possibility of protecting natural features and views shared by more than one development. Perhaps the street systems of neighboring projects can be linked to facilitate public bus or school bus service. Perhaps the buildings and civic spaces in a project can be designed to complement rather than compete with adjacent developments. Perhaps shared facilities, such as schools and libraries, can be developed. Timing issues and competition among developers may make reaching private agreements on such matters difficult. But a number of developers in the same area who identify mutually beneficial opportunities might work to convince public officials to establish policies for multiproject coordination.

The two projects described next—Gap Creek in Sherwood, Arkansas, and the new downtown for Southlake, Texas—show that design quality can more than pay for itself in price premiums as well as in cooperation (rather than animosity) with public officials and neighbors, making for a smoother development process. Furthermore, developers who are mindful of their civic visibility and proud of place making will gain respect from contributing to community sustainability while making money.

Metropolitan Realty & Development at first proposed a conventional single-family subdivision for its 130-acre Gap Creek development. But the grid layout on steep slopes would require costly cut and fill, so the developer drew up a new plan that respected hillsides and kept the tree cover. Under

the new plan, Gap Creek's streets are designed to fit the terrain. A relatively narrow road—27-foot pavement on a 50-foot right-of-way—with 30- to 50-foot green buffers on both sides is used in place of a wide collector street. Streams buffered by greenbelts are retained to provide natural drainage. Trees are retained close to curb lines, and sidewalks, which wander in and out of the street right-of-way, connect to trails that run along the streams and through the greenbelts. Virtually no clearing and grading were needed to accommodate streets and lots.

The site-sensitive plan created 17 more lots than the conventional plan, many of which back up to the development's 23.5 acres of green space. The amount of piping needed for drainage was cut by a third. The development cost per lot dropped from $16,326 to $11,507. And the value of a typical Gap Creek lot came to exceed that of comparable lots in nearby subdivisions by $3,000.

In the rapidly growing Dallas/Fort Worth suburb of Southlake, Cooper & Stebbins acquired a 130-acre site for development as a standard power center and business park. However, based on the area's demographics—household incomes averaging almost $90,000 a year and a core market area of almost 100,000 people—and Southlake's clear lack of an identifying place, the developer recognized an opportunity to do more (and better). Using a plan by architect David Schwarz, Cooper & Stebbins in collaboration with the city of Southlake is developing a place-making and architecturally varied downtown instead of a run-of-the-mill suburban commercial and business center.

Southlake's downtown, centered around a town square, emphasizes high-quality design and

▲ **A conventional subdivision plan for Gap Creek in Sherwood, Arkansas, was revised to respect the site's hilly terrain. The new plan (shown here) protected hillsides and tree cover, lowered construction costs, and created 17 additional lots.**

David Schwarz/Architectural Services Inc.

▲ **Distinctive architecture and a pedestrian-orientation make the Southlake town center outside Dallas more than just another suburban greenfield commercial strip.**

corporate smart-growth principles. Local governments have found that expediting the project approval process for smart-growth developments can be a powerful incentive. Many communities have adopted policies and programs that stimulate the types of development that may be considered to represent smart growth (or at least smarter growth). The following sections describe some commonly used regulatory incentives targeted for or resulting in smart growth.

Predictability in Planning and Zoning

The fundamental policies and regulations that guide community development are generally established in a community's comprehensive plan (or general plan) and its zoning and subdivision ordinances. Plans usually identify areas in which it has been determined that specified types of growth would be desirable, and almost as frequently they identify areas in which urban development would be undesirable. Zoning regulations enforce plans by identifying what specific uses are permitted and establishing requirements pertaining to the amount and character of new development. Subdivision regulations establish standards for the layout of lots and the design of streets and other community facilities in new subdivisions.

Planning and zoning are policy and regulatory tools that should be used to establish a constructive public context for private development. And this context should be one that supports smart-growth goals, and does not further conventional suburban patterns of development.

Innovative development needs first and foremost a stable policy environment. Thus, community plans and development regulations must be based on reasonable expectations for future growth, a broad consensus on community goals and the desired character of the community, and recognition of regional needs. Local governments must move beyond wishful thinking to establish a direction for future community development.

accommodates a mix of uses. Two-story buildings have retail shops on their lower floors and office and service uses on the upper floors. City government offices are housed in a building on the town square and a post office is around the corner. The city created a tax-increment financing district to pay for the government center and is contributing $6.7 million for infrastructure improvements. The first 275,000 square feet of the $65 million center opened in 1999 and the second and third phases consisting of 68,000 square feet of retail and office space were completed in late 2001.

Regulatory Incentives

Local governments can promote smart growth in greenfield areas by using incentives to motivate developers to undertake smart developments. On the most basic level, they can revise current development policies and regulations so that developers are at least allowed to undertake projects that in-

Once a direction is established, communities can adopt comprehensive plans and zoning regulations that encourage developers to build smart projects. They can, for example, designate areas for compact growth and mixed uses, include a mix of residential uses and promote transit-friendly development in their plans, allow for and even encourage clustered development in their zoning, and allow design flexibility in their subdivision regulations. In such ways, communities can establish a constructive climate for smart growth that helps developers to do the right thing and helps to insulate the development process from naysaying NIMBYists.

Another aspect of planning and zoning that is important for motivating developers to build smart is predictability. Too few communities closely adhere to their adopted comprehensive plans, choosing instead to revise plans and amend zoning based on negotiations with developers. This method of development permitting introduces much uncertainty into the project approval process. Sometimes routine small revisions accumulate to the point that major policy changes occur, in a process known as creeping incrementalism. Sometimes communities underzone (allow by right only low-density uses) in order to force developers to seek rezoning. During the rezoning process, these communities can negotiate revisions to development proposals and exactions from developers.

Communities that engage in frequent plan and zoning revisions signal a reluctance to put the force of community policies behind the realization of smart-growth goals. Developers will hesitate to take on the risk of innovative development when competing developers easily can have the rules rewritten. Communities that forthrightly hold by their adopted growth policies and regulations, on the other hand, promise some certainty in the development approval process that can motivate developers to design for long-term value.

Lincoln, Nebraska, provides an example of how having clear and certain policies on growth can influence developers' choices. City officials in Lincoln decided decades ago to manage city growth by keeping development contiguous to the urban edge and they implemented that decision through tight control over utility extensions and zoning. The firmness of the city's growth management policies convinced developers to focus on projects within the urbanizing area and to avoid hopscotching to sites in the rural surroundings.

Another example is provided by Carlsbad, California. That city's resolute policies laying out funding responsibilities for infrastructure to be made available as development proceeds (see page 110)

give developers a predictable road map for planning new projects.

Flexible Zoning

Conventional zoning defines what uses are permitted and what form development can take in terms of lot sizes, setbacks, building heights, street standards, and so forth. It can be a straitjacket limiting proposals for innovative compact, mixed-use development. Flexible alternatives to conventional zoning have been adopted in many communities to encourage more imaginative and well-designed development. These include planned unit development (PUD) zoning, specific planning, traditional neighborhood district zones, and overlay zones. Some communities have incorporated performance standards into their zoning ordinances to encourage better-quality development.

Floating Zones and Overlay Zones

Some communities offer options to the official zoning depicted on their zoning maps in the form of floating zones, which establish certain standards for desired forms of development—say planned unit developments or traditional neighborhood districts—or, in the case of specific planning in California, call for customized planning and zoning. The regulations go into effect only when projects are officially approved on a project-by-project basis for designation on the zoning map. Floating zones therefore can provide more flexibility in regulating development.

For example, St. Johns County, Florida, recently amended its comprehensive plan to allow the development of new towns in the rural fringe outside defined growth areas. The amendments spell out basic requirements for desirable locations, range of densities, mix of uses, and other factors, but rely on developer proposals to identify specific sites that will be designated for new town development. Developer plans for proposed new towns must be quite specific in that they provide the basis on which the county commission designates sites for new town development and provides the appropriate zoning.

Planned unit development (PUD) zoning provisions, which sometimes are incorporated in subdivision regulations, are a common zoning technique for allowing the designers of relatively large projects to vary the spacing and density of development to some degree. For example, a PUD ordinance may allow development to be clustered at fairly high intensities on part of a site to retain open space elsewhere on the site. Some PUD ordinances allow a variety of uses as well, although many pertain only to residential uses.

To obtain approval for a PUD, developers usually submit a master plan for the overall project and a specific subdivision plan for the first phase of development. The approved master plan guides the design of subsequent phases. Communities may include in their PUD zoning project criteria that promote smart-growth goals for density, mix of uses, layout, open-space conservation, and other aspects of development. PUD zoning can thus provide the kind of regulatory flexibility that allows smart growth in greenfields.

Many California communities and some communities in other western states use an allied approach —the specific plan. Specific planning is based on local regulations that allow developers to draw up detailed project plans that may include innovative site layouts, innovative combinations of uses, and even innovative building designs. After reviews, hearings, and negotiations, local officials amend the general or comprehensive community plan and the zoning ordinance to incorporate the specific plan and its implementing regulations.

Many developers of master-planned communities and other large-scale projects use specific plans to provide long-term entitlements for phased developments. Developers of complex smaller projects, such as town centers, may use specific plans to define public/private roles and responsibilities. Specific planning is essentially customized planning and zoning. Both public officials and developers have found it to be a valuable method for realizing high-quality development that is attuned to community needs and desires.

Floating PUD type zoning districts that facilitate the development of projects embodying the ideas of new urbanism and traditional neighborhood design have become popular. Under conventional zoning and subdivision regulations, the developers of such projects must go to great lengths to obtain approval, which often involves obtaining multiple zoning amendments, exceptions, and variances. Traditional neighborhood district zoning, on the other hand, incorporates standards that permit the small lots, specific architectural features, street

layouts, streetscape designs, and fine-grained mix of uses advocated by new urbanists.

York County, South Carolina, for example, enacted an ordinance in January 2000 creating a traditional neighborhood district (TND) as a floating zone that requires interested developers to apply for a rezoning. The district allows all types of residential uses and requires a variety of other uses "intended to serve the daily needs of the residents while also fostering a sense of community among the residents." To qualify for rezoning as a TND, proposed projects must be at least 80 acres, have direct access to at least one arterial road, and plan to use public water and sewer facilities. A minimum of half the gross land area must be permanently allocated to open space. (Half of the required open space may be located off site.) At least 5 percent of the gross land area must be allocated to civic facilities. Residential densities in the neighborhood vary from five units per acre at the perimeter, to 20 units per acre throughout most of the neighborhood, to 25 units per acre at the center. Streetfront setbacks are minimal and front porches and bay windows may encroach on this space. Narrow streets and sidewalks are specified. Alleys are encouraged.

In its spread nationwide, TND zoning sometimes incorporates quite specific requirements for architectural features, but it offers developers opportunities to design clustered, compact, multiuse development. Wisconsin launched an interesting experiment in this regard in its 1999 smart-growth law, which, among other provisions, requires all cities and villages with a population of 12,500 or more to enact a model traditional neighborhood development ordinance as an option to conventional development.

Related to floating zones are overlay zoning districts. Overlay zones create another layer of zoning over one or more conventionally zoned districts. Communities may, for example, designate certain areas—for example, emerging regional business centers in suburban locations or the area around transit stations—for special regulatory treatment. An overlay zone may be established for specific areas to remove the impediments of conventional zoning and provide incentives for developing smartly.

Performance Zoning

Performance standards represent another aspect of adaptable zoning. Zoning ordinances often include performance standards to control noise, glare, emissions, and other factors in industrial districts. They may also use performance standards—floor/area ratios or open-space ratios—to control density. Appropriate land uses also can be determined according to their performance in meeting specified criteria and standards, but because performance standards can be somewhat complex to articulate and administer, only a few communities have adopted them as a basic means of determining appropriate land uses throughout the community.

Communities that have adopted performance standards as a means of encouraging high-quality, innovative development usually provide performance-based zoning as an option to conventional zoning. Performance-based zoning establishes standards that will be applied to development, such as the amount of traffic generated, the noise level, the amount and speed of stormwater runoff, and the compatibility of the architecture. Any use that meets the standards is permissible.

The rapidly growing city of Fort Collins, Colorado, has managed growth for more than two decades using flexible zoning techniques. Located along the Front Range of the Rocky Mountains about 65 miles north of Denver, Fort Collins began its growth spurt in the 1970s, fueled by increased enrollment at Colorado State University, an influx of high-tech industries, and the flourishing economy of the Denver region.

In 1981, the city adopted a development guidance system that allowed developers to choose special zoning—a combination of PUD procedures and performance standards—as an alternative to conventional zoning. Under the special zoning, any use could be considered in any area, subject to the performance criteria spelled out in the ordinance. Points were earned for meeting the criteria, and to gain approval development proposals had to earn sufficient points. The development guidance system was widely used for large-scale projects, which were popular among the area's developers.

As Fort Collins grew, however, its residents began to demand more control over assuring that development would be compatible with adjoining uses. Also, it became clear that most developers were less interested in having the freedom to propose any use anywhere than they were in the predictability of the development process. Based on what

the city had learned about the relative importance of the various criteria and standards that had been guiding development, the city council overhauled the development guidance ordinance in 1997. The new ordinance spells out desired locations and design qualities for new development and makes the approval process less discretionary, although many optional design possibilities have been retained.

Cluster Zoning

Many communities allow the clustering of development to conserve open space. Developers in greenfield areas are increasingly taking advantage of such regulations in order to make the best use of their sites. Clustering allows the amount of development permitted on a site to be grouped compactly in one section to conserve natural areas (and provide open space) on the remainder of the site. Clustering has been touted by developers, builders, and planners for decades as a means of reducing development costs and saving open space.[5] It is, however, frequently opposed by neighbors and community activists fearful of what they believe is higher-density development.

The clustering approach is becoming more common in greenfields development, largely on the strength of its environmental benefits. So-called "conservation developments" have shown initial and long-term value in the market and thus are increasingly popular among developers and homebuyers as well as public officials. Rural communities interested in the conservation of their open space should look to ordinances facilitating conservation developments rather than engaging in mostly futile efforts to stem the tide of development with large-lot zoning.

Coffee Creek Center (see profile on page 84) represents a contemporary approach to cluster development. Another recent conservation development demonstrating aspects of smart growth on a greenfield site is the New Century development located in Maplewood in the Twin Cities region of Minnesota. Developed by Robert Engstrom, New Century is on a 55-acre site assembled from 13 parcels (some with houses) situated just inside the I-494/I-694 beltway about a ten-minute drive from downtown St. Paul. It offers a mix of housing styles—80 single-family homes on lots that average about a quarter acre, 16 duplex units called twinhomes, and 85 townhouses—in an area where conventional subdivisions are the rule. Amenities

include a central park, extensive plantings along the streets, and access to an adjacent city park and woodlands. The overall density of New Century is 3.3 units per acre.

Density Bonuses

Many communities have crafted zoning provisions that allow developers to increase the development density of projects in return for incorporating special features or qualities into those projects. Developers usually consider such bonuses to be an attractive incentive. Density bonuses have been used mostly to improve the quality of downtown development or to stimulate the production of affordable housing. They can be used also to promote compactness and a mix of uses in greenfield projects.

In Anne Arundel County, Maryland, a new ordinance establishes four mixed-use development (MXD) districts in which allowable densities are higher than for the districts they will replace. The four MXD districts are 1) for primarily residential use, 2) for primarily commercial use, 3) for primarily employment use, and 4) for transit-oriented uses. Working with landowners and developers to identify parcels of an appropriate size and location, the county is preparing sector plans that will designate specific areas for the mixed-use districts.

For development that achieves a real mix of uses, these districts provide the option to develop at densities substantially higher than the underlying standard zoning. In the MXD-residential district, for example, housing can be at a density of seven units per acre (compared with the standard one unit per acre). In the MXD-transit district, the allowable floor/area ratio (FAR) is 2 (compared with the standard FAR of 0.1).

Anne Arundel's ordinance lists the uses permitted within each mixed-use district. Allowed within the MXD-residential district, for example, are all types of residential uses except apartment hotels, many types of retail and service operations (excluding some, like car dealerships, that clearly are unwanted in residential areas), and professional and general offices. The other three districts allow almost all types of commercial and service uses, most residential uses, and offices.

The ordinance also specifies proportions of various uses in order to assure a real mix of uses within the mixed-use districts. In the MXD-residential district, for example, at least 50 percent but no more than 80 percent of the floor space must be residential uses, 10 to 25 percent retail and service uses, and 10 to 20 percent office uses. In addition, the ordinance requires a specific phasing of the mix: no more than half of the commercial and office space can be constructed until at least 25 percent of the dwelling units are under construction, and no more than 75 percent of the commercial and office space can be constructed until at least 50 percent of the dwelling units are under construction.

Anne Arundel County's mixed-use districts ordinance contains provisions that require compatibility and connections with adjoining uses, the preservation and enhancement of natural features, the integration of buildings and open space, and high-quality building designs. It also establishes detailed rules pertaining to the design of parking, pedestrian circulation, landscaping and buffering, and signs.

Among the density bonus programs adopted by communities to encourage developers to provide affordable housing, that of Montgomery County, Maryland, stands out. The county has initiated various programs to produce housing for low- and moderate-income residents to offset high housing prices (caused by the county's residential desirability and, some say, its restrictive regulatory climate).

The centerpiece of Montgomery County's affordable housing effort has been an inclusionary housing requirement: all residential developments of 50 units or more must include a proportion of moderate-cost housing. In return, developers are awarded density bonuses on a sliding scale to relieve the financial burden of providing such housing. Strict design standards are enforced so that the lower-cost units cannot be identified as such. Resale restrictions keep the housing available to lower-income residents. This and other county programs have produced more than 35,000 below-market-price housing units.

By-Right Zoning for Smart Development

When communities adopt development regulations that involve flexible zoning and discretionary approval procedures, they generally require project proposals to undergo special reviews and hearings. Public officials tend to think that the greater the flexibility in development regulations the closer the oversight of specific proposals should be.

In so-called discretionary approval systems the approving authority has a considerable amount of leeway in interpreting the requirements of the ordinance. Certain kinds of provisions—those that call for, say, integrating buildings with the pedes-

trian circulation system or for landscaping that enhances vehicular patterns and open spaces—leave much room for judgment and for disagreements that can delay decisions. Such discretionary systems also allow public officials to impose additional (and perhaps costly) conditions on the proposed development—such as off-site infrastructure improvements, density reductions, or design modifications. Although many communities adopt flexible zoning and discretionary approval systems in order to incentivize smart development, the approval process often deteriorates into arguments over the reasonableness of requests and requirements that at some point may outweigh any incentives in the ordinance for innovative design.

To avoid this problem, communities should write provisions and map zones in ways that allow compact and multiuse development by right. Administrative review and standard permitting procedures should suffice; special approval processes should not be required. This will not be an easy job. To write specific provisions that can guide growth to achieve certain design and development qualities requires vision, imagination, and concise description of desired outcomes. To designate in advance areas to which these provisions can apply requires an agile balancing of competing resident and community interests.

Whereas smart development in Anne Arundel County's mixed-use districts (see preceding section on density bonuses) is intended to be a by-right option, subject to administrative reviews but not additional hearings, Boulder, Colorado, has adopted a variety of mixed-use zoning districts that allow mixed-use development by right but also provide for discretionary reviews for variations from certain standards.

The city's mixed-use redeveloping district, for example, which was adopted in 1985, allows a variety of residential, retail, and office uses on the same lot or in the same project. The intention of the district is to stimulate the development of high-density housing and preserve historic structures along Pearl Street. It establishes an array of acceptable uses, allows additional uses if at least half of the proposed floor area is for residential uses, and makes available still more uses after special review. To help retain historic structures, the district has no minimum setback, sideyard, or building width requirements, and balconies may be counted toward the open-space requirement. According to Bob Cole, director of current planning in Boulder, a number of projects have been constructed within this and similar mixed-use zoning districts, about half of them by right without special reviews for variations in standards.

Charlotte, North Carolina's zoning districts for mixed-use development furnish another example. The Charlotte ordinance, which was adopted in 1992 and has been amended, includes four urban residential (UR) districts intended for use in urbanizing areas as well as in older areas that might benefit from revitalization. (Charlotte's ordinance also creates a mixed-use development district bordering downtown and three mixed-use districts for large-scale development.) Within the UR districts, a mix of uses is allowed by right. This improves the opportunity for developers to build mixed-use projects without incurring undue delays and expenses because of the approval process.

The UR districts are designated on zoning maps according to neighborhood plans. They allow a range of development densities and a variety of use mixes. The UR-1 district, for example, allows a mix of housing types. The UR-3 district permits business or office uses as long as they take place in structures that are no larger in floor area than twice the building footprint.

All four UR districts have development standards that allow flexible design. The minimum lot size is only 3,000 square feet. Yards—front, side, and rear—can be small. The size of structures with more than three housing units is regulated by floor/area ratios. Allowable building heights may be increased by expanding sideyards and rearyards. In addition, developers can earn density bonuses by preserving historic structures and by providing certain amenities and design features, such as public open spaces, pathways, fountains, and roof areas that are usable as open space.

Smart Siting and Design of Public Buildings

Local governments can locate and design public buildings in ways that promote smart growth. Public buildings—schools, libraries, courthouses, government offices, post offices, and the like—are activity generators that are often overlooked as an element of community design. As urban critic and journalist Roberta Gratz writes, public buildings can be "anchors [that] work as integral pieces of

a whole place, not separate from it. They don't draw away from their surroundings, but weave into it. They are part of the ordinary workaday life and fabric of a place. Most importantly, they generate activity and diversity."[6]

Too often the locations of new public buildings are chosen on the basis of site costs, a consideration that ignores the many potential benefits of developing such facilities as part of existing or planned neighborhoods. To cost-conscious decision makers, inexpensive sites at the edge of town or outside the town seem attractive. That development in outlying locations will contribute to sprawl and may inconvenience employees is not taken into account.

Communities investing in new or expanded public facilities should treat them as opportunities for supporting multiuse centers of activity. Properly sited, designed, and programmed public buildings can fit into and help bring about the evolution of walkable, compact, and distinctive centers of activity. Educational facilities, libraries, and civic centers should be planned to make positive contributions to the livability of their communities.

The potential smart-growth role of standard community facilities—the schools and community centers found in every neighborhood—should not be overlooked. School buildings and community libraries should be sited in ways that make them conveniently accessible by foot to nearby residents, not just accessible by school bus and car. If such facilities are designed as elements within a community retail or business center they can add life and place-making value to such centers.

Lower Infrastructure Costs

Communities can promote smart development in greenfield areas by lowering its infrastructure costs—making smart development more economical than unsmart development. Lower infrastructure costs may be offered in a variety of formats, including:

▲ flexible or alternative standards for infrastructure and adequate public facility requirements;
▲ waived or reduced impact fees; and
▲ the establishment of special taxing districts to finance infrastructure improvements (or the direct public funding or construction of infrastructure).

Standards and Requirements

Many communities are experimenting with revised infrastructure standards that lower development costs even while they result in superior site design. A number of the programs and projects that have been profiled in this chapter include or have taken advantage of revised infrastructure standards. York County, South Carolina's traditional neighborhood district zone (see page 90) allows narrower than standard street pavement widths. The developer of Gap Creek (see page 87) redesigned the main collector street as a parkway with a narrower pavement than otherwise would have been required. Coffee Creek Center (see page 84), a conservation development, uses natural drainage channels for stormwater management instead of expensive pipes and curb-and-gutter street drains.

(Coffee Creek Center also requires a smaller linear amount of streets and of water and sewer pipes by virtue of its cluster design than would similar noncluster developments. Allowing clustering is another action that communities may take to reduce infrastructure costs for development.)

Many localities have adequate public facilities requirements, which means that approvals are based on there being enough roads, sewer capacity, and so forth to support proposed development. Such localities can promote development in priority development areas by reducing infrastructure capacity requirements for development in those areas. Florida, for example, requires all local jurisdictions to determine the concurrency of proposed development with adequate facilities before they approve new developments, but the state also allows municipalities to establish what are called concurrency management districts, or areas in which growth is allowed to take place despite congested road conditions.

Another example is offered by Montgomery County, Maryland, which found that strict applications of its adequate public facilities requirements frequently prohibited intense development around transit stations, which is where the county hoped to encourage development. The county therefore now lowers or even waives level-of-service standards in locations where it desires to promote growth.

Impact Fees

Many communities levy impact fees on new development to help finance the infrastructure needed to support it—usually off-site facilities such as high-way and intersection improvements, water mains, and parks that may serve several developments. Lowering these fees in effect reduces developers' infrastructure costs.

Some local governments waive or reduce such fees for types of development that serve particular community objectives. Impact fees may be waived, for example, for affordable housing projects or for projects located in inner-city areas in need of revitalization. Various types of development representing smart growth, such as compact development, multiuse development, and conservation development, also could be recognized by communities as meriting reductions in impact fees. Development that is smartly located—in designated growth areas or near developed areas for which some public services are already provided—could be rewarded with lower fees. (Charging developers higher fees for projects located outside such areas is justified because public services there must be provided from scratch.)

Austin, Texas, has established a desired development zone (including highway corridors, transit-station areas, and the inner city) within which fees are waived and other inducements such as infrastructure enhancements and modifications of parking requirements are provided to attract development.

The small city of Altamonte Springs, Florida, which is ten miles north of Orlando, has a fee-incentive program to attract development to its central business district. For projects over a threshold size, fees for building inspection, plan review, and transportation are waived and sewer and water connection fees and the wastewater treatment facility charge are halved. Several major projects have been developed in the downtown since these incentives were first offered and plans are in the works for several more. The city expects to recoup the forgone building fees from additional tax revenues in less than five years.

Special Taxing Districts

Many communities that are starved for funds to build basic infrastructure have allowed developers to establish special taxing districts for financing infrastructure through bond issues. The bonds are repaid through annual assessments over a 15- to 20-year period on properties within the district. Such an arrangement saves development costs, which usually translates to lower housing prices or better-quality houses.

A variation on this theme is the tax-increment district. Many communities use tax-increment financing (TIF) for infill and redevelopment projects, and it can be equally useful in greenfield areas. TIF involves the establishment of districts within which all increases in property taxes after the district's creation are committed to paying for infrastructure improvements. Because this prospective tax revenue is guaranteed by local governments, it can collateralize revenue bonds used for the front-end financing of improvements.

In most states, special taxing districts must be approved (and often administered) by local governments. Communities can use the opportunities afforded them by the power to create special districts to give preference to development planned with smart-growth features, as was done in Hanover Park, Illinois, and Southlake, Texas.

The Chicago suburb of Hanover Park recently established a TIF district encompassing a number of infill parcels around a transit station. The goal of the district is to promote the development of a mixed-use town center. The TIF revenues are expected to pay for the infrastructure improvements that will be needed to support transit-oriented development.

The government center and extensive infrastructure improvements for Southlake's new downtown development (profiled on pages 87–88) are being funded through a 408-acre tax-increment reinvestment zone. The tax-increment district in this case and many others provides a mechanism for long-term investment in improvements needed to support public and private investment.

Promoting the Conservation of Open Space
Open-space conservation is a key principle of smart growth. Communities can promote it through incentives aimed at individual property owners and nonprofit organizations with a mission to protect open space. (They may also acquire open space, an option that is further discussed under "Regulatory Requirements" later in this chapter.)

Conservation Easements
Conservation easements permanently protect land from development and cost less than full acquisi-

tion of the land. They are being used increasingly for open-space protection. Landowners retain the right to farm land under conservation easement or to keep it in its natural state. The land is kept on the tax rolls and taxpayers can deduct the value of donated easements from taxable income.

Private conservancy organizations like the Nature Conservancy, the Trust for Public Land, and the Conservation Fund purchase many conservation easements. According to a survey by the Land Trust Alliance, an alliance of private nonprofit land trusts in the United States, local and regional land trusts by 1998 had purchased or established 7,392 conservation easements that protect nearly 1.4 million acres of open space, representing almost a fourfold increase in the amount of easement-protected acreage in just a decade. Land trusts and conservancy groups often partner with developers to conserve open space within developments.

A conservation easement received by the Lowcountry Open Land Trust on a 314-acre former cotton plantation located on Wadmalaw Island a dozen miles southwest of Charleston, South Carolina, provides an example. Existing zoning would have allowed approximately 70 houses on this site. The landowner agreed to cluster development—amounting to no more than seven houses—on a 30-acre parcel, and to leave more than 85 percent of the farm permanently undeveloped and available for forestry, agriculture, and recreational uses. This was the 15th such easement received by the Lowcountry Open Land Trust on Wadmalaw Island, bringing the land conserved there to more than 2,500 acres. Lowcountry Open Land Trust has conserved 24,917 acres of open space on the South Carolina coast.[7]

Planning Ahead
States and local governments in undeveloped and developing areas should plan ahead for open-space conservation. They should identify significant natural features and conservation areas in advance of development and encourage the formation of entities that can assume the ownership or management of conserved open spaces.

The advance identification of conservation areas provides incentives for smart growth in two ways. First, it notifies landowners and developers that the community wants certain land to remain undeveloped, and thus helps them make decisions about the location of development and the design of development sites. Knowing ahead of time what land is considered sensitive helps developers not to choose sites or lay out their sites in ways that may embroil them in lengthy controversies. Second, knowing the location of conserved open space enables those developers for whom the marketing advantage of locations near open space is important to choose their sites judiciously.

Three diverse programs—the state of Maryland's GreenPrint program, southern California's Natural Communities Conservation Planning program, and the Phoenix region's Desert Spaces Plan—exemplify governmental efforts to plan ahead in order to promote the conservation of open space.

In May 2001, Maryland launched its GreenPrint program with $35 million in first-year funding. GreenPrint aims to preserve the state's green infrastructure—that is, the land deemed necessary to support diverse plant and animal life and perform important natural processes like filtering water and cleaning air. The state used satellite imaging technology and input from many organizations and agencies to map its important unprotected green infrastructure. GreenPrint includes a plan for coordinating public and private land protection activities that constitutes an open invitation to landowners, conservation groups, land trusts, and public agencies to use an array of tools—land acquisition, easements, and other set-asides—to accomplish the goals of the program.

In southern California, developers, conservationists, landowners, and federal, state, and local governments are working to implement a plan for the coastal sage scrub ecosystem that extends from Santa Barbara to the Mexican border, providing habitat for a number of endangered species, including the California gnatcatcher and least Bell's vireo, both songbirds, as well as the Stephens' kangaroo rat. More than 70 percent of the original ecosystem has been depleted by development.

Developed under the auspices of the state's Natural Community Conservation Planning (NCCP) program, the southern California plan seeks to identify and protect essential habitat for all species within the sage scrub ecosystem. The main objective of the plan is to reconcile conflicts between development and conservation proactively and on a regional basis. It combines the land use powers of

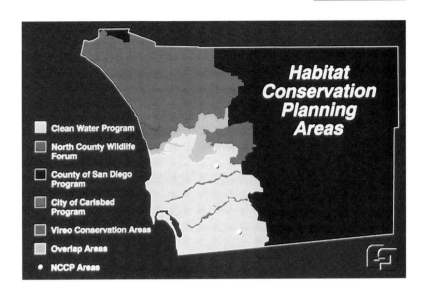

local communities and the enforcement powers of the federal Endangered Species Act within the framework of a state government planning program. By identifying areas where development can occur, the plan should provide certainty to developers, and by setting aside critical habitat in perpetuity, it should assure environmentalists that habitat will not be lost bit by bit as projects are developed.

San Diego adopted a Multiple Species Conservation Plan (MSCP) in 1997, a key NCCP subregional plan. (Sections of San Diego County are covered as well by two other plans—the Multiple Habitat Conservation Program and the Multiple Habitat Conservation and Open Space Program.) The San Diego region, one of the most biologically diverse environments in the continental United States, is home to some 1,700 species of plants and more than 400 species of birds.[8] Rapid growth in the region over many years has led to fragmentation and loss of habitat. Currently, more than 200 plants and animals are listed, or proposed to be listed, as endangered, threatened, or rare species by the state or federal government.

The 1997 MSCP covers about 900 square miles in southwest San Diego County, about half of which is planned for development and the other half for permanent habitat. Much of the land is publicly owned. Under the MSCP, developers will be required to set aside about three-fourths of their property as natural habitat or buy into a local mitigation bank. For their part, government agencies will buy about 27,000 acres, which will cost upward of $540 million.[9] Thus far, federal, state, and local governments

▲ Multispecies planning in San Diego County, an exceptionally rich and fragile environment, has provided greater predictability for development and conservation.

have purchased 13,348 acres of habitat in the San Diego region, mostly in the MSCP area.[10]

In Phoenix, the Maricopa Association of Governments (MAG), which consists of 27 jurisdictions within Maricopa County, launched another approach to the advance identification of sensitive lands in the form of its 1995 Desert Spaces Plan. The MAG region encompasses 9,200 square miles, of which about 30 percent is privately owned.

Rapid growth has consumed much of the region's open space, particularly in the Sonoran Desert. The aim of the Desert Spaces Plan is to create a regional open-space system. Member governments are enlisted to protect the open spaces that define the character of the valley while allowing for growth and development. The plan calls for preserving and in some cases enhancing the floodplains of major rivers and washes (dry river beds) that thread through the region, canals and cultural sites, upland desert vegetation, wildlife habitat, and scenic landscapes.

Existing parks and protected open space form the basis for an interconnected system of parks and open space that are regionally significant from a scenic, biological, archeological, or recreational perspective. The Desert Spaces Plan recommends specific management policies for such regionally significant open spaces. The plan also proposes a regional network of trails mostly along rivers, washes, and canals.[11] Increased coordination among local, county, state, and federal jurisdictions in acquiring and conserving open space is the plan's primary means of implementation. Set-asides of open space made by developers as part of the development approval process are included in this coordinated effort.

Management of Conserved Land

Communities can provide an incentive for the conservation of open space by working with conservancies, land trusts, and other environmental and civic organizations to establish management approaches for conserved lands. Developers can deed the open space they set aside to a community association, but they may wish to assure its long-term conservation by arranging for its management by a land conservation organization.

Developers and land conservation groups increasingly are working together to preserve and manage open space that is part of development projects. For example, a number of local land trusts—voluntary organizations that work with landowners to conserve land of scenic, habitat, historic, or other value—have promoted or taken part in conservation developments. More than 1,200 local land trusts exist in the United States, up from about 750 in 1985. Collectively, their land acquisitions (both easements and fee simple) have helped protect a total of more than 4.7 million acres of land.[12]

Transferable Development Rights

The transfer of development rights (TDR) from property that communities want to keep undeveloped to property that communities want to see more intensely developed can accomplish two smart-growth goals simultaneously—protecting open space in greenfields and increasing development densities in urban or urbanizing areas. TDR programs, like easements, treat the right to develop land as a commodity separate from the land itself. Allowing property owners to sell valuable development rights for use on properties in designated receiving areas compensates them for regulations that limit their development opportunities. The purchasers of these development rights are allowed under TDR programs to use them in designated areas to develop at higher than normal densities.

TDRs rely on market forces rather than regulations to protect open space, which is a major advantage of this incentive. The sale and transfer of development rights are market transactions that must be supported by public policies and programs.

TDR programs are not without problems. Many jurisdictions have found them difficult to administer. They are complex, and thus difficult for small planning staffs to implement and for landowners to understand and accept. People who live near or in receiving areas may object to increased project densities in their neighborhoods. The strength of the market for the development rights depends on the strength of development pressures in the receiving areas. Furthermore, if developers can readily obtain rezonings or variances to develop at higher densities in the receiving areas, they have no incentive to purchase additional development rights.

San Luis Obispo County, California, uses a form of TDR to protect Monterey pine forest habitat from development. An antiquated subdivision covering part of this habitat in the coastal city of Cambria created small lots that in many cases are located on steep and highly erodible slopes. The county's voluntary transfer of development credits (TDC) program features a revolving fund that allows the acquisition of undeveloped lots in the pine forest (sending area) for the sale of their development credits to property owners in receiving areas who want to build homes larger than allowed by zoning. More than 200 transfers have been completed and the county has recently expanded its TDC program to the whole county for the preservation of agricultural land and for the protection of severe fire-hazard areas.[13]

Montgomery County, Maryland, adopted a TDR program in the early 1980s that has become one of the most well known and successful of such programs in the country. The county has designated large tracts of agricultural land as rural density transfer zones, which are downzoned from one dwelling per five acres to one dwelling per 25 acres. Owners of land in the transfer zones can sell development credits based on the original zoning. Owners of land in receiving areas that are designated in the county's general plan can buy the development credits and use them to increase development densities. Montgomery County's TDR program has transferred credits equivalent to 4,300 dwelling units from more than 40,000 acres of farmland.[14]

Washington Township, located near Trenton, New Jersey, recently established a TDR program that is associated with its plan to create a traditional town center. Township officials working closely with developers designed a multiuse town center that includes 900 to 1,000 housing units around a commercial complex containing 250,000 to 300,000 square feet of retail and office space, as well as parks, gardens, pathways, and two lakes.

Washington Township placed restrictions on rural development to encourage density transfers to the center. According to township planner Robert Melvin, development rights for 52 housing units had been transferred to the town center site as of late 2001 and negotiations were underway for the transfer of 250 to 500 more units. Melvin reports that townhouses in the center are selling at prices more than 20 percent above similar houses elsewhere in the township, and that more residential and commercial development has been approved.

Proactive Transportation Choices Programs

Generally, in greenfield areas, the car is king. Developers expect to cater to the automobile in their choice of sites and in designing their projects, and their expectations usually are supported by public policies and regulations giving priority to road construction and paying scant attention to other modes of travel. Communities concerned

◀ These single-family detached and attached dwellings adjoining Orchard Park are part of one of several new housing projects clustered around new parks and natural areas in Washington Township, New Jersey's planned town center.

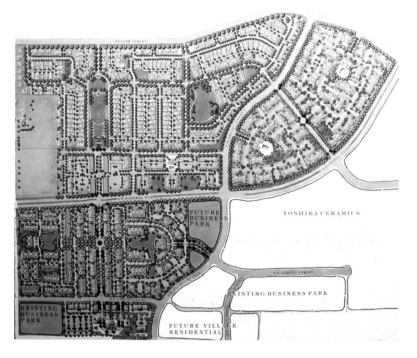

▲ Designation of Orenco Station as a town center in Portland Metro's 2040 plan started the ball rolling for this transit-oriented and pedestrian-oriented development. The project, which covers 190 acres, includes 1,834 housing units and retail and office space.

with promoting smart growth can encourage developers to consider site designs and facilities that can widen opportunities for nonautomobile travel.

In communities that impose standards for adequate public facilities as a condition for development approvals, highway congestion can lead to development moratoriums. Developers will try to avoid moratoriums by looking for ways to reduce traffic generated by their projects, in particular for ways to broaden travel choices. Furthermore, projects that provide access by means other than automobiles can increase their market penetration, which is an opportunity that many developers welcome. To successfully broaden travel choices, developers need guidance on best practices in designing projects that can accommodate multimodal travel possibilities.

Among the programs communities can undertake that can provide incentives for developers to expand travel choices are the following:

▲ plans and guidelines for trail and pathway systems for pedestrians and bikers;
▲ planning for extensions of bus and rail systems and related development;
▲ design standards for bus- and rail-access points; and
▲ transportation demand management (TDM) programs.

Trail Planning

Communitywide plans for walking, biking, and hiking routes and trails indicate how existing trail networks can be extended and interconnected throughout the community (and even the region). That such a plan exists in a community evidences public support for pathway systems and prompts developers to consider them in project designs. Trail plans usually provide guidelines for the incorporation of pedestrian and bike pathways into projects and suggest that these be connected to the external network of trails. Such plans often provide design and construction standards covering widths, materials, and other aspects of trails.

Federal and state funding is available for planning and building trail systems. Bicycle trail and pedestrian pathway projects account for 54 percent of the $3.27 billion in federal funding awarded since 1992 for transportation enhancement projects.

The Yakima, Washington, greenway plan illustrates effective trail planning (see photo on page 35). Yakima City and County updated its greenway plan in 1995 and subsequently adopted it as part of the Yakima urban area comprehensive plan. The greenway plan assures that the ten-mile greenway corridor will be preserved as the urban area is developed. This corridor includes recreation areas, parks, wetlands, and other environmentally sensitive lands along the Yakima and Naches rivers, and it provides facilities for bicycle and pedestrian travel. City and county agencies, the Yakima Greenway Foundation, and private property owners cooperated in establishing the greenway, which in some sectors is bordered by commercial, residential, and industrial uses. The foundation, acting as a land trust, manages the corridor land.[15]

Transit Service Extensions

Advance planning for the extension of bus and rail transit systems—even though far in the future—acts as an incentive for developers to pay attention to opportunities for transit-oriented development. If the future location of rail lines and stations is known, developers can choose sites incorporating or accessible to future transit service, and they can design their projects to be transit friendly.

Ordinarily transit follows rather than precedes development and it is hard to predict service availability in developing areas. Nevertheless, since rail-transit extensions generally require an eight-to ten-year lead time for design and development, current plans may well identify greenfield sites that will be accessible to rail service. Bus service is more readily extended and also somewhat more predictable, especially along major routes in regions where transit agencies are aggressively expanding.

Portland, Oregon, is a community that plans well in advance of transit service in order to promote transit-friendly forms of development. For example, transit and regional planning agencies worked with jurisdictions along the proposed westward extension of the light-rail line to prepare plans for fairly dense development around future rail stations. Thus, when service on the extension began in 1999, a number of transit-oriented projects were already completed and others had started construction. This gave an immediate boost to ridership.

Most of these transit-oriented developments also exhibit other important smart-growth characteristics, namely compactness, a mix of uses, and a pedestrian-orientation. Orenco Station, for example, in Hillsboro, is a 190-acre, transit-oriented new community that will feature 1,834 residential units—single-family houses, townhouses, apartments, loft units, and accessory units—and a multiuse town center that includes some apartments over retail uses. Small lots, alley parking, and narrow streets help make the neighborhood pedestrian friendly. A network of streets and walkways and parks provides convenient, attractive access to the transit station.

Bus Stop and Transit Station Standards

Published design standards for bus stops and rail-station areas can help developers relate their projects to transit options. The Metropolitan Transit Development Board in San Diego in 1993 issued *Designing for Transit*, a publication that shows ways of integrating land development with public transportation. Recognizing that it is usually cheaper and easier to design for transit needs in advance than to retrofit for transit later, *Designing for Transit* offers guidelines for creating pedestrian- and transit-oriented communities and specific design standards for bus and light-rail transit facilities.

The publication's design standards for bus facilities include, for example, bus dimensions and turning templates, bus stop dimensions and layout, and standards for various types of bus shelters. For light rail, *Designing for Transit* provides standards for placement of the rail line—down the center of streets, along the side of streets, or in separate rights-of-way—and for different types of station shelters.

The Metropolitan Transit Development Board's design guidelines appeared a year after the city of San Diego published design guidelines for transit-oriented development that focused on achieving patterns of development that can support transit service. These two publications give developers the tools they need to plan and design projects that will take advantage of transit opportunities and bolster transit use.

Transportation Demand Management

By putting together transportation demand management (TDM) programs, communities often stimulate developers to provide more multimodal transportation features in their projects. (See pages 52–53 for a general discussion of TDM.) TDM programs typically target major employers, encouraging them to compensate employees for using transit (instead of free employer parking), to promote vanpools and carpools, to provide storage and changing facilities for bikers, and to include pathways and bus stops in their projects. Developers of business parks, in turn, may find that putting TDM elements into their projects helps them to attract employers to that location.

The developer of Hacienda Business Park in Pleasanton, California, for example, was stimulated by the city's 1984 trip reduction ordinance to take a number of steps that have helped minimize the traffic impacts of the business park. The developer formed an association of property owners and tenants to implement a trip reduction program for the business park. This included designing preferential parking for carpools, installing bicycle racks, and appointing transportation coordinators to help workers find new ways of commuting.

Expedited Approvals

Projects that advance smart-growth ideals need help in overcoming approval problems. These typically include a lack of consistent guidelines and standards, duplication and conflicts within and among the agencies involved, time-consuming consecutive reviews, and uncertainty about the appropriate length of reviews. Planner/architect Mark Hinshaw, director of urban design for LMN Architects in Seattle, observes that "in many cities, land use codes are a morass of lists, tables, diagrams, definitions, subsections, subparagraphs, cross-references, amendments, and footnotes" that require attorneys to decipher them.[16]

As was noted earlier in this chapter, the kinds of flexible zoning techniques that communities adopt for promoting smart development often entail special approval processes that can be particularly long and uncertain in outcome. Proposals submitted under planned unit development and similar zoning provisions usually require detailed plans and specifications, special hearings, and even separate reviews by design commissions. So do most proposals using mixed-use zoning, density bonuses, traditional neighborhood district zoning, and clustering provisions. The requirements can become so onerous that they outweigh any advantages developers might accrue from playing by smart-growth rules. Says Hinshaw: "we need regulations that are more direct, more explicit, more qualitative in their intent, and much more concise."

Communities that have successfully streamlined or otherwise reformed their development regulations have focused on some or all of the following techniques:

▲ Clarify the organization and language of ordinances and coordinate the provisions and procedures specified in different ordinances.
▲ Periodically update provisions, weeding out unnecessary or unworkable requirements and reevaluating standards and guidelines.
▲ Establish procedures for interpreting questions.
▲ Specify conditions for the routine approval of minor permit applications.
▲ Spell out standards and criteria for discretionary approvals.
▲ Publish guidebooks and checklists for applicants.
▲ Hold preapplication conferences for complex projects.
▲ Establish a central information center to supply basic information and to route requests and questions to appropriate departments.
▲ Train the members of boards and commissions who deal with development permits.
▲ Provide fair and consistent rules for hearing procedures and official decision making.

Short of comprehensively revamping codes to simplify requirements, communities can expedite the

approval process, with a focus on moving qualified smart-growth proposals quickly through reviews and hearings. Austin, Texas, for example, has promised to streamline permitting for development in the city's desired development zone (see page 95). Some communities treat highly desirable economic development projects this way, sometimes assigning a staff person to virtually hand-carry the application through the process. Communities can improve the process for proposals exemplifying smart growth by means of some or all of the following measures:

▲ Designate a single agency, such as the planning department or economic development department, to coordinate interagency reviews and keep projects moving through the pipeline.
▲ Make administrative decisions rather than hold special hearings on routine waivers and exemptions from development regulations.
▲ Prepare simplified checklists and other easy-to-read guidelines to inform applicants about procedures and requirements.
▲ Before plans are formally submitted, arrange conferences between agencies and developers to discuss the development concepts and the steps required for approval.

Mill Creek, a suburb of Seattle, Washington, successfully expedited the approval process for development proposals meeting its criteria for the SR527 corridor subarea plan around the town center. An advance review of the environmental impacts of specific types of projects (called "planned actions") was performed prior to the submission of actual proposals. The understanding thus obtained of potential impacts reduced the time necessary to approve projects that fit the description of planned actions. As a result of this streamlining, three developments totaling 774 housing units made it through the approval process in four months. The combination of the predictability provided by an approved subarea plan and prior evaluation of environmental impacts significantly speeded up the approval process.[17]

Regulatory Requirements

Communities need not limit themselves to offering incentives for smart development. They also can adopt policies and regulations that require smart development. Regulations requiring specific forms of development can be powerful tools for promoting smart growth in greenfield areas, but they are tools that must be used constructively.

Used constructively, regulatory requirements for smart development can establish a level playing field for all developers. Fair standards can promote good development and restrain poor development. Fair standards help to maintain the value of public and private investments for many years. Used less constructively, regulatory requirements for smart development may actually become disincentives for innovative development and they may raise the costs for smart development to the point where it benefits only well-to-do households.

All community decisions about growth and development should seek a point of balance between establishing a reasonable threshold of development quality and serving a wide range of development needs. Strict standards for the design and construction of housing might be adopted to maintain the community's long-term value. But adopting these standards can raise housing costs, which in effect deprives lower-income households of opportunities to live in the community. Communities need to pay careful attention to where they draw the lines. And they need to draw them on their own terms, understanding that each possible outcome has both winners and losers.

Homebuilders in the competitive entry-level homeownership market, for example, often oppose any regulations, like open-space requirements, that even slightly increase their development costs. Unlike the buyers of upscale housing who will pay premiums for green open space, their buyers are often looking for the lowest possible price. In competitive metropolitan markets, affordable homebuilders often cannot raise prices to cover higher costs. Therefore, they are inclined to cut costs rather than add quality. Some communities offer affordable housing developers quid pro quos for higher-quality design and construction, such as density increases that lower land costs, assistance with financing costs, or faster permitting. A more viable solution would be to establish minimum standards for entire regional housing markets, but fragmented governance within metropolitan areas makes this a quixotic solution as well.

Requiring Compact, Multiuse Development

Techniques for requiring compact and multiuse development are of very recent origin. Their introduction here and there has flown in the face of regulatory tradition in most U.S. communities, with its emphasis on maximum densities and heights, minimum lot sizes and setbacks, and segregation of uses. Regulating for compact and multiuse development also runs counter to the tendency of most Americans to think of the ideal suburban form of development as loose bundles of similar uses spread over the landscape.

Nevertheless, some communities have begun to require urban patterns of development—even on greenfield sites. Among the techniques they have brought to this task are urban growth boundaries and urban service limits, minimum density policies, and mandatory mixed-use zoning.

Growth Boundaries and Service Limits

An urban growth boundary is a line drawn around an area—a city, a town, or an urban region—to distinguish between land suitable for development and land that will remain mostly undeveloped. Urban growth boundaries are like superzoning in that they establish broad policy about the desired location of growth.

Comprehensive plans and zoning promote urban development densities within growth boundaries, and supportive infrastructure systems are provided. Downzoning to very low densities discourages development outside growth boundaries, as do limits on extending water and sewer services. Land outside urban boundaries is generally restricted to resource uses, such as farming and timbering.

Urban service limits, which communities have used for decades, differ somewhat in scope and intent from urban growth boundaries. Urban service limits designate areas to which specific urban services—roads, schools, sewer and water lines, and so forth—will be extended. Although zoning that restrains development outside the areas planned for urban services may be used to buttress these limits, the usual focus of such policies is the orderly expansion of urban service systems rather than smart forms of development and open-space conservation.

But the differences between growth boundaries and urban service limits are not necessarily clear-cut.

The so-called "blue line" that establishes limits on water supply on the upper slopes of the mountains surrounding Boulder, Colorado, has become a de facto urban growth boundary. Boulder's aggressive open-space acquisition program supports the blue-line policy, as does a joint city-county comprehensive plan that limits the number of subdivisions outside the boundary that would need urban levels of services.

Urban growth boundaries and service limits are generally designed to accommodate the growth that is projected to occur over a specified period of time, usually 20 years. They are supposed to be reviewed periodically and expanded if necessary. Some communities designate areas outside the boundary as urban reserves to indicate where development potentially might occur in the distant future.

Appealing in their simplicity, urban growth boundaries have become increasingly popular as a technique for limiting urban sprawl. Oregon's 1973 growth management law requires all municipalities to adopt growth boundaries. A number of other states—including Florida, Washington, and Maryland—require counties, cities, and towns to designate growth areas. A wave of growth-boundary setting has swept through California in recent years. (But proposals to establish state requirements for municipal growth boundaries failed to win voter approval in recent referendums in Colorado and Arizona.)

To the extent that growth boundaries designate in advance areas where development will be allowed, they improve the predictability of the project approval process. They have other important benefits as well: they discourage land speculation in rural areas, help prevent leapfrog development, facilitate the conservation of open space, and make the provision of public services more cost-effective.

Urban growth boundaries are not sufficient in themselves to produce smart development. Long experience demonstrates—in Oregon's municipalities, Minnesota's Twin Cities region, Florida's Sarasota County, and Kentucky's Lexington-Fayette County—that boundaries do not necessarily prevent urban sprawl, which may continue within the lines. To be truly effective in promoting smart growth, boundaries must be accompanied by programs that specifically encourage infill and redevelopment, compact and multiuse development, affordable housing, and multimodal travel choices. These programs can include density bonuses, expedited permitting for smart development, and minimum density requirements.

Portland, Oregon's urban growth boundary is perhaps the most well known UGB in the United States. Established in the 1970s, it closely reflected the urban service area established by the regional sewer agency and quickly became the region's prime mechanism for managing growth. Metro, the regional planning and service agency (approved by voters in 1978 and made a state-chartered agency with new powers in 1990), has used the boundary to direct growth. Working with the region's counties and municipalities, Metro has concentrated on promoting compact infill and redevelopment, transit use, an affordable mix of housing, and the conservation of regional open space. Metro's 2040 strategic plan calls for substantial development and redevelopment within the presently designated urbanizing area and it does not call for significantly expanding the urban growth boundary.

The possible effects of urban growth boundaries on land prices and housing affordability are a matter of some controversy. Developers and builders claim that Portland's boundary, for example, pushed housing prices in the 1990s up to levels that are unaffordable for many of the region's households. Data published by the National Association of Home Builders in 1999 supporting that claim received wide notice, although some critics argued that NAHB's analysis was based on faulty methodology.

Metro's planning staff argues that the rise in Portland's housing prices occurred after a long period of unusually low prices, and that it was propelled by a surge in demand for upscale housing in the midst of an economic boom. And the Metro planners point out that Salt Lake City, a region with no growth boundary, has been experiencing a similar problem with housing affordability. Growth boundaries no doubt can exert some pressure on housing prices, but other factors, such as an increase in market demand, probably play a larger role in rising prices.[18]

Minimum Densities

Minimum density standards set high enough and applied to designated areas could promote compact development. Portland, Oregon, may be the only region in the United States that has established minimum densities to encourage compact growth and the production of affordable housing.

Portland's density standard, which is a policy rather than a mandate, is contained in a metropolitan housing rule formulated by Metro, the regional planning and service agency, pursuant to a state goal for affordable housing. The rule requires the region's counties and municipalities to plan for at least half of new housing construction to be in the form of multifamily or townhouse units, and to aim for minimum housing densities—of ten units per acre in the city of Portland and six to eight units per acre in most suburban areas.

According to studies conducted in 1982 and 1991, the rule has stimulated dramatic increases in the amount of land zoned for multifamily and townhouse uses and in the production of multifamily and townhouse units. These studies also reveal that small-lot houses make up a growing share of all single-family houses. By the early 1990s, housing development in Portland was almost at the targeted density levels, although single-family development was consuming more land than desired.[19] (Noncompact single-family development is a trend that seems to be continuing as Portland experiences high levels of growth.)

Mandatory Multiuse Zones

Some communities promote compact, multiuse development by mandating it for transit-station areas, new town centers, and traditional neighborhood districts. Some compact, multiuse development is occurring through joint public/private project initiatives.

The Orenco Station development (profiled on page 101) was designed to implement the city of Hillsboro's plan mandating mixed-use development around light-rail stations. The 2040 plan for the Portland region designated the site as a town center and established a residential density gradient from the station and a requirement for mixed uses. After a two-year period of discussions and negotiations, the city of Hillsboro created a custom-tailored zoning district (station community residential village) for which design guidelines were established that would assure an urban mix of housing types and land uses.

A number of communities have adopted provisions allowing traditional neighborhood design (TND) projects as an option to conventional zoning, and some have mandated TND development as the only type of subdivision that will be permitted. Huntersville, North Carolina, is one of several suburban communities in the Charlotte region that have replaced conventional zoning and subdivision provisions with TND requirements.

Chapel Hill, North Carolina, amended its comprehensive plan in the early 1990s to initiate a small-area planning process designed to prepare detailed land use plans for undeveloped parts of the town's urban service area. In 1992, the town council adopted a plan for the southern area that specified a TND pattern of development and called for implementation through a conditional-use zoning process. Now a project, Southern Village, is under construction—a 312-acre mixed-use TND development.

Public/private mixed-use town centers and transit-oriented developments (TODs) are becoming more common in suburban communities. Often located on public land or involving some public land, these developments often start out as requests from public agencies for proposals from developers. Whatever approach to their development is used, public/private town centers and TODs usually begin with a public statement of desired uses, densities, and other characteristics of the planned complex. Typically the program statement specifies a mix of uses and requires an overall design that is compact and pedestrian-oriented. Community solicitations for specific forms of development are a direct way of assuring smart growth in areas in which communities see significant opportunities.

Having seen nearby communities succumb to sprawl, public officials in Towamencin Township, Pennsylvania, 15 miles from Philadelphia, decided to take matters in hand. The small township (population 17,000) used a state grant to hire a planning consultant to help produce a blueprint for maintaining and enhancing the historic character of the township. More than 100 public meetings went into the making of the plan. The plan envisions a high-density, mixed-use village designed to be walkable and with more than one-quarter of the area dedicated to open space and civic uses. An overlay zoning district was created to guide development and a land use and design manual was prepared to help developers understand the quality of development desired by the township. This entrepreneurial planning effort has won Towamencin Township numerous awards.[20]

Requiring Open Space

Communities use a variety of techniques to restrict development in order to conserve open space—ranging from straightforward planning, zoning, and subdivision regulations that identify areas to be protected from development (see "Promoting the Conservation of Open Space," pages 96–98) to the superzoning of urban growth boundaries (see "Growth Boundaries and Service Limits," page 103). Public acquisition of land is a direct method of protecting open space. The acquisition of development rights through conservation zoning and agricultural zoning is another frequently used technique, as is requiring developers to include open space in subdivisions.

Land Acquisition

Governments at all levels conduct land acquisition programs. The federal government purchases open space for a variety of purposes—national forests, parks, recreation areas, wildlife sanctuaries, wilderness areas, and other natural areas. States have become quite aggressive in funding the acquisition of open space.

Florida, for example, in 1979 established a program, Conservation and Recreation Lands, to conserve unique natural areas, endangered species habitat, unusual geologic features, wetlands, and significant archaeological and historical sites. In 1990, the state enacted Florida Preservation 2000, a ten-year land and water conservation program, to pump more funds into land acquisition. And in 1999, voters approved a successor program, Florida Forever, which authorizes $3 billion in bonds to be issued over ten years for the acquisition of natural areas.

New Jersey is another state with a major land acquisition program. A constitutional amendment was approved in 1998 to raise the state sales tax by 0.25 percent to provide $98 million annually for 30 years to acquire and manage conservation areas, protect farmlands, and preserve historic sites and buildings.

At the local level, many programs to acquire open space for a variety of purposes have been insti-

tuted. Boulder, Colorado, launched its well-known program in 1967. Funded by a 0.4 percent sales tax that has supported more than $60 million in bond issues for open-space acquisition, the Boulder program has preserved more than 22,000 acres on the mountainsides surrounding the city. Austin, Texas, provides another example. Over the past decade, that city's voters have approved bond issues totaling more than $130 million to create parks and greenways and protect critical watershed lands.

Small communities also acquire land for open space. The Lincoln, Massachusetts, open-space program was described in chapter 3. An aggressive acquisition program initiated in 1996 by Pittstown, New York provides another example. Conservation of open space to protect the character of the town had been a planning goal for many years, and in 1987 Pittstown adopted one of the state's first mandatory cluster development ordinances to help save open space. But in the mid-1990s, the town's population reached 25,000 and development was consuming open space at a rapid pace.

Pittstown imposed an 18-month moratorium on subdivisions and prepared a plan revision that called for the protection of almost two-thirds of the town's undeveloped land. A detailed inventory and evaluation of 95 land parcels larger than five acres identified 2,000 acres for priority attention. Based on this information, the town prepared an action plan, Greenprint for the Future, that proposed 1) acquisition by the town of development rights on seven farms totaling 1,200 acres and 2) cluster development regulations and special incentives to protect another 800 acres. Acquisition would be funded through a $10 million bond issue. The Greenprint for the Future contained a fiscal analysis reporting that this program would save residents money on property and school taxes. By the end of 2001, the town had acquired development rights on six of the seven farms and was negotiating for purchase of the seventh, and it had protected 600 acres through clustering and other regulatory incentives.[21]

Conservation and Agricultural Zoning

Zoning to deter suburban style development is a technique used by many agricultural and rural communities to conserve open space. Such zoning imposes requirements for large minimum lot sizes and limits uses to agricultural, conservation, and related activities. Conservation or agricultural zoning generally is intended to implement policies contained in comprehensive plan. It often goes hand in hand with growth boundaries or urban service limits.

To provide a sufficient deterrent to development, conservation zoning must set lot sizes large enough to make purchase for residential use too expensive for most households. Thus, the appropriate minimum lot size depends on local land prices and housing markets. Examples follow of minimum lot sizes in conservation or agricultural zoning around the United States:

	Minimum Lot Size
Land outside Portland, Oregon	5+ acres
Lexington-Fayette County, Kentucky	10 acres
Agricultural preservation area, Montgomery County, Maryland	25 acres
Rural areas of Baltimore County, Maryland	60 acres
Agricultural land outside Minnesota's Twin Cities	40 acres

Many variations of agricultural zoning are on the books. In Lancaster County, Pennsylvania, 39 of 40 municipalities have adopted agricultural zoning.[22] Loudoun County, Virginia's 1991 plan restricts development in the county's rural area but allows farmers to cluster development in hamlets. Frederick County, Maryland, allows the development on farm properties of three lots plus one additional lot for each 50 acres of property.

Many suburban communities adopt agricultural zoning to protect open space, but not necessarily to protect farming. The frequent result is improperly designed and implemented agricultural zoning, which can, unfortunately, actually promote sprawling low-density development. Agricultural zones with two-acre, five-acre, or ten-acre minimum lot sizes are not uncommon, and even ten-acre lots are not large enough to discourage residential development in most urbanizing regions. Such zoning often results in the proliferation of estate housing developments and hobby farms to the detriment of truly agricultural use.[23]

Conservation zoning is somewhat rarer than agricultural zoning. This is because landowners can still make economic use of their land by farming under agricultural zoning, whereas most economic uses of land under conservation zoning are prohibited. Some communities, however, do adopt zoning to preserve important natural and environmental features, such as stream valleys, hillsides, mountain slopes and ridges, wetlands, and floodplains —and to preserve views.

Scottsdale, Arizona, for example, has established an overlay zoning district covering 134 square miles of the McDowell Mountain slopes on the city's border. For steep slopes (25 percent and greater), unstable slopes and soils, desert wash areas, unique natural landmarks, and exposed rocks, the zoning district imposes a sliding scale of development densities. One housing unit per 40 acres, which is the lowest density on the scale, is allowed on slopes of 35 percent or more. Set-asides of open space are required, ranging from 20 percent on relatively flat terrain up to 80 percent on steep hillsides and 95 percent on unstable slopes. The regulations encourage density transfers and clustered development.

Open-Space Requirements in Subdivisions

Subdivision regulations in most communities provide for the preservation of open space. For example, they quite commonly require developers to set aside natural buffers along streams and to leave steep slopes undeveloped. Subdivision regulations frequently reflect federal laws protecting wetlands, floodplains, and wildlife habitat. Subdivision site planning provisions are used often to promote the conservation of a wide variety of designated natural features, including woods, ponds, rock outcroppings, mountain ridges, and views.

Requiring Infrastructure

Beginning in the 1960s, growth management on the local level has been characterized by increasingly stringent requirements for development-related infrastructure such as roads, parks, sewer and water service, and schools. Many public officials, beset by mounting traffic congestion, overcrowded schools, and rising demand for water and sewer services, have become convinced that managing infrastructure—keeping facilities and services in line with growth—is the most significant task in managing growth.

Refusing to address infrastructure capacity problems is certainly not a smart way to manage growth. Smart growth needs smart infrastructure policy. Smart growth, therefore, requires communities to keep facilities and services in line with growth, as follows:

▲ establish reasonable standards for infrastructure facilities;
▲ frame and abide by schedules of capital construction related to sources of funding;
▲ make development approvals contingent on the availability of adequate facilities; and
▲ adopt policies and regulations that assure a fair sharing of costs.

These are not easy tasks. Most communities need not only to meet current and future needs, but also to make up for longstanding deficits in infrastructure capacity and quality. Furthermore, demand for new and upgraded infrastructure is continuing to climb and costs are rising because of higher standards of quality. In the meantime, taxpayers are resisting higher spending for infrastructure and federal spending for local facilities has declined.

Capital Improvements Programs

Programs for facility investments (capital improvements) have been a staple of local planning for decades. Such programs provide public schedules of planned maintenance and expansion, usually for six-year time periods. They also identify the sources of funding for improvements.

A major benefit of effective programs for facility investments is the certainty they provide that facilities will be available when they are needed. This helps create a constructive environment for community development. Long-term facility programs must be more than an assemblage of departmental wish lists. They must be shaped by fiscal realities. And even though program priorities are subject to revision and the projections of revenue may be too high, local officials must use the long-term capital improvements programs in making their annual budget decisions in order to promote a predictable pattern of facility investments.

Adequate Public Facilities Requirements

A predictable capital improvements program provides a solid base for development regulations that make approvals contingent on the capacity of existing and planned facilities to support growth. Such regulations are known as adequacy of public facilities requirements or concurrency requirements (meaning the concurrency of facility capacities with development).

The concept of an adequate facilities requirement is one of the earliest growth management techniques to be declared reasonable by the courts (in a 1971 New York case, *Golden* v. *Planning Board of the Town of Ramapo)*. It makes good sense, but applying adequate facilities requirements in developing communities has proved troublesome. Four kinds of standards and policy determinations, and a complex set of relations among them, are involved, as follows:

▲ **Measures of facility needs.** How many trips (and by what travel modes) are generated by different kinds of development? How many school seats will be required per unit of different kinds of housing? How much water is used in different types of development? And so forth.
▲ **Capacity measures.** What are the desired level-of-service standards for different roads? How much school space should be provided per student? And so forth.
▲ **Definition of available capacity.** At what point in the process of planning infrastructure is its funding and construction certain enough to warrant a commitment as to its being available for planned development?
▲ **Contingent factors.** To what extent will facility needs or capacity be affected by alterations in the patterns of development, including those alterations caused by other growth management policies? For example, to what extent will more compact development reduce projected vehicle use? To what extent will water conservation measures reduce projected water use?

These determinations might appear to be technical in nature, but in practice they are highly political because such determinations are influenced by concerns about the quality of facilities, cost implications, the rate of community growth and change, the short- and long-term effectiveness of growth management measures, and other considerations. The determinations that are made on these standards and policy issues can, experience has shown, allow development to proceed with little constraint despite real capacity shortages; or they can slow or even stop development due to deficiencies in one or another type of facility.

Development moratoriums resulting from adequate public facility requirements are dreaded by developers and can roil a community's political waters. More to the point for smart growth, they also may prevent development in the areas defined by public policies as most desirable for development and drive it to rural areas. Many communities elect to avoid potential moratoriums by relaxing standards. For example, Orlando, Florida, and Montgomery County, Maryland, both reduced their level-of-service standards for roads in congested core areas where they wish to concentrate growth. Making adequate facility requirements work for smart growth requires coordinating them with and customizing them for other growth policies.

Shared Public/Private Funding

Communities have been shifting more of the costs of constructing infrastructure facilities to the private sector. (In the process, they have also given up some control over the design and timing of infrastructure improvements.)

Not all, but most communities require developers to provide (design, fund, and construct) the on-site portions of essential infrastructure systems, including roads, sidewalks, sewer and water lines, and drainage facilities. Communities often require developers to provide a certain amount of common open space—parks, recreation areas, and conservation areas. They also may require that land be set aside for schools, fire stations, and the like (for future purchase and facility construction by the relevant agency). Communities that are highly attractive to developers may be able to require that they dedicate school sites, build fire stations, and construct other expensive improvements. In most communities, developers are responsible for any necessary connections of on-site systems (water lines, sewer lines, stormwater drains) with existing off-site systems.

Developer responsibility for off-site infrastructure is not as widespread or as clear-cut. Many communities require developers to build (or pay for) improvements that will be needed as a direct consequence of the development—for example, new lanes on bordering streets, traffic signals at nearby intersections, and enlargements to water mains and sewer interceptors. They may require developers to contribute funds for community parks and recreation areas—in lieu of requiring them to provide small, unconnected open-space elements in their projects. Communities that are highly attractive to developers may be able to require developers to build interstate highway interchanges and pay for other expensive improvements.

Impact fees are an increasingly used method of making development pay for off-site infrastructure facilities. (Costs incurred by developers in directly constructing facilities covered by impact fees can offset the fees.) Impact fees in some communities cover a wide range of facilities, up to and including government administration buildings, police stations, and fire trucks.[24] Additional off-site investments may be triggered by state and federal regulations that require developers to mitigate damage to environmentally sensitive land by contributing to mitigation banks or purchasing and restoring or enhancing off-site wetlands and habitat areas.

The legal standard for both on-site and off-site investment requirements is that the improvements must be directly related to the proposed development. That is to say that the improvements would not be needed in the absence of the development. It is not legal to require developers to pay for making up past deficits in improvements. If developers are asked to pay the whole cost of facilities that will benefit other developments, existing or future, the other developers should have to reimburse the original developer(s).

The reality, however, is that many communities find themselves unable to finance needed improvements. The reasons are many, including legislated limits on property tax increases in some jurisdictions, general taxpayer resistance, and policies inspired by slow-growth and no-growth advocates. Furthermore, procedures for reimbursing developers for oversized improvements are frequently unreliable, especially over periods of many years. Thus, many developers are left with no options but to shoulder the financing burden for major off-site improvements or to postpone development.

Some communities demand exactions of land and facilities, a practice that adds more uncertainty to the development process. Exactions may represent requirements over and above those spelled out in regulations, and often they are left undefined until the project has its final hearing. Developers working in communities that impose exactions may try to negotiate terms during the approval process, but they remain vulnerable to changes up to the time the permit is granted. To the extent that exactions cut into a project's bottom line, they may well diminish the quality of the finished product—hardly a smart-growth solution.[25]

Putting It Together

In the interest of smart growth, communities should take care to establish a predictable who, what, and when of infrastructure expansion and funding. Who does what and when should be clear and enforceable. Their tools for accomplishing this will be a credible program of capital improve-

ments linked to requirements for adequate public facilities and policies that reflect a fair sharing of facility costs.

Carlsbad, California's program for funding and constructing facilities in line with projected development is highly structured and provides an example. Carlsbad is a rapidly growing suburban community north of San Diego. After several false starts, it fashioned an infrastructure program in 1986 that is designed to accommodate projected development at a reasonable pace. Carlsbad's approach to infrastructure financing may seem complex, but for developers it promises some welcome certainty about the city's infrastructure needs and financing expectations.

The Carlsbad program lays out a citywide facilities improvement plan. The first element is specified performance standards for each of 11 types of public facilities (see figure 6-1). The second element is estimates of thresholds of development at which facilities will require improvement to continue meeting performance goals. And the third element is detailed plans for 25 zones in the city identifying needs for public facility improvements and funding. This combination of standards, thresholds, and zone plans provides an overall management plan for developing infrastructure concurrently with growth and for evaluating the timing and cost-sharing requirements for proposed development projects.

Requiring Travel Choices

By preference and necessity, cars will remain the king among mobility choices in suburban greenfield areas. This does not mean that communities should ignore techniques for expanding short-term and long-term transportation choices in such areas. Some proactive transportation facilities programs were described in the "Regulatory Incentives" section (pages 99–101). In addition to adopting programs like these, communities can include provisions in their zoning and subdivision regulations that can promote travel choices and help reduce road congestion.

Communities should seek to improve the connectivity of street systems. Whereas local street and highway systems once were planned to allow travelers multiple route options, the street systems in new developments are being planned to minimize connections with adjoining develop-

Figure 6-1 Public Facilities Performance Standards, Carlsbad, California

City Administrative Facilities
1,500 square feet per 1,000 population must be scheduled for construction within a five-year period.

Libraries
800 square feet per 1,000 population must be scheduled for construction within a five-year period.

Wastewater Treatment Capacity
Adequate for at least a five-year period.

Parks
Three acres of community park or special-use area per 1,000 population within the park district must be scheduled for construction within a five-year period.

Drainage
Facilities as required by the city must be provided concurrent with development.

Circulation
No road segment or intersection in the zone nor any segment or intersection out of the zone impacted by development in the zone shall be projected to exceed service level C during off-peak hours, nor service level D during peak hours ("impacted" means 20 percent or more of the traffic generated by the zone will use the road segment or intersection).

Fire
No more than 1,500 dwelling units outside a five-minute response time.

Open Space
15 percent of the total land area in the zone, exclusive of environmentally constrained nondevelopable land, must be set aside for permanent open space and must be available concurrent with development.

Schools
Capacity to meet projected enrollment within the zone as determined by the appropriate school district must be provided prior to projected occupancy.

Sewer Collection System
Trunk line capacity to meet demand as determined by the appropriate sewer district must be provided concurrent with development.

Water Distribution System
1) Line capacity to meet demand as determined by the appropriate water district must be provided concurrent with development.
2) A minimum ten-day average storage capacity must be provided prior to any development.

Source: City of Carlsbad, California.

ments. Gated communities deliberately do without connectivity in order to promote exclusivity and security. The residents of neighborhoods adjacent to developing tracts oppose proposed connections that would bring traffic onto their streets. In fact, it is hard to refer collectively to the streets in many developing areas as street systems. These systems boil down to a repeated pattern of local streets intersecting with a single collector street that funnels traffic onto a major arterial. More isolating than the unconnected streets in many newly developing suburban areas is the fact that residences are fenced off from adjoining land uses—commercial, office, civic, or recreational—so that they are impossible to access other than by car.

Communities can add provisions to their zoning and subdivision regulations requiring projects to make street and pathway connections with adjoining property. For example, subdivisions can be required to provide at least one street connection to existing or future streets in adjoining subdivisions for each cardinal direction (north, south, east, west). In addition, they can be required to provide pathways to adjoining neighborhood-oriented uses such as schools, other civic buildings, and neighborhood shopping centers.

Jurisdictions seeking to promote linkages throughout the community are likely to meet strong opposition from residents of existing neighborhoods who are fearful of potential traffic and other impacts from new development. Various types of traffic-calming devices to reduce speeds on local streets (and discourage cut-through traffic) can make connectivity more acceptable to neighbors.

Community subdivision regulations can also incorporate standards and design requirements relating to transit friendliness, trails, and general walkability. The portion of the St. Johns County, Florida, comprehensive plan dealing with new town development contains relevant requirements, as follows:

▲ a pedestrian/bicycle system consisting of sidewalks, bike paths, and/or trails linking villages to each other and the town center;
▲ a design that accommodates potential internal transit and linkages to external transit; land set aside for transit purposes; and location of future potential transit stops in the town center close

to high-density residential developments, and in or near the village centers;
▲ sidewalks on both sides of all streets (on arterial roadways, a sidewalk separated from the roadway by a landscape strip may be used); and
▲ bicycle lanes on both sides of collector and arterial roads (or a bike path separated from the roadway by a landscaped strip).

These types of requirements can establish opportunities for satisfying travel needs by means other than cars. So can requirements that promote development that meets smart growth's compactness and multiuse goals.

Requiring Affordable Housing

Smart growth's ideal mix of housing includes affordable housing, and the production of affordable housing generally requires public support to supplement market forces. A number of communities have determined that affordable housing is a priority that is to be promoted by regulatory actions, not just housing policies and programs. Many suburban (and resort) communities that are succeeding in attracting economic development are finding it difficult to provide adequate housing for the workers on which their booming economies depend. These communities are prime candidates for affordable housing requirements.

The Montgomery County, Maryland, requirement that developers of projects with 50 or more housing units include affordable units in return for density bonuses (see page 93) provides one example. Massachusetts and New Jersey require local jurisdictions to provide their fair share of affordable housing, and many jurisdictions in these states use techniques similar to Montgomery County's.

Massachusetts's 1969 anti-snob legislation and subsequent state regulations urge that at least 10 percent of the housing stock in communities be available to low-income households. Local governments are allowed to issue a comprehensive permit for publicly subsidized housing that overrides all other required permits and may be approved despite conflicts with existing zoning. Lincoln, an affluent town outside Boston where housing prices have risen steeply, met its 10 percent goal by negotiating the development of affordable housing as part of project approvals and enacting a bylaw to permit accessory apartments in cluster developments.

In the 1980s, some cities that were experiencing robust commercial development in their downtowns began to require contributions to affordable housing production as a condition of approval for new commercial construction. Office developers in downtown Boston or San Francisco, for example, could build housing or donate fees to housing trust funds established to finance low- and moderate-income housing. Under most such programs, the housing could be built anywhere in the city.

Housing requirements could be made a condition for the approval of commercial projects in growing business centers in greenfield locations as well. Such requirements could support the production of affordable housing as well as other housing needed by employees. However, since suburban governments compete for shopping centers, business parks, and other valuable ratables, they are unlikely to reduce their competitiveness by adding such a requirement to commercial development, unless directed to do so by state legislation like that in Massachusetts and New Jersey.

Communities can require employers to contribute to the provision of employee housing. This requirement is imposed in some resort areas in remote locations where decent affordable housing is hard to find. In many resort communities, high housing prices make attracting workers problematical. Workers in Aspen and other Colorado ski resort towns, for example, where houses cost $1 million and more, typically must double up in poor-quality units or commute long distances from the towns in which they can afford to live. Resorts in Eagle, Pitkin, and Summit Counties in Colorado import up to 44 percent of their workers, according to an Associated Press report in September 2000.

Melanie Mills, public policy chief with the Colorado Ski Country USA trade organization, told Associated Press that "resorts realize that providing housing is a cost of doing business." Many resort communities require employers to contribute to the development of employee housing. Vail Resorts, which operates ski resorts in several areas, is spending $54 million to add 700 beds to its employee housing, and Aspen plans to increase the number of beds it offers from 150 to 300.[26]

Many universities in high-cost housing markets provide faculty and student housing. The city of Seattle helps its employees and the employees of

several medical and other institutions afford housing by arranging below-market loans for them.

Smart Growth in Rural and Remote Areas

Can the principles of smart growth guide non-metropolitan development—the development that occurs in small villages and towns beyond the urban fringe, in stand-alone new communities in the countryside, and in resort locations? Are the ideas of compact and multiuse development, transportation choices, open-space conservation, and community livability applicable for development in rural and remote areas?

Emphatically yes. Rural areas and small towns can benefit from well-designed and appropriately located development that follows the principles of smart growth. In rural areas, the development of master-planned communities, for example, can provide residential and economic opportunities for residents. Developers are attracted to areas where the low cost of land can offset the high costs of infrastructure and the rich array of amenities provided in master-planned communities. The development beginning in the 1960s of Columbia and Reston in the Washington, D.C., region added high-quality living environments and work opportunities on the then-outskirts of the urban region. Through their large scale and superior design these new towns met most of the principles of smart growth long before the principles were articulated.

Small towns also can benefit from using smart-growth concepts to guide their expansion. Even if development occurs slowly, it should be planned to retain the character of existing development (with particular attention paid to its compactness and mix of uses), to conserve open space around the town, and to provide opportunities for future travel choices to regional employment centers.

Resort, second-home, and retirement developments can be designed to satisfy smart-growth standards while they provide people access to nature's attractions. Bonita Bay in Bonita Springs, Florida, and Shenandoah in Virginia's Blue Ridge Mountains demonstrate how the development of recreation-oriented projects can respect the environment.

However, remote development raises problems for smart growth. It can involve long commutes. It can also use up or otherwise threaten land that might better serve as regional open space. And to the extent that remote development draws substantial growth from existing urban centers, it can weaken regional concentrations. Large-scale projects in remote locations could represent some of the highest-quality development in the region, but they also could be land-scraping and cost-cutting building of the worst kind. Development around small towns and villages could bring welcome economic growth, but it could also spill out into low-cost rural lands and create a microcosm of metropolitan sprawl.

Resort development by its nature tends to occur in fragile and environmentally important locations. Extensive resort and second-home development on the Atlantic and Gulf coast barrier islands, for example, raises many issues relating to flood damage, beach stabilization in developed areas, limited public access to beaches, and harm to ecosystems. Nature-oriented primary- and second-home development throughout forested areas in the Mountain states has increased the threat of forest fires (and exposed more houses to that threat).

Smart growth requires encouraging an appropriate amount of remote growth of an appropriate character. How much and what kind can only be answered in the context of specific conditions in the area under consideration, including the pattern of urban and exurban development and the extent and character of environmentally sensitive land. A few states with growth management programs have established processes and criteria that suggest an appropriate quality of development outside designated growth areas.

Vermont and Florida both require special analyses of developments of regional impact (DRIs), which include large-scale developments. DRI reviews endeavor to determine the potential multijurisdictional effects of proposed projects and recommend revisions to mitigate adverse impacts. The reviews frequently specify special conditions and standards for DRIs.

Growth management laws in Oregon and Washington require the designation of urban growth areas around existing communities but also allow the development of resorts and new communities outside existing cities and towns. In Oregon, destination resorts must be located at least 24 miles from

the urban growth boundaries of cities of 100,000 or more. Such resorts must be at least 160 acres in size, and at least half the site must be dedicated for permanent open space. The Oregon law also specifies minimum standards for different types of development.

The Washington law allows counties to authorize new fully contained communities outside of designated growth areas, provided that the proposed community provides all new infrastructure, pays impact fees, implements transit-oriented site planning and traffic demand management programs, installs buffers for adjoining development, protects natural areas, and provides a mix of uses and affordable housing.

Oregon, Washington, and New Jersey also regulate the expansion of small towns through their growth-area designation processes. Maryland's Smart Growth law allows growth in small towns outside county-designated growth areas if the proposed development is contiguous and related to existing development.

According to the states that have established procedures and policies to guide development in nonmetropolitan areas, then, the appropriate characteristics of such development would include the following:

▲ fits within overall plans for local jurisdictions and the region;
▲ reflects best practices in design and development;
▲ provides or finances infrastructure systems to support proposed development;
▲ designs and phases new development to avoid fiscal impacts on local governments; and
▲ protects and, if necessary, restores environmental resources.

Adopting criteria similar to these characteristics would constitute a reasonable (and smart) approach for allowing development in areas outside the metropolitan sphere of influence. Two projects, Bonita Bay on the Gulf coast of southwest Florida and Shenandoah in the foothills of the Blue Ridge Mountains about 90 miles from Washington, D.C., exemplify the kinds of qualities that smart growth calls for in rural and resort development.

In some ways, Bonita Bay is a typical upscale golf course community with pleasant residential areas

Just north of Naples, Florida, in a relatively rural area, Bonita Bay is a recreational and second-home development that preserves a significant amount of wetlands and other open space.

and lavish amenities. It is a 2,400-acre master-planned community that offers many styles of single-family houses and high-rise condominiums. Among its amenities are five private championship golf courses, two clubhouses, 18 tennis courts, three waterfront parks, a beach park and marina, and 12 miles of secluded walking and biking paths.

But developer David Shakarian and his successor David Lucas had a greater vision for Bonita Bay, one that would set standards in environmentally responsible development. The guiding principle for the development's design was the preservation and enhancement of the site's natural, historical, and archeological features. Planning work began in 1981. Planners identified 40 habitat types on site and mapped 22 drainage basins.

The Bonita Bay master plan preserves natural wetlands, organizes development around the site's topography and vegetation, and establishes a storm-water management system that uses native vegetation to filter out silt, nutrients, and pollutants. One-half of the site will remain as open space, including the golf courses, parks, and trail systems. Wherever possible, flora and fauna are left undisturbed, as are specimen tree stands and important archaeological and ecological sites. New landscaping is required to be at least 50 percent native species.

Bonita Bay's environmental features have created strong demand and some housing prices have been pushed up to $2 million and more. Prospective homebuyers, surveys show, value the development's standard amenities (its golf courses, swimming facilities, and tennis courts) less than they value its hiking and biking trails and the opportunities offered for viewing wildlife.

Shenandoah is an active adult community being developed by Ray Smith of the Dogwood Development Group. About 2,300 housing units will be developed on a 1,000-acre site around a state-owned fishing lake. Smith expects that the project will attract both retirees and second-home purchasers (many of whom may plan to retire there).

More than half the site will be retained in open space, with 16 miles of nature trails but no golf course. Designed specifically to achieve certification as a habitat community from Audubon International and the National Wildlife Federation, Shenandoah's main theme is the preservation of habitat to increase biodiversity. It will feature native plants, small lawns, and the use of water elements and vegetation to enhance natural habitats. Smith is certified by the National Wildlife Federation to teach people how to construct backyard wildlife habitats and has a Master Naturalist certificate from the Audubon Society.

Although neither of these projects has the kind of urban character that is at the heart of smart-growth principles, both serve significant markets for residential and recreational activities and both protect and enhance land, habitat, and water quality. Each demonstrates that rural and remote developments can fulfill some of the important goals of smart growth.

Getting the Job Done

In conclusion, current forms of development in most greenfield areas are in many respects antithetical to the principles of smart growth. As long as developers and communities continue to develop and manage growth in conventional ways using conventional practices, they will not get the job done.

Growing smart in greenfield areas requires an evolution in the way development is practiced and regulated. It will take time and effort for developers and public officials to make the necessary adjustments in their approaches and priorities. Developers need to learn and be convinced that smart growth can only help to achieve the goal of producing high-quality, marketable development. Public officials need to learn and be convinced that smart growth can only help to further community development that benefits current and future residents.

Suburban communities have taken many steps to encourage and even require the kinds of development that make for smart growth, and these initiatives have been discussed in this chapter. And suburban developers have designed and built projects with many smart-growth characteristics, and these projects have had market success. There is experience from which to learn and build.

Notes

1. Kerry Tremain, "Redesigning the Burbs," available at: sustainable.state.fl.us/fdi/fscc/news/world/0008/confcnu.htm (Web site of the Florida Sustainable Communities Center, posted 28 August 2000).

2. For more information, see the case study on Fairview Village in David J. O'Neill, *The Smart Growth Tool Kit* (Washington, D.C.: ULI–the Urban Land Institute, 2000), pp. 101–105.

3. For more information, see David A. Ross, "A New Village Center for Reston, Virginia," *Urban Land*, December 1997, pp. 21–22.

4. Christopher Leinberger, "The Connection between Sustainability and Economic Development," in *The Practice of Sustainable Development*, ed. Douglas R. Porter (Washington, D.C.: ULI–the Urban Land Institute, 2000), p. 61.

5. See, for example, *Innovations vs. Traditions in Community Development*, Technical Bulletin 47 (Washington, D.C.: ULI–the Urban Land Institute, 1963) and Welford Sanders, *The Cluster Subdivision: A Cost-Effective Approach*, Planning Advisory Service Report 356 (Chicago: American Planning Association, 1980). The current champion of clustering is Randell Arendt; see his *Conservation Design for Subdivisions* (Washington, D.C.: Island Press, 1996).

6. Roberta Brandes Gratz, with Norman Mintz, *Cities Back from the Edge* (New York: Preservation Press, 1998), p. 237.

7. See Lowcountry Open Land Trust homepage at: www.lolt.org.

8. "Natural Habitats in the San Diego Region," *INFO* (San Diego Association of Governments), January/February 1995, p. 1.

9. William Fulton, "Natural Habitat Set-Aside Plan Wins in San Diego," *Planning*, March 1997, p. 24.

10. San Diego Association of Governments, *Report on Natural Community Conservation Program Land Acquisition Activities* (San Diego, California: Agenda Report no. 99-7-22, 23 July 1999).

11. Maricopa Association of Governments, *Desert Spaces: An Open Space Plan for the Maricopa Association of Governments* (Phoenix, Arizona: 1995).

12. See Land Trust Alliance homepage at: www.lta.org.

13. Sierra Business Council, *Planning for Prosperity: Building Successful Communities in the Sierra Nevada* (Truckee, California: 1999), 32.

14. Montgomery County Environmental Assessment page at: www.co.mo.md.us/services/dep/Assessment/agriculture.htm.

15. Washington State Office of Community Development, *Achieving Growth Management Goals: Local Success Stories* (Olympia, Washington: 2000), pp. 34–35.

16. Mark Hinshaw, "Planning Practice: Simplified Zoning," *Planning*, June 2000, p. 14.

17. Washington State Office of Community Development, *Achieving Growth Management Goals*, pp. 2–3.

18. For more information on this debate, see Arthur C. Nelson et al., *The Link between Growth Management and Housing Affordability: The Academic Evidence* (Washington, D.C.: Brookings Institution Center on Urban and Metropolitan Policy, 1995), especially pp. 25–26.

19. 1000 Friends of Oregon and Home Builders Association of Metropolitan Portland, *Managing Growth to Promote Affordable Housing: Revisiting Oregon's Goal 10*, executive summary (Portland, Oregon: 1991).

20. Fred McCaffrey, "Small Town Planning: Thriving with—Not Just Surviving—Growth," *Urban Land*, May 2000, pp. 16–17.

21. James Andrews, "Planning Awards 1998: Pittstown's Greenprint Initiative," *Planning*, April 1998, pp. 6–7; and Bill Carpenter (planning director of Pittstown, New York), interview by author, 16 February 2002.

22. Tom Daniels, remarks at a conference entitled "Rebuilding Nature's Metropolis: Growth and Sustainability in the 21st Century" (American Collegiate Schools of Planning, Chicago, 21–24 October 1999).

23. Tom Daniels, *When City and County Collide: Managing Growth in the Metropolitan Fringe* (Washington, D.C.: Island Press, 1999), p. 151.

24. The legal basis, fee calculation procedures, and administrative processes for impact fees are fully described in James C. Nicholas, Arthur C. Nelson, and Julian C. Juergensmeyer, *A Practitioner's Guide to Development Impact Fees* (Chicago: American Planning Association, 1991).

25. For more about the technical, legal, and administrative issues raised by the use of exactions and impact fees, see Douglas R. Porter, *Managing Growth in America's Communities* (Washington, D.C.: Island Press, 1997), pp. 133–141.

26. Associated Press report, 23 September 2000.

Growing Smart through Infill and Redevelopment

7

Directing more of the growth that needs to be accommodated in metropolitan regions to existing towns and cities can attain important efficiencies in development and further many of the principles of smart growth. Accommodating growth through infill development and the redevelopment of vacant and underused properties means less need to expand infrastructure systems and convert rural land to urban uses.

However, anyone conversant with the history of urban development in the United States knows that few cities have been able to stem the flow of people and jobs from old city cores to suburban jurisdictions. At least since the 1920s, few central cities and older suburbs have been able to attract the reinvestment needed to maintain and improve their neighborhoods and business centers.

Indications are that these long-term population/job migration and inner-neighborhood disinvestment trends are turning around. Developers are reconsidering the attractions of urban locations and the hopes of public officials in urban jurisdictions have been raised. This chapter provides examples of the return of long-neglected sites and buildings to profitable and productive uses, and it suggests the kinds of public programs that can be undertaken to support the revival of languishing urban areas.

Viewing Urban Land as a Valuable Resource

People often fail to sufficiently appreciate the potential resource value of underused urban land. The availability of underused land in built-up urban and older suburban areas will be very important in future efforts to achieve smart growth. And this land resource offers significant opportunities for profitable development and for the creation of more livable communities.

Smart growth encourages more growth in urban areas (and thus less growth in nonurban areas) because growth in urban locations conserves resources, makes efficient use of existing capital assets (buildings and infrastructure), and adds to the quality of life in metropolitan regions in several ways:

▲ Urban locations are highly accessible.
▲ Revitalized residential and commercial neighborhoods make distinctive places.
▲ The use of existing infrastructure capacity means less construction of new facilities.
▲ The revitalization of existing outdoor assets (waterfronts, parks, historic districts, scenic streets) provides recreational opportunities.
▲ Important cultural facilities and civic institutions, such as concert halls, museums, and theaters, gain support from a denser popula-

tion and are, in turn, more readily available to more people.

Smart growth's clarion call for growth in existing neighborhoods and communities echoes attempts throughout much of the 20th century to attract development to American cities to halt the debilitating loss of housing and jobs. In the early part of the century, civic leaders launched ambitious programs to replace teeming tenements with better housing. In the middle years of the century, cities embarked on urban renewal to clean out or clean up crumbling industrial districts and depressingly shoddy downtowns. As inner-city neighborhoods continued to decay, cities initiated urban redevelopment programs in the hope of arresting this decline.

Some of these efforts succeeded. Development was attracted and many inner-city locations became choice again. Some imposing civic facilities occupied land that had been cleared of decaying buildings. However, in many cases the renewal and redevelopment programs tore down expanses of housing, disrupted neighborhoods, and wrought other destruction that was not healed by new construction. Redevelopment frequently left land vacant for years, blighting surrounding areas. Or it gave rise to poorly designed development that was little better than what it replaced.

In the 1970s, drastic cutbacks in federal funding for renewal programs left communities with few resources to use against further deterioration. In the last decades of the century in many cities, while commercial cores experienced a remarkable revival inner-city neighborhoods continued to empty out. Demand for close-in locations continued to fall and many inner suburbs began to feel the pinch also. Shopping strips and residential areas developed in the post–World War II period showed many signs of underuse and wear and tear.

A century of outmigration of people and jobs and mostly failed redevelopment efforts left cities with a stock of boarded-up and obsolete buildings, acres of vacant lots, and numerous contaminated sites and tax-delinquent properties. Today these properties represent opportunities. From a smart-growth perspective they represent a valuable resource. A variety of structures, many of them architecturally distinctive, await reuse. Well-located vacant sites—in areas served by basic infrastruc-

ture facilities and near major employment centers —await development.

City planner Anne Vernez Moudon, in commenting on the initial draft of this chapter, observed: "While the supply of infillable or redevelopable land in most cities seems small—on the order of 10 to 13 percent of total usable land—the development capacity of this land is amazingly substantial." Such land as zoned, says Moudon, could accommodate as much as 40 percent of the new development expected over several decades if the forces of demand and supply come to recognize that in-city sites offer opportunities for livable communities and profitable development.

That recognition began to dawn in the closing years of the 20th century, spurred by the aging of the baby boom generation, the increasing diversity of households, and the emergence of revitalized urban cores as stronger centers of employment, culture, and government. Renewed interest in central locations for jobs, housing, and amenities is being felt in many cities and inner suburbs, where historic buildings are being adapted for new uses, ramshackle housing is being replaced or restored, and derelict commercial centers are springing to life. Empty spots in the urban fabric are filling in. Contaminated sites are being cleaned up to make room for new development. And the redevelopment process is being aided and moved along by local governments in many ways.

Demographics Driving Development

Profound changes underlie the renewal of interest in urban neighborhoods. Families with two adults and kids represent less than a quarter of the demand for housing today. The dominance of less traditional households—single persons, childless couples, unrelated adults, empty nesters, and single parents—in housing markets is growing. Interest in urban amenities (and in shorter commutes as well) is growing. Interest in large yards and excellence in school systems is declining. Bob Levey's Mrs. Sweetness (see box on opposite page), who is thinking about moving back to the city, is, as he says, "part of a trend."

Changing consumer demographics and global economic shifts have transformed markets for non-residential development as well, providing support for mammoth regional shopping centers and dis-

New Life in the City for a "Classic" Couple

"You want classic, I'm classic," said the woman on the phone. "Born in Washington, D.C., in 1940, married my sweetness in 1964, had three kids, lived all that time in Silver Spring, in the same little paintbox of a house. I've done it right and done it predictably all these years. Now my sweetness and I are seriously thinking about moving back into the District of Columbia."

After a pause, I said, "Why assume I'm going to think you're nuts for wanting to move into D.C.?"

"Because," she said, "my generation spent its time, money, and energy trying to move out of D.C. Maybe it was the old bit about having a nicer,

newer house, or a back yard for the kids. Maybe it was racism—subtle, or not so subtle."

"And now you're finding that in an empty nest, the burbs feel a little, well, hollow?"

"Exactly. There's nothing going on here. People mow their lawns and wash their cars, and that's it. All the cultural stuff we want to do is in the city. All the good restaurants are downtown. Access to the airport is much easier from downtown. Plus, if you don't have kids, you really feel out of it in the suburbs."

"If it's any consolation, ma'am, you're part of a trend. You know how housing sales have spiked over the last year or so? One of the reasons is

people like you, looking to live closer to the action. Besides," I said, "you feel a sense of affinity for the District of Columbia, a sense of appreciation for the place itself. So many people who move to Florida or Rehoboth Beach are looking for peace and quiet, but what they really mean is a white-bread non-community, a place with no surprises. I'd welcome surprises, especially if I had had the freedom to take advantage of them the way you do."

"Bob Levey," said Mrs. Sweetness, "I'm calling the real estate agent right away."

Source: Excerpted with permission from "Bob Levey's Washington," Washington Post, 20 July 2000.

---

count centers, big-box retailers, suburban mixed-use projects, urban entertainment centers and districts, and a range of hotel formats.

A sign of the times is the strong reverse commute—from residences in city cores to suburban job locations—in a number of metropolitan travel corridors. Another sign is the surprising gains in housing construction experienced in large cities and downtowns during the 1990s. According to an analysis from the Brookings Institution, the number of housing permits in large cities more than doubled between 1991 and 1998, "growing at a faster rate than that of suburbs and metropolitan areas in general."[1] The opportunities for adapting old buildings and developing new housing in in-town locations are catching the attention of developers across the nation.

In cities and older suburbs across America, infill development, redevelopment, and adaptive use have become thriving industries. A surprising fact: $100 billion to $200 billion is spent on housing rehabilitation each year in the United States, according to a recent study from the Center for Urban Policy Research at Rutgers University. Spending for residential rehabilitation thus approaches total annual spending for housing construction and it constitutes about 2 percent of the nation's economic activity. Capturing more of this spending

for infill and redevelopment projects would give smart growth a powerful boost.

Reuse Projects

Not so many years ago, trying to save old structures—historic or not—from decay and demolition was an uphill fight. Old buildings generally were considered obsolete and unstylish. Developers generally considered them expensive to renovate and lacking in market appeal. Today, however, recycling old buildings has become a respectable (and profitable) market niche in many cities and older suburbs.

Buildings and neighborhoods with interesting spaces and unusual appearance are particularly attractive to many people and developers. Old neighborhoods have an ambience, often a storied past, and unique design features, as well as locations near jobs and cultural institutions and convenient access to stores and services—aspects that appeal to people who are unsatisfied with suburban lifestyles.

With intricate facades, wide-open floors, and large expanses of glass, many old urban industrial buildings are adaptable for any number of uses. As a result, many of these buildings have been converted to new uses and in combination these conversions have created new multiuse residential and enter-

▶ **Converted tobacco warehouses at West Village create a stylish living environment in Durham, North Carolina.**

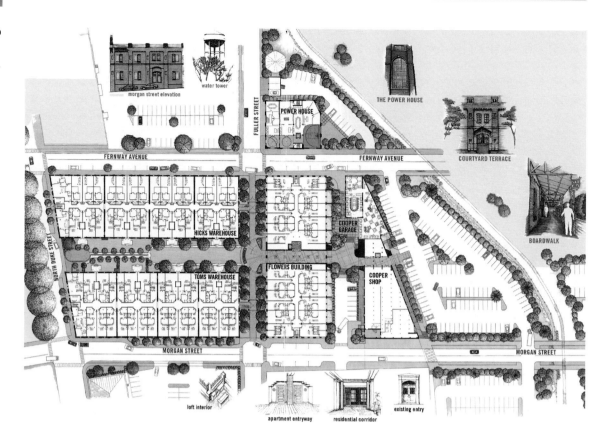

tainment districts—for example, the warehouse district in Tucson, the railroad/industrial corridor in Wichita, Denver's Lower Downtown, Portland's River District, the Flats in Cleveland, Charlotte's South End, Chicago's West Side, and Philadelphia's Old City.

The recent emergence of a multiuse neighborhood in Durham, North Carolina, began with West Village, an industrial building reuse project that was completed in late 2000. West Village demonstrates the serendipitous combination of growing market interest in alternatives to suburban living and the availability of centrally located, adaptable structures in a thriving region. A local development partnership, Blue Devil Ventures, spent $40 million to convert five historic tobacco warehouses in Durham's declining core to 243 loft apartments. This sparked considerable additional investment in the city's historic industrial district—including other adaptive use projects, a new civic center, a restored theater, and a new park.

Blue Devil Ventures carefully defined the target market for West Village—20,000 faculty and staff members at the Duke University campuses and medical center located a mile west of the site, 38,000 workers at Research Triangle Park acces-

sible via the nearby Durham freeway, and thousands of employees in downtown Durham located a few blocks east of the site.

The red-brick tobacco warehouses were built from 1900 to 1926. They feature high ceilings and large windows. Decorative window frames, cornices, and ornate chimneys adorn the exteriors of two of the buildings. The project designers took full advantage of the architecture and formal grouping of the buildings to create a variety of dramatic apartments and open space. Rentals have been strong, with many units having been rented during the construction period.

Knickerbocker Lofts, a few blocks from downtown New Rochelle, New York, provides an example of a smaller adaptive use housing project, the conversion of the 1890 Knickerbocker Press Building to 46 rental lofts and a small retail shop. Sitting on a hillside, the three- and four-story L-shaped building has large clear spans, high ceilings, and great quantities of glass. No two apartments are alike and the building was fully occupied in less than four months after it opened for occupancy in late 1999, despite its relatively isolated location in a rundown industrial area. Downtown New Rochelle is now experiencing substantial redevelopment.

The range of opportunities for building reuse and adaptive use in cities and close-in suburbs is broad, as the following snapshots of other successful projects indicate:

▲ The Cotton Mill, New Orleans. An 1882 cotton mill with 323,000 square feet of floor space in six structures located in the warehouse district was rehabilitated as 287 rental and condominium units. The buildings ring an entire city block, creating a large courtyard in the interior. The original wood flooring and 5-by-12-foot windows were restored.

▲ South Tryon Square, Charlotte. A 40-year-old, 15-story office tower in downtown was wrapped into a $55 million mixed-use project developed by Spectrum Properties. The structural shell of the building was preserved and a four-story granite base unites the old and new buildings and is topped by a garden.

▲ Liberty Tree Building, Boston. Conversion of this 1850 landmark building to use as the Massachusetts Registry of Motor Vehicles rescued it from imminent destruction. The building is above a subway station, making it a desirable office location, and its restoration helped spark a recovery of its neighborhood.

▲ Humble Oil Company office building, Fort Worth. The former Humble Oil building was restored as a Marriott Courtyard hotel, one of several such conversions sponsored by Marriott International in different cities.

▲ Denver Dry Goods Building, Denver. A six-story structure built in 1888 was gutted and made into a mixed-use complex that includes affordable housing, market-rate housing, retail uses, and office uses. Developed by Jonathan Rose working with the city of Denver, the project features energy-efficient window glass and energy-efficient HVAC.

▲ Conversions to housing, Baltimore. Many of Baltimore's mostly vacant Class B office buildings and some retail buildings are being adapted to meet strong demand for downtown rental housing. Baltimore has a substantial inventory of older commercial buildings. A former Hecht's department store, for example, has been converted to 172 residential units. In the last three years, state and local tax-abatement and gap financing programs established to support such projects have contributed to the completion of more than 500 housing units, and another 1,000 units are under construction or planned.

▲ The Prince George, midtown Manhattan. Common Ground, a nonprofit housing organization, refurbished a once grand turn-of-the-century residential hotel to provide housing and supportive services for homeless and low-income individuals seeking to become self-sufficient. The $39 million project, which opened in March 2000, involved extensive restoration of ornamental plaster ceilings, marble and mosaic floors, and a lobby that is said to have once been the largest hotel lobby in Manhattan.

▲ Belmont Dairy, Portland, Oregon. A vacated and run-down dairy building located in a mature residential neighborhood was half rehabilitated and half torn down and new construction was added to provide 19 market-rate loft units, 66 affordable, energy-efficient rental apartments, and 26,000 square feet of retail space (see pages 22–23).

▲ Bass Lofts, Atlanta. A former high school set in the funky but newly fashionable Little Five Points neighborhood was adapted as 103 luxury loft apartments, and 30 new units were constructed as part of the project. Many of the school's original features, including the gymnasium's 30-foot ceiling, stage, and bleachers, were retained to secure historic-preservation tax credits and create unconventional living spaces.

Some developers who do renovation work prefer buildings that have not been designated as historic landmarks, in order to avoid the restrictions that preservation agencies often attach to the renovation process. (For the same reason, some developers opt to not seek historic-preservation tax credits for their projects.) Many of the adaptive use projects taking place in Chicago's West Side, for example involve distinctively designed—but not landmarked—buildings that can be freely reconfigured for new uses. The Thrush Realty Company, for example, restored a heavy timber and masonry building, the Barrett Bindery, as the centerpiece of an apartment and townhouse infill development known as Block Y. Each of the 65 apartments in the restored building was outfitted with a gracious balcony that would not have been permitted under the strict rules of historic preservation.

Some misconceptions about preservation and adaptive use are prevalent. One is that historic preservation costs more than new construction. Of course, costs will vary widely from one project to another, but renovation costs for buildings qualifying for historic-preservation tax credits may be up to 60 percent less than the cost of comparable new construction. (Historic-preservation tax credits are discussed later in this chapter.) A complete rehabilitation, including exterior repairs, roof replacement, and replacement of all systems may cost more than equivalent new construction. However, the architectural distinction and design details of historic buildings often make up for higher project costs.

Another misconception is that buildings cannot be profitably converted to new uses. Adaptive use may require skillful and imaginative redesign, but many projects around the country show that it can be successful. Buildings intended for office uses do not always require expansive floor spaces; many office tenants, especially in downtown areas, are looking for small spaces. In most cities, in fact, three-quarters or more of office tenants have fewer than 20 employees.

The renovation or adaptive use of old buildings and historic buildings often entails unusual headaches for the developer and usually takes extra time, effort, and imagination to carry out successfully. For example, there follows a recounting of some of the problems encountered in developing

some of the projects listed above as success stories. Just because such projects are difficult does not make them unprofitable. Indeed, when they are well conceived and well designed they can, by virtue of their individuality and character, beat out much of the competition in the marketplace.

▲ **The Cotton Mill.** Months of design studies, and even a full-size mock-up of roof design details, were needed to obtain approval from preservation officials on the massing of the rooftop construction. Air-conditioning units had to be hidden in a specially built trough within the condominium roofline and separated from the condominium walls by several inches of sound-deadening concrete. The mill's extensive exterior and interior brickwork was pressure-washed, with attention paid to containing the water on the interior to avoid damaging the wood floors. The interior wash did not remove all of the 100-year-old lead-based paint, and what remained had to be repainted with a special lead-encapsulating coating. To comply with National Park Service standards for historic preservation, the more than 1,200 large cypress-framed windows were removed and shipped out of state for chemical paint stripping, then repaired on site (in a workshop with nine workstations established for this purpose), and reinstalled.

▲ **Bass Lofts.** The ten-foot-high windows at the Bass high school also received special treatment. To retain the window frames and sashes, each window required a double reglazing. A large amount of asbestos was discovered in the window caulk and more lead-based paint than had been expected was discovered on the frames. Both the asbestos and the lead required careful and costly removal. Abating these types of environmental hazards cost twice what it had originally been estimated to cost.

▲ **Denver Dry Goods Building.** The restoration of this building required the removal of more than 30 layers of lead-based paint from the exterior brick, sandstone, and limestone surface.

Infill Projects

Developers are finding vigorous market support also for the construction of new buildings on old sites in cities and older suburbs. Infill uses run the gamut, most often focusing on housing but also involving retail, entertainment, office, and mixed uses. Among the sites available for such develop-

▶ Many architectural features of the historic Cotton Mill in New Orleans were retained in the adaptation of the buildings for residential use.

Rick Olivier

ment are skipped-over parcels of land, land formerly in industrial use, closed military bases, and the lots left after the demolition of abandoned housing. Also, underused parcels with buildings that can be rehabilitated or replaced are candidates for infill projects.

Infill projects gain value from their locations near and connections with existing urban land uses—revitalizing downtown cores, gentrifying urban neighborhoods, transit stations, colleges and universities, and so forth. Some infill developments are quite large additions to existing neighborhoods. Others consist of one or a few buildings folded into the urban pattern. The wholesale redevelopment of residential neighborhoods that are in decline—often by means of mixed-income housing projects—is a form of infill development that is gaining prominence. The redevelopment of retail districts as well is gaining ground as a type of infill development. These four categories of infill development are discussed in the following sections.

Large Neighborhood-Building Developments

Three projects—Addison Circle in Dallas, East Pointe in Milwaukee, and Playa Vista in Los Angeles—exemplify the kinds of major neighborhood-building projects that are transforming and reinvigorating cities across the nation. Addison Circle is being developed on parcels that remain in a suburb that is almost completely built out, East Pointe was developed on a nine-block area that was cleared in the 1960s for a highway that was never built, and Playa Vista is going up on a former industrial site. These three different locations suggest the range of opportunities open to developers. These and other large-scale infill developments such as the Lowry Air Force base redevelopment in Denver (see page 23), Harbor Town in Memphis, and Battery Park City in New York City testify to strong demand for housing and associated uses in cities and inner suburbs.

Addison, Texas, is a suburban town of 12,300 people located northwest of Dallas. It is about 80 percent developed in conventional style with low-density houses, commercial and business parks, and commercial strips. Addison Circle is a phased town center project by Post Properties in partnership with a local developer, Gaylord Properties, with the remaining phases expected to be completed between 2003 and 2005. Occupying an 80-acre

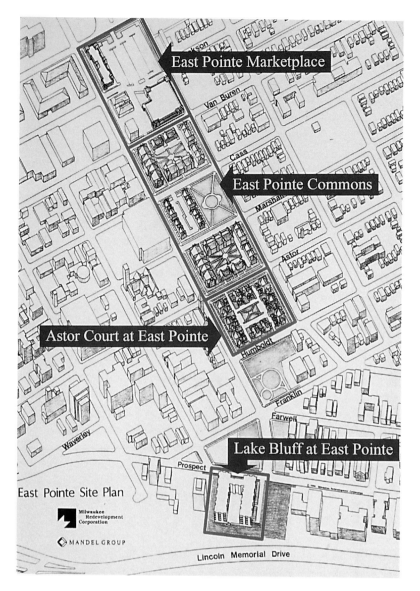

East Pointe Marketplace

East Pointe Commons

Astor Court at East Pointe

Lake Bluff at East Pointe

East Pointe Site Plan

Milwaukee
Redevelopment
Corporation

MANDEL GROUP

Lincoln Memorial Drive

▲ **East Pointe, a 438-unit residential development, was designed to fit into an existing neighborhood just north of downtown Milwaukee and to not block views of Lake Michigan.**

for the project is provided by a civic circle that acts as the visual center for the development, building courtyards, and pocket parks.

Located just north of downtown Milwaukee, the 17-acre East Pointe site became available for redevelopment in the mid-1980s when officials decided to scrap a planned freeway. The phased development of the $57 million project was managed by the Milwaukee Redevelopment Corporation, which formed a partnership with Barry Mandel, a local developer, to plan and construct the project. East Pointe is decidedly urban in design, with 438 market-rate rental apartment and condominium townhouse units and a neighborhood retail center.

This development is clustered so that almost half the site is conserved in open space. Most residences come with underground parking. East Pointe broke ground in late 1990 and was completed in 2000. The apartments rented up quickly and sales at the retail center are almost double what was expected. About one-third of the patrons of the retail center walk to shop, a travel mode that is made attractive by pedestrian-friendly street design and street connections to the surrounding neighborhood.

Sited on 1,087 acres of former Hughes Aircraft Company property just south of Marina del Rey in the Los Angeles area, Playa Vista is planned to include 13,000 residences, an employment campus, 2.5 million square feet of commercial and retail space, and community facilities. Demand for housing in this centrally located area is soaring, and Playa Vista's initial development phase, which broke ground in 2000, will help meet this demand with about 3,200 residential units. A varied mix of housing will be offered—76 different floor plans have been proposed and many architectural styles. The design incorporates neighborhood qualities that will sustain market attractiveness over time.

Smaller Infill Developments

Smaller projects that recycle vacant and underused properties are perhaps less dramatic but no less important. Many such projects are driven by rising demand for housing, and especially demand for affordable housing, in central locations. Eight projects described here exemplify an uncountable number of small infill developments that are occurring in cities and inner suburbs across the United States:

parcel adjacent to a DART (Dallas Area Rapid Transit) station and close to the town's conference and theater center, Addison Circle contains a mix of uses.

In the first three phases, completed in 2000, 1,315 dwelling units, 75,000 square feet of retail space, and 340,000 square feet of office space were developed. Currently under development is a mixed-income residential neighborhood with almost 3,000 dwelling units, mostly rental, in mid-rise buildings interspersed with neighborhood-serving retail uses, parks, and civic spaces. This development is at a density of 75 units per net acre—three times the density of typical apartment projects in north Dallas. A section of Addison Circle adjacent to the North Dallas Tollway is being developed for high-density office and commercial uses with a total of up to 10,000 employees. Public open space

▲ Pearl Court Apartments, Portland, Oregon;
▲ Richmond City Center, Richmond, California;
▲ Toscana Apartments, Sunnyvale, California;
▲ Kellytown development, Charlottesville, Virginia;
▲ Block Y, Chicago;
▲ Gramercy on Garfield and Greenwich on the Park, Cincinnati;
▲ 59th Street Terminal, Chicago; and
▲ Pacific Place, Seattle.

Developed jointly by Prendergast & Associates and the city housing authority, Pearl Court Apartments adjoining downtown Portland provides 199 affordable housing units on a one-acre site that is part of the redevelopment of 70 acres of vacant railroad yards. Its market is households earning 40 to 60 percent of the region's median income. Because it was expected that many residents with jobs in downtown would not need to drive to work, the development was required to provide only 18 parking spaces. Money saved on parking requirements went into a library, a formal two-level lobby, numerous small lounges and outdoor decks, and a large bicycle storage room. A landscaped interior courtyard is provided. Construction began in fall 1996 and full occupancy was reached in early 1998.

The multiuse Richmond City Center, developed between 1993 and 1996 by BRIDGE Housing Corporation and the Martin Group on a site cleared for a regional shopping mall that was never built, transformed a blighted area with a history of failure into a livable city center. Richmond was one of the most economically depressed communities in the San Francisco Bay area, and decades of federal and state economic assistance had failed to alleviate distress and crime in its core area. Development of the city center gave Richmond a new image. Included on the 11-acre site are a 64-unit rental apartment complex, 34 townhouses, an 82,000-square-foot neighborhood retail center, and a park providing much-needed play areas. A police substation is located on the ground floor of the apartment building. Special financing arrangements make the housing affordable, and it was quickly occupied.

The Toscana Apartments complex in the heart of housing-starved Silicon Valley was completed in 1999 by AvalonBay Communities. The site had been planned for a high-rise residential building that was in the early stages of construction when it was halted in the late 1980s by the real estate recession. Toscana Apartments includes 710 units in 12 three-, four-, and five-story buildings, providing a variety of market-rate rental units. The buildings are grouped into several neighborhoods, each with its own design style, paint schemes, and courtyard layouts. Almost all parking is under the buildings, which makes more space available for landscaping, play areas, and walking paths. Some 50,000 jobs are available within three miles of Toscana. About 40 percent of Toscana residents work at home at least one day a week and another 10 percent work full-time at home.

Kellytown is a single-family neighborhood in Charlottesville near the University of Virginia. It was established after the Civil War by freed slaves. A growing demand for housing has prompted infill development in Kellytown. Developer Tom Hickman purchased two large undeveloped parcels in Kellytown and initiated a 16-month collaborative planning effort with neighbors and town officials to prepare a place-sensitive site plan. Among the key elements in this plan are the retention of original structures still on the site, the preservation of a forested area for wildlife habitat and flood mitigation, new development that is compatible with existing houses in the community, and small lots in order to retain open space. Hickman designed the housing to echo the style of the turn-of-the-century farmhouse on the property in which he had grown up. As of early 2002, 30 of 32 planned houses have been completed on 40-by-50-foot lots, sales have been brisk, and prices have gone up from between $150,000 and $170,000 in the initial phase to $250,000 and up today.

The Thrush Realty Company's Block Y project in Chicago's West Side, part of which entailed the adaptive use of the Barrett Bindery building for housing as described on page 121, grouped two new apartment buildings and five rows of townhouses around the former bindery to create a 255-unit development.

In Cincinnati, two mid-rise rental apartment buildings—the 148-unit Gramercy on Garfield and 64-unit Greenwich on the Park—developed from 1991 to 1996 by Towne Properties on a city-owned site provide housing on the northern edge of the central business district. These buildings include retail space, indoor parking, and a proportion of affordable units. Additional buildings are planned in the phased development.

Inner cities often have extensive underused railroad yards, some of which are finding new life as locations for housing and retail uses. Most such infill sites require substantial cleanup before they can be redeveloped. Some redeveloped railyards, like the 132-acre former Penn Central Railroad railyard in Chicago's South Side, retain their industrial character. This railyard was transformed into the 59th Street Terminal intermodal center, a $40 million cargo-transfer facility with the capacity to accommodate 600,000 transfers a year between trucks and trains.

Pacific Place exemplifies successful commercial infill development. Occupying a full city block in downtown Seattle that once was used for parking, this 335,000-square-foot retail and entertainment center has a six-level underground parking garage and five floors of retail shops and entertainment uses. A skybridge extends from the third floor directly into Nordstrom's new flagship store located in a renovated building across Sixth Avenue.

Residential Neighborhood Redevelopment

In many cities, mixed-income housing projects are being encouraged, supported, and developed as a tool for reviving distressed inner-city neighborhoods. Various federal, state, and local funding programs are generally involved in such projects, including the U.S. Department of Housing and Urban Development (HUD) Section 8 subsidy program, federal grants that may be used to supplement state and local housing finance programs (for example, HUD community development block grants, urban development block grants, housing development action grants, and HOME (Home Investment Partnership Program) grants), various debt-subsidy programs such as the Federal Home Loan Bank's affordable housing program, and federal low-income housing tax credits.

Neighborhood redevelopment is a particular focus of HUD's HOPE VI program. Created in 1992, this initiative is designed to replace worn-out and partially vacant public housing projects with attractively designed projects that include public, affordable, and market-rate housing units. As a public housing initiative, HOPE VI aims to retain public housing in central locations, but to end its segregation into public housing precincts by fostering

projects that achieve successful mixes of market-rate housing and housing targeted to low- and moderate-income households. HOPE VI projects generally are joint ventures involving traditional public housing agencies, nonprofit providers, and private developers.

The three projects described next—The Terraces in Baltimore, Park DuValle in Lexington, Kentucky, and the Villages of Parklands in Washington, D.C.—illustrate mixed-income housing development to upgrade urban neighborhoods, The first two examples have a public housing component, while the third does not, but it takes advantage of government housing finance programs to provide affordable housing.

Lexington Terrace near the center of Baltimore provided public housing for hundreds of families, but the project's dilapidated and mostly unoccupied high-rise buildings were torn down in 1996. With HOPE VI funding, Lexington Terrace has been reborn as The Terraces, a mixed-income neighborhood with 203 rental townhouses for public housing residents, 100 for sale townhouses, an 88-unit apartment building for seniors, a business center, and a community recreation and daycare center. The lot and block pattern at The Terraces continues the pattern of adjacent rowhouse neighborhoods, and public housing and market-rate units are designed to be indistinguishable. Public housing residents receive case assessment and referral services, vocational training, and other services. The joint venture team of Struever Brothers, Eccles and Rouse of Baltimore, and Edgewood Management of Bethesda, Maryland, developed and manage the property for the city of Baltimore's housing authority.

Park DuValle is a $160 million mixed-income neighborhood that is under development on a 130-acre site in Louisville, Kentucky, that once contained 1,100 run-down two-story public housing units. At completion, Park DuValle will have 1,650 units divided among small apartment buildings, duplexes, and single-family houses, with one-third occupied by public housing tenants, one-third by moderate-income families, and one-third by middle-income families.

The Villages of Parklands, located in the relatively downtrodden Anacostia section of the District of Columbia, is the redevelopment by a private devel-

The Townhomes of Oxon Creek, with 210 for sale units targeted to households at or below median income, is part of a larger neighborhood-building development in inner-city Washington, D.C., that also includes the renovation of 1,400 rental apartments.

oper, William C. Smith & Company, of a 50-acre site that had been occupied by a 1,400-unit garden apartment complex rife with crime and violence. Working with Parklands residents, neighborhood leaders, and local government agencies over a period of nine years, the developer fashioned a comprehensive program aimed at making the neighborhood safe and hospitable and launched a phased campaign to upgrade the neighborhood.

Among the initiatives taken and improvements made: tenants engaged in illegal or antisocial activities were (and continue to be) evicted; more than $25 million was invested in the extensive renovation of 900 apartments; defensive-design features and new landscaping (including the planting of almost 20,000 tulip bulbs) were installed; and Splashpark, a $1 million state-of-the-art water recreation facility, was constructed. Splashpark was independently financed by William C. Smith & Company, which also is raising money for the ARC, a recreation and performing arts center for the community.

The developer worked with local school officials and invested more that $300,000 in physical upgrades for two schools, including Garfield School, which has since seen its academic ranking increase from 100th (out of 270 schools in the city) to 13th.

The developer has since "adopted" (made substantial building repairs on) five additional schools and the local library. The developer operates a shuttle bus to the nearest Metrorail and bus station and to nearby shopping facilities.

The last phase of development at the Villages of Parklands was the Townhomes of Oxon Creek, a 210-unit townhouse development on 15 acres, which is targeted to first-time homebuyers with incomes at or below the area's median income. The Parklands redevelopment has succeeded in establishing a sense of community for this neighborhood and a secure residential environment that promises stability and long-term value.

Retail District Development and Redevelopment

In many cities and built-up suburbs, the development and redevelopment of retail districts is a growing priority. One particular type of opportunity in this respect concerns the stretched-out strips of commercial development that are found throughout urban America. ULI has proposed ten principles for energizing these kinds of commercial strips and transforming them into more positive components of community life.

Many commercial strips contribute to their local economies and provide important community ser-

▲ Bethesda Row in the evolving suburban activity center of Bethesda, Maryland, has transformed an area of low-density service and industrial uses into a retail and entertainment attraction.

vices. But typically they present a chaotic appearance and are poorly integrated with the rest of the community, even cut off from bordering development. Frequently they engender traffic congestion. Their spread-out nature, dependence on access by car, and lack of distinction violate important tenets of smart growth. Furthermore, business at many older strip malls is languishing.

But realizing that commercial strips are here to stay, urbanists have struggled to find ways to improve them. In 2000, ULI sought expert opinions on solutions to the problems presented by commercial strips, and came up with the following ten principles for community action:[2]

▲ Establish leadership forums and partnerships that can coordinate public and private improvement efforts, stay on top of traffic and security issues, and take steps to make parking a less prominent element of the landscape.

▲ Anticipate the evolution of retail market demographics, which are making walkable and stylish settings, a mix of uses, and place-making amenities increasingly marketable.

▲ Know the market for individual centers on commercial strips, recognizing the market forces at work in the area and the position of the centers in the hierarchy of retail locations.

▲ Reduce the amount of land zoned for retailing to maintain the value of existing locations, stimulate reinvestment in existing locations, and avoid promoting discontinuous and inefficient new development.

▲ Establish "pulse" nodes of development spaced out along strips—in a peaks and troughs pattern

—to pump new life into strip districts. Use key intersections or major transit stops as locations for higher-density, pedestrian-oriented commercial development.

▲ Reduce traffic congestion along commercial strips by balancing and accommodating needs for through traffic and destination traffic, improving pedestrian and transit access, and reducing traffic conflicts. Methods for reducing traffic conflicts include limiting access points, linking parking lots, allowing for shared parking, and redesigning intersections.

▲ Make strips into distinctive retail settings. Place-making methods include providing attractive walkways and a continuous streetfront experience; installing attractive lighting, street furniture, and landscaping; and designing informative and consistent signage.

▲ Diversify the character of commercial strips by rezoning to promote higher densities and the inclusion of nonretail uses such as housing and offices.

▲ Take steps to eradicate ugliness. Strive for design excellence as individual properties are developed and redeveloped. Use design guidelines to promote pedestrian-scaled streetscapes. Work with utility companies to place power lines underground. Be more creative in the placement and design of parking lots.

▲ Target public investment and change development regulations to support the reinvention of commercial strips. Support place-making goals and the evolution of pulse nodes by investment in public facilities and services. Implement zoning and other development standards that promote high-quality, place-making designs. Provide fiscal and regulatory incentives to encourage multiparcel and public/private ventures.

In cities across the country, urban retail development is increasingly occurring in mixed-use formats. Bethesda Row in downtown Bethesda, Maryland, and Phillips Place in Charlotte, North Carolina, provide examples. Another trend on the retail development front is the discovery by stores and developers of considerable buying power in bypassed inner-city and inner-suburban areas. Among recent projects capitalizing on this discovery are the renovation of the Lee-Harvard neighborhood shopping center in Cleveland, Ohio, and the redevelopment of the Lakewest Town Center in West Dallas, Texas.

Federal Realty Investment Trust's Bethesda Row project in downtown Bethesda, Maryland, an affluent close-in suburb of Washington, D.C., is creating a mixed-use retail district. Much of downtown Bethesda has been reconstructed over the past 15 years with substantial new office and retail development focused around a centrally located Metrorail station. The Bethesda Row development is providing new shopping streets at the edge of this expanding suburban activity center near a cluster of new high-rise apartments and densely designed townhouses. The site is a seven-block area two blocks from the Metrorail station.

The multiphase project involves the rehabilitation of some former light-industrial buildings and the infilling of vacant lots. The first three phases feature 110,000 square feet of office space (mostly located over shops), 190,000 square feet of retail space, and 40,000 square feet of restaurants. An office building under construction will also house art-movie theaters. All uses at Bethesda Row front along the existing streets and most back up to a 1,000-car county parking garage. The development includes tree plantings, new street lighting, and widened sidewalks to make the district attractive to pedestrians and to encourage shopping and outdoor dining.

Phillips Place in Charlotte, North Carolina, offers another example of a new multiuse retail district.

Located on a 35-acre site in the upscale SouthPark area of the city, Phillips Place features 130,000 square feet of retail space, a 124-room hotel, a multiplex cinema, and 402 residential units. The housing is provided in a variety of formats: three-story apartment buildings, apartment and townhouse units over retail uses, and lofts over two-story townhouses. The commercial component is configured as an open-air retail village along a main street. It is designed to invite pedestrians to stroll along the storefronts. The $80 million project began construction in late 1995 and was completed in spring 1998.

After bypassing inner-city markets for decades, retail development is again making an appearance in cities around the country. Crime, lack of buying power among poor residents, and complex zoning often dominated by local politics are reasons given for why retailers have avoided inner-city markets. Their return to inner cities is profit-driven. For example, the Super Stop & Shop in Boston's South Bay Center is the top-grossing store in the 186-store chain and the Foot Locker store in Harlem is among the company's most successful stores, with sales exceeding $1,000 per square foot, according to the *Washington Post*.[3]

With their generally dense concentrations of housing, inner-city neighborhoods often represent considerable purchasing power within small areas.

Inserted into a built-up suburban location in Charlotte, North Carolina, Phillips Place, a traditional style town center, provides a distinctive shopping and residential environment.

Combined, inner-city neighborhoods in small and large U.S. cities wield around $331 billion in retail purchasing power, according to a 1999 HUD study.[4] Furthermore, every city contains neighborhoods of moderate-income households that most often are underserved by retailing. Many inner-city residents have to drive to suburban stores for their shopping needs. According to the HUD study, retail sales in 48 inner cities examined fell short of residents' retail purchasing power by $8.7 billion.[5]

The extensive renovation of the 16-acre Lee-Harvard neighborhood shopping center in Cleveland exemplifies growing interest in inner-city markets. The center was reconfigured to reestablish it as a profitable retail center and focus of community life in a neighborhood of middle-income homeowners. The shopping center had fallen on hard times. Deferred maintenance and a poor retail layout had diminished its attraction for businesses, and the potential loss of anchor stores loomed as a threat to its future. Led by a nonprofit community development organization, Lee-Harvard's reconfiguration involved reducing the amount of floor space and reshaping it to form a more attractive and accessible shopping center. The project included upgrades to noticeably deteriorated structures, associated parking and entryways, and signage. These renovations succeeded in retaining the center's existing anchors.

Lakewest Town Center in West Dallas represents another success story for inner-city shopping center redevelopment. In 1990, a ULI advisory services panel identified the Dallas West retail center (as it was then known) as a potential catalyst for neighborhood revival. Although it was in a prime location with no other shopping center within five miles, the center was half empty, the parking lot was potholed, and the lighting was so bad that merchants had to close at sunset. In 1992, a public/private development group was formed to undertake redevelopment. The developer constructed a new roof and new storefronts, repaired and replaced lighting, repaved the parking lot with concrete, and added new signage—at a cost of $2.6 million. A Carnival supermarket was brought in as an anchor tenant, and the refurbished center attracted a mix of national and local retailers. By 1996, Lakewest Town Center (as it was renamed) had achieved a 97 percent occupancy rate and its profitability had improved dramatically. The success of this project has stimulated related development in the West Dallas area.

Issues and Obstacles

This may be an auspicious time for infill and redevelopment: market forces appear to be aligning with community efforts to promote the revitalization of central cities and inner suburbs. But it is important to understand that the kinds of community-transforming reuse and infill projects profiled in the last section are occurring only in some parts of some cities—chiefly in the favored quarter of some metropolitan regions (see "Conditions for Project Success" section on page 133 for a discussion of the favored quarter) and in some inner-city neighborhoods that have been targeted for substantial public investment and subsidy programs.

Already there are signs that the most attractive historic buildings and the most developable vacant sites in some cities have been snapped up. Maintaining the current momentum of infill and reuse and widening opportunities for the redevelopment of buildings and areas will require smart-growth advocates and communities to devote attention to the removal of obstacles to in-city development. Their aim should be to create a level playing field for development: cities and inner suburbs should be as attractive for new development as are greenfield locations.

A survey of Atlanta housing developers conducted by Robert Charles Lesser & Co. in connection with an October 2000 ULI forum on infill housing identified eight significant barriers to the development of infill housing. The barriers these developers had encountered were, in order of importance:

▲ high land costs;
▲ neighborhood opposition;
▲ complex zoning and permitting processes;
▲ inferior quality of in-town schools;
▲ inflexible zoning restrictions and regulations;
▲ the need to design new projects to fit into existing neighborhoods;
▲ (for high-density projects) the high cost of decked parking; and
▲ lack of popular and market support for and knowledge of higher-density and mixed-use projects.

The obstacles faced by infill developers in Atlanta —high costs, lack of acceptance, and regulatory constraints—are similar to the problems that the developers of infill and redevelopment projects encounter in many other communities. These obstacles are not insurmountable, especially in a robust market. After the following comments on high costs, neighbor resistance, regulatory complexity, and financing difficulties for infill and redevelopment projects, some steps that developers can take to improve project feasibility ("Conditions for Project Success") and steps that communities can take to reduce or eliminate obstacles to infill and redevelopment ("Promoting Infill and Redevelopment") are discussed.

High Costs

Cost issues cause developers to look twice at in-city properties as opportunities for development. Land prices in built-up areas tend to be high by comparison with prices on the urbanizing fringe. Furthermore, the redevelopment of previously used sites or the reuse of buildings entails costs not encountered in greenfield development, for example, the cost of demolishing structures, the cost of cleaning up toxic wastes, or the cost of remediating lead paint. Developers practiced in constructing projects on large and largely unobstructed parcels must customize their building designs and construction methods to cope with various site restrictions. Parking needs can add considerably to the cost of urban projects. And the infrastructure advantage of urban locations (which is a factor in higher land prices) may turn out to be illusory as expensive upgrades (or replacement) become necessary.

Land

Land prices are one of the most troublesome aspects of in-city development. Sites for pioneering infill and redevelopment projects usually exhibit known deficiencies, including untested market interest. They also pose the risk of various unknown problems, including contamination. Site deficiencies and risks enable developers who are interested in deteriorated areas that are showing early signs of revival to find sites priced well below land prices in other areas. These developers, in effect, trade off potential risks for cut-rate land.

As reviving areas attract more development, however, and developers become more confident of overcoming locational risks, land prices tend to escalate. Developers buying into areas in a later phase of revitalization may find land prices pushing up development costs to levels that require increased densities or even changes in types of development. In Chicago's booming West Side, for example, prices for historic buildings and vacant sites have increased to the point that commercial developers are outbidding residential developers.

Parking

In-town sites often have little room for surface parking—and the land is too valuable to use for surface parking. But providing structured parking is expensive. Making the numbers work for structured parking requires high densities or high rents and sale prices, or both. In-town housing projects that hope to attract suburban households generally need to provide secure parking spaces, especially if they are located in marginal neighborhoods. For many infill and redevelopment projects, the parking solution is a sizable element of the developer's pro forma.

Infrastructure

One of the presumed advantages of developing within built-up areas is the availability of infrastructure. Urban and inner-suburban developers often find to their chagrin that the infrastructure systems serving their sites have not been well maintained or are not sized to provide adequate capacity for new development. The repair or replacement of infrastructure systems is expensive.

In many neighborhoods, infrastructure has been allowed to fall into disrepair, the result of long-term decline, the moving away of civic activists, and cuts in maintenance dollars. The infrastructure problem is generally more acute when areas formerly used for warehousing and industry are redeveloped for housing. Local streets may need repair, underground utilities may require upgrading, and other facilities may be insufficient to serve the new kind of development.

If local governments do not respond to infrastructure needs in a timely manner, developers are left with the choice of living with old, crumbling systems or doing the job themselves. Furthermore, for many adaptive use and infill projects the so-called Christmas tree effect comes into play: opportunistic neighborhood activists or elected officials require various neighborhood-serving infrastructure improvements—many ornaments on the tree—as a condition of development approval.

Developers have found their projects saddled with requirements for parks, open space, and transportation improvements that serve the neighborhood more than the development itself. Such requirements can unreasonably escalate development costs and ultimately make projects financially infeasible.

Resistant Neighbors

Neighborhood acceptance is one of the most knotty problems facing redevelopment and infill projects, which, by their very nature, will make significant changes in their neighborhoods and communities. Infill developers tend to think that the effects of their projects will be mostly positive:

▲ new buildings and uses will replace blighted buildings and empty lots;
▲ property values in surrounding areas will rise;
▲ the community's tax base will expand;
▲ the new activity generated will improve local housing and retail markets; and
▲ new residents will generate support for improved public facilities and community services.

For these reasons, elected officials frequently support proposed developments.

The people who live near or own a business near proposed projects, however, frequently are less enthusiastic about the benefits. Often suspicious of any changes in their surroundings, they tend to think that the effects of any given project will be mostly negative:

▲ traffic congestion and parking problems will worsen;
▲ new people, new buildings, and new activities will change the character of the neighborhood (unpredictably, but probably for the worse);
▲ increased property values will cause an increase in property taxes;
▲ street patterns and views, trees, open space, historic or architecturally significant buildings, or other desirable elements of the neighborhood will be disturbed;
▲ vacant lots serving recreation, gardening, or other desirable purposes will become unavailable;
▲ construction activities will disrupt the neighborhood, and for large projects such disruption will go on for a long time.

In neighborhoods that have had recent experience with undesirable development—unattractive buildings, for example, or unneighborly uses—residents may have become more resistant to change, as well as organized and politically savvy. Neighborhood organizations are fully capable of convincing elected officials to put costly conditions on proposed projects or to decide against approval, even if the officials support the type of development being proposed and even if adopted policies and plans promote such projects.

Development Regulations

Developers tend to consider the zoning and building codes of most jurisdictions as obstacles to development, but the jurisdictions that offer the most opportunities for redevelopment and infill—namely, central cities and older suburbs—are among the most difficult regulatory environments in the nation. Central cities and older suburbs often use ossified and restrictive zoning ordinances and building codes administered by bewildering bureaucracies to regulate development, and they complicate the process by adding advisory roles for numerous committees and commissions.

It is common for infill parcels to be zoned for uses that no longer are economically viable. Their rezoning can take months or years. Regulations may require that properties available for redevelopment be decontaminated and toxic waste cleaned up, and the cleanup process is rarely without controversy, which extends the development period. Old buildings being adapted for new uses usually must meet code provisions that were devised for new construction, and meeting those provisions often requires a complete makeover of basic systems. For historic buildings, renovators encounter another layer of state and federal rehabilitation standards.

In addition, city code administrators or city councils often approve final permits only after many conditions have been attached—and many of these conditions need to be resolved through further discussions and negotiations. Labor laws and certain construction requirements in cities are likely to make the construction of urban projects more expensive compared with similar projects in developing suburban areas.

Regulatory complexity in central cities requires more effort on the part of developers to get projects approved, lengthens the duration of the approval process, and increases project risk. Developers in growth-happy metropolitan fringe areas would not tolerate such regulatory conditions. The achievement of smart growth through infill and redevelopment, therefore, depends on establishing a less hostile environment for development in central cities and inner-suburban areas through the overhaul of regulations and the regulatory system.

Financing

For a number of reasons, obtaining financing for reuse, infill, and redevelopment projects often is more difficult than obtaining financing for projects in greenfield locations. Lenders prefer the tried and tested. They avoid pioneer projects. Risk and uncertainty are anathema to lenders, and few locations seem riskier or more uncertain than areas in which little development has taken place in recent years and areas that have become known as undesirable places to live in, work in, or visit.

Lenders are leery also of customized projects, projects that differ from conventional off-the-shelf packages.[6] Projects that are cleverly designed to fit infill sites or that propose new uses for old buildings usually are not conventional enough for lenders' tastes. And the high land and development costs associated with some in-city projects ring more alarm bells for lenders, who tend to discount the likely future value of the location and the new use.

Lender caution often forces the developers of in-city projects to assemble funding from a mix of public and private financing sources. The assembly of financing packages usually requires complex negotiations and agreements that may not fall into place in a timely manner.

Conditions for Project Success

A range of site and use options are available for developers looking for infill and redevelopment opportunities. In infill and redevelopment, the key to success is fitting the product to the location—and, as is the case for all real estate, location is the primary factor driving market responses. Most infill and redevelopment activity is occurring in urban and suburban business centers and in neighborhoods located in an area that real estate economist Christopher Leinberger calls "the favored quarter" of metropolitan regions.

Clusters of high-income housing and high-end employment that have evolved historically in cities and towns in combination constitute a particularly desirable sector of urban regions—the favored quarter—where most new and relocating jobs settle. "Employment locations," Leinberger says, "tend to be driven by proximity to executive housing (the bosses make employment location decisions) and by access to the regional freeway network."[7]

Demand for locations in the favored quarter creates incentives for infill and redevelopment. Lots skipped over during the first wave of development become choice building sites. Properties with steep slopes or peculiar shapes attract developers willing to tailor building designs to constraining conditions. Badly maintained buildings in newly desirable neighborhoods offer opportunities for upgrading or replacement. The land under small detached houses offers sites for the development of large houses, townhouses, or apartment buildings, so the small houses, even if perfectly sound, are demolished. Commercial strips are redeveloped with multistory office buildings and more intensive commercial uses.

Many kinds of locations that are outside the favored quarter can also attract infill and redevelopment. Locations adjoining or near hot market areas can serve as spillover areas providing (less expensive) expansion room for development. Areas of distinctive character can attract special segments of the market. Some neighborhoods—every metropolitan area has one or two—attract infill on the strength of their reputations as funky addresses where artists, musicians, and other nonconformists congregate. Neighborhoods of historic value—which are found in every city and many suburbs—can support infill development, as can university neighborhoods.

In the absence of strong demand, infill sites tend to linger on the market—for good reasons. As Real Estate Research Corporation (RERC) put the problem in a 1982 publication on infill development strategies: "What remains after the other parcels are developed are typically those that have problems—difficult soil/drainage or other physical conditions, odd shapes, ownership problems, poor access, land damaged by a pre-urban use (quarries, landfill sites, wrecking yards), or other characteristics. For a long time these problem parcels were ignored or tabled on a community's agenda and not worth the effort for developers who had other options."[8]

Much has not changed in the 20 years since RERC made its observation. Impediments still stand in the way of the development of infill sites—and underused properties available for redevelopment. In addition to the problems listed by RERC, land assembly (involving properties under multiple ownership) can be difficult and expensive for developers wanting to put together a sizable project. Too often infill sites hide nasty surprises, like toxic wastes or hard bedrock.

But although the impediments remain, much of the land available for infill has one advantage it did not enjoy 20 years ago: a sought-after location. Rising market interest in central locations accessible to employment concentrations, culture, shopping, and entertainment is altering the cost-benefit equation for potential infill properties. Whereas the impediments to development have long been decisive for many developers who chose to avoid inner-city neighborhoods and business districts, the rising market for infill is now making it worthwhile for many of these developers to seek to develop infill properties despite their impediments.

However, the product must fit the market. This is true in the favored quarter and especially true outside the favored quarter. Identifying products that fit a location and shaping products to a site's locational attributes demand all the acuity developers can command. They must understand geographic shifts in consumer demand, track emerging markets for specialized products, and keep their eyes open for opportunities emanating from rezoning or new public investments. Once developers have defined market interest in a particular product and location, they must find a site that fits that product.

In evaluating the fit of an envisioned project to a given infill or redevelopment site, developers must take certain steps to assure project feasibility, including the following:

▲ Examine site conditions, specifically focusing on identifying the site conditions that likely deterred others from developing or redeveloping the property. These deterrents may have included geologic or topographic problems, toxic waste concerns, the presence of obsolete struc-

tures, the shape and size of the parcel, infrastructure issues, and adjoining uses. The main point of this examination is to determine what the problems may be and estimate what it will cost to overcome them.
▲ Examine legal records and possible legal problems, including land ownership records, deed restrictions, tax liens, and past attempts at development.
▲ Study zoning and building code requirements to determine how they might constrain (or support) the type of development under consideration for the site and how they might affect development costs.
▲ Plan a project that in its function, design, and layout blends with the neighborhood rather than offends the neighbors.

Planning the restoration or adaptive use of historic buildings, especially if the use of historic-preservation tax credits is contemplated, requires even more careful preparation. Donovan D. Rypkema, a real estate economist who specializes in renovated buildings, offers the following steps for success in renovation projects:[9]

▲ Use architects and building contractors who have successfully renovated old buildings. For tax-certified historic rehabilitation projects, use architects and contractors who have successfully worked on projects that adhered to National Park Service standards for historic preservation.
▲ Expect that the project will take more time to complete than normally required. Rehabilitation almost always encounters structural and regulatory surprises that need attention.
▲ Contact local building officials and, for tax-credit projects, representatives of the state historic-preservation office at the outset of the project before the option agreement is signed, to clarify requirements that will affect project feasibility.
▲ Before the property is acquired, estimate costs for curing structural problems, removing lead paint, abating asbestos, and remediating any other environmental problem, based on structural and environmental analyses of the property.
▲ Emphasize the building's unusual features in marketing. The individual character of old and historic buildings is often their principal attraction to tenants.
▲ Seek allies in local preservation groups. Members of such groups can supply valuable information

about a building's history, possibly provide access to financial resources, and help obtain political support for the project.
▲ Be prepared to obtain financing from multiple sources, including public sources of subordinated funding.

To overcome NIMBYism, it is important for developers to identify within the community potential advocates for and opponents of the development they want to propose for a particular infill site, and to evaluate their influence. They should identify influential neighborhood organizations, civic groups, special-interest groups, and business organizations in the area. Developers also should be prepared to offer a compelling case for developing the proposed project—showing its benefits to the community and the neighborhood compared with leaving the site undeveloped or in its current use.

Promoting Infill and Redevelopment

A wide array of techniques and programs have been tried by city and town governments, often working with nonprofit groups and developers, to improve neighborhoods and business districts. Valuable experience has been gained about what does and does not work. For example, at least four lessons emerged from experience with 1960s style urban renewal projects:

▲ Making sites available for development by wholesale clearance—the bulldozer approach—severely disrupts entire neighborhoods, and has effects that ripple throughout the community and continue into succeeding generations. Large-scale clearance for redevelopment is inequitable and increasingly infeasible politically.
▲ Assembling sites before having formulated a strategy for attracting redevelopment that is both economically viable and socially conscious is in general a recipe for immense outlays of money with few constructive benefits.
▲ Local governments must find ways to work with rather than against the residents of the community if they hope to mend a disintegrating urban fabric.
▲ Infill and redevelopment will not succeed without a nurturing context, which involves a long-term commitment to the conservation of whole neighborhoods. As everyone who has been involved in community renewal efforts knows: Rome was not built in a day.

The past and continuing efforts of innumerable local housing, redevelopment, and economic development agencies to stimulate infill and redevelopment properly deserve a great deal of credit. Local agencies have built supportive policy frameworks and generated constructive projects that have helped bring development back to cities. They have been aided in such efforts by community development block grants and other federal funding mechanisms and by funding from state housing and economic development agencies.

Resources for community redevelopment are always limited. The effective use of available resources to stimulate and support infill and redevelopment begins with defining strategic approaches. Communities have learned the value of focusing programs and investments in the following ways:

▲ Target specific neighborhoods and business districts with a battery of coordinated, mutually reinforcing programs. Such actions leverage the assets of target areas to the greatest effect.
▲ Build on economic and social forces at work in the community to take full advantage of untapped or unfulfilled markets and consumer needs.
▲ Cast a wide net to assemble federal, state, and local governmental funding, plus corporate and community assistance, to promote investment in targeted areas.
▲ Establish a collaborative process for decision making and community investment. Involve government, civic, business, and other interests in the revitalization of the community, ideally through an interlocking, multilayered network.

A collaborative process, building on an existing market, and multilayered financing are among the techniques used in the successful renovation of the Lee-Harvard shopping center in Cleveland (see page 130) The New Village Corporation, one of dozens of community organizations working to revive Cleveland neighborhoods, wanted to halt the deterioration of the Lee-Harvard center because the center's decline was reducing the livability of its working-class neighborhood. (The nonprofit New Village Corporation is the real estate development subsidiary of Neighborhood Progress Inc. (NPI), one of Cleveland's premier organizations promoting neighborhood conservation and development.) New Village had been involved in the renovation of several small centers.

After acquiring the center and assessing the tasks before it, New Village teamed up with Amistad Community Development Corporation, the local neighborhood improvement organization. The community organizations sought the support of the local member of the city council and the mayor's office and also brought on board an experienced developer of shopping centers, Forest City Enterprises. Forest City, which is headquartered in Cleveland, agreed to join the team as a merchant developer, to advise on a development strategy and financing sources and to manage the design and construction. This team drew up a plan for a $26 million reconstruction aimed at improving the structural condition, retail function, and appearance of the shopping center.

Many sources of funding were lined up. Amistad secured a $1 million loan from the city and a $500,000 federal grant arranged by U.S. Congressman Louis Stokes. Networking among local community groups brought in $3.5 million in low-interest, long-term loans with initial principal payments deferred. The sources of this patient money were the Cleveland Development Partnership (an organization of corporate leaders), the Village Capital Corporation (a financing affiliate of NPI), and the Neighborhood Development Investment Fund (a city fund to support business expansion in neighborhoods). Forest City was instrumental in arranging a $12.3 million first mortgage loan from a consortium of three banks. The final piece of the funding puzzle fell into place when Fannie Mae's American Communities Fund came up with $1,875,000 in equity investment and a $961,000 bridge loan to help with construction financing.

Now virtually complete, the redeveloped Lee-Harvard shopping center has retained more than

30 local businesses and 650 jobs with payrolls of about $12 million. The city estimates that annual tax revenues from Lee-Harvard will increase by $1.5 million. And, the livability and long-term vitality of the Lee-Harvard neighborhood have been significantly improved.

Cities and inner suburbs should take a variety of approaches to the task of promoting infill and redevelopment. Various kinds of programs and process reforms can help remove obstacles to these kinds of development and support the market for infill and redevelopment. The following sections discuss many of the approaches communities are using to provide incentives for in-city development, including:

▲ constructive efforts to defuse NIMBYist opposition;
▲ site assembly;
▲ assistance in the cleanup of problem sites;
▲ various programs to help reduce development costs;
▲ financial assistance for homebuyers and renters;
▲ the marketing of in-town development;
▲ various programs to promote downtown redevelopment;
▲ programs to promote neighborhood conservation; and
▲ streamlining regulations and regulatory processes.

Defusing NIMBYism

Not-in-my-backyard (NIMBY) opposition often is one of the highest hurdles faced by the developers of infill and redevelopment projects. It is par for the course for local residents to object stridently to proposed projects. They complain about the effects on already congested roads and school systems, about incompatible project designs and densities, and about the failure of past efforts to manage growth. Sometimes there is truth in their telling, but more often their exaggerated claims and fears are merely an expression of their anxieties about change.

A redevelopment plan proposed recently for a neighborhood shopping center in an established suburb of Washington, D.C., for example, is a paragon of smart development, calling for a mix of uses with 40 townhouses and 40 loft apartments over retail uses grouped in a classic main street design—plus a tree-lined hiker/biker path. But a member of a local homeowners association was not impressed with the plan's smart-growth aspects: "A complete change in the nature of the center . . . on this small corner is neither desired by, nor compatible with, the existing community or its needs."[10]

In another example of NIMBYist opposition to a smart-growth project, the town council of Mount Pleasant, South Carolina, a community located just outside Charleston, turned down an application to develop I'On Village, a traditional neighborhood design project on a 243-acre infill site. The plan called for a mix of housing types, a neighborhood commercial and civic center, and considerable open space in the form of lakes, parks, and greenways. The town council rejected the application in 1995, fearing its high density and multifamily housing.

I'On Village developers Tom and Vince Graham, supported by the South Carolina Coastal Conservation League, fought for 14 months to reverse the decision. After a nasty political battle that resulted in a major turnover in the town council, approval was obtained for a reconfigured plan that allowed less commercial space, eliminated a planned elementary school, and confined residential uses to single-family houses. With 762 homesites clustered to preserve the site's important environmental resources, I'On Village has won several awards for building design and environmental conservation and it will no doubt become a major asset for Mount Pleasant. However, as Sam Passmore, land use director of the South Carolina Coastal Conservation League, told a Sensible Growth Symposium audience in Chicago in late 2001: "What could have been a real contribution to smart growth is likely to become an exclusive rather than inclusive community."

How can communities ward off or come to terms with the almost knee-jerk opposition to proposals for new development in existing neighborhoods? In the first place, it is important to anticipate neighborhood concerns and attempt to define mitigation measures that can be incorporated into proposed projects. Mitigation requires conciliation and compromise, but quite often mitigation demands are raised during rancorous hearings. It is better to try to arrive collaboratively at an understanding before final hearings are held and official decisions are made. Another approach to defusing NIMBYist opposition is to establish mechanisms related to new development for funding community improvements desired by project neighbors.

From the NIMBYist perspective, elected leaders tend to value proposed projects for benefits they provide for the community at large, including tax dollars and general revitalization, but they tend to fail to account for the impact of proposed projects on neighboring properties. Major new developments may contribute to the vitality of the whole community, but they may also add traffic to already congested streets, further tax the capacity of already inadequate local public facilities (schools, playgrounds, libraries, and other facilities), and increase the property taxes of residents with limited incomes.

In some communities, neighborhood groups are powerful enough to exact significant "donations" from project developers. Such donations are seen as compensation for the hardships suffered by neighbors because of the project. For example, the proposal for an upscale mixed-use project next to the Friendship Heights Metrorail station in Montgomery County, Maryland, ran into a buzzsaw of neighborhood opposition and went through a lengthy review process and multiple hearings. During the review process, the developer incorporated a donation into the project—a 20,000-square-foot community center to be managed as a county facility. Later, when the project was in the final design stages, a neighborhood watchdog group argued that county standards require a minimum of 24,000 square feet for such facilities and insisted that "we are entitled to the same benefits that people in the rest of the county get."[11]

This type of ad hoc bargaining for developer donations or contributions is unfair and its results are unpredictable.

A more constructive approach would be the establishment of a compensation mechanism for neighborhoods affected by infill and redevelopment. For example, increases in local tax revenues from new development could be earmarked to fund neighborhood improvements. This would be like the tax-increment financing (TIF) districts that many local governments use to fund infrastructure upgrades in redevelopment areas or the tax-increment reinvestment zones in Houston and San Antonio from which tax revenues are channeled to developers to repay them for the front-end costs of infrastructure improvements.

Local governments could set up a formal compensation procedure whereby they would estimate projected revenue from infill and redevelopment projects during the project planning discussions and then determine what percentage of that revenue will be used to fund improvements desired by local residents—parks and playgrounds, for example, or streetscape improvements, or better police and fire services. Such a commitment to improve neighborhood facilities could spell the difference between rejection and acceptance of infill projects by neighbors.

Site Assembly

Communities can help prepare the way for infill development and redevelopment by identifying potentially developable parcels and by assembling and conveying sites. They can search their databases to provide brokers and developers with lists of vacant and tax-delinquent properties, including information on size, current assessments, and any tax or legal problems attached to the property records. And, as many communities have done, they can formally acquire tax-delinquent properties by foreclosure and package them for development.

Unused city-owned parcels can be combined with tax-foreclosed properties to create developable sites. Public agencies frequently hold unused properties that can be declared surplus for city needs and sold for infill and redevelopment. The city of San Antonio conveys such properties to the San Antonio Housing Trust, which acts as a clearinghouse to make properties available to nonprofit housing agencies for nominal fees.

Chicago's housing department aggressively assembles vacant and unused parcels for redevelopment.

Under its New Homes for Chicago program, the housing department conveys sites to developers—for as little as $1—for the construction of single-family and two-flat houses and condominiums for low- and moderate-income families. In its newest program, HomeStart, the housing department manages the construction and sale of market-rate housing on sites that are retained in city ownership through the development period.

The city of Dayton, Ohio, scrapped a long-standing plan to clear and redevelop the historic Wright-Dunbar neighborhood, a residential neighborhood that had been ravaged over many years by abandonment and demolition. The scrapped plan was replaced by a plan to renovate houses and build new ones. Under this plan, the city acquires abandoned properties, primarily through foreclosure, and sells them for $1 for housing development. Buyers are given one year in which to build or restore a house.

Planning to launch a similar program, the city of Houston is creating a land bank of tax-delinquent properties to be redeveloped for market-rate housing. The program is made possible by 1997 state legislation allowing state tax liens on foreclosed properties to be waived. Houston's redevelopment authority will be the repository for the tax-foreclosed properties and the broker for their resale to homebuilders.

Cities can focus land acquisition programs on nonresidential land uses as well, for example, on the revitalization of declining business districts. Programs by which cities acquire selected properties in order to remove a blighted land use and initiate redevelopment, improve streetscapes, construct parking garages, and support business development can attract private development investment to the district.

The redevelopment program pursued by Suisun City, California, demonstrates the use of public land acquisition to stimulate the development of a mixed-use town center. Located 44 miles northeast of San Francisco, Suisun City is a historic inland port that had fallen on hard times. Surrounded by classic suburban sprawl, the retail and industrial core was decaying, unable to expand or attract high-quality development. But the city of 26,000 residents reinvented its downtown core through a series of redevelopment projects.

Beginning in 1990 with the city council's adoption of a specific plan, the city's redevelopment agency purchased empty lots and old warehouses in order to build a waterfront plaza that would make Main Street an activity-filled town center, acquired and restored a historic building to create a centerpiece of commercial activity on Main Street, funded the development of a public marina adjacent to the plaza, and assembled sites in a dilapidated neighborhood just east of downtown for the construction of nearly 300 residential units in a traditional neighborhood development. Suisun City's land assemblage program required a great deal of political will in the face of landowner resistance, but it was a key element in sparking the new development that has turned the city's fortunes around.[12]

Cities could become more aggressive in undertaking to assemble sites for infill development and redevelopment, in particular by making greater use of eminent domain to acquire properties. The forcible taking of property by local governments for any use has always been a politically ticklish proposition. Urban renewal disasters in the 1960s and 1970s helped make politicians especially wary about acquiring property for private redevelopment.

According to a recent survey, cities continue to be reluctant to use eminent domain to assemble properties for redevelopment or to round out private assemblages. Among 36 cities responding to the survey, only four indicate a definite willingness to use the power of eminent domain for encouraging commercial redevelopment. In most of the remaining cities, city councils are unwilling to make a definite commitment or they favor condemnation only in cases when developers are prepared to proceed with redevelopment.[13] More aggressive public actions to assemble sites for redevelopment would help promote infill in the most desirable locations and redevelopment of the most desired uses.

Reducing Brownfield Risks

Brownfields—land formerly in industrial or commercial use—represent a significant but problematical source of infill and redevelopment sites. Brownfield properties are potentially contaminated by toxic wastes. According to some experts, more than 500,000 brownfield properties in the United States may contain contamination—from buried industrial wastes of unknown toxicity to leaking underground gasoline tanks—that requires

containment, removal, or other actions before the property can be reused.

The detection of toxic substances is often difficult and their treatment expensive. Furthermore, governmental agencies often disagree about remediation standards and procedures. These problems make lenders reluctant to finance development on brownfield sites because of the potential loss of collateral value and potential liability if contamination is discovered.

The prevalence of questionable brownfield sites in many cities constitutes a serious challenge for redevelopment. Many communities have come to understand this and with state and federal assistance have fashioned programs to clean up brownfield sites or to reduce liability risks for their development. Many cities have taken on the job of assessing the cleanup needs of significant sites and helping to fund remediation. Developers, in the meanwhile, have learned to factor into their project analyses the possibility of contaminated buildings and soil, and specialists are widely available for treating such conditions. Developers also have gained experience in working with public agencies to determine cleanup requirements and methods.

Still, risks remain and developers can encounter many problems when they try to reuse old buildings and redevelop previously used sites. Cleanup costs often are unpredictable and they can be astronomical. City agencies are generally reluctant to assemble lists of brownfield sites that might interest developers seeking sites, because property owners are leery of publicizing even the possibility of contamination problems on the properties. Despite the risks and problems, the rising marketability of in-city sites is promoting greater use of brownfield properties.

Washington's Landing in Pittsburgh, a mixed-use residential and commercial development, occupies one of several brownfield sites that the city has redeveloped through public/private efforts. Washington's Landing is on Herr's Island, a severely contaminated 42-acre area formerly used for manufacturing and offering a prime opportunity for redevelopment because of its location just two miles from downtown. The Pittsburgh Urban Redevelopment Authority (URA) purchased the land in 1983, devised a plan for a mix of residential and commercial uses, and managed a two-year cleanup effort that used city and state funding sources. The URA also constructed basic infrastructure systems, a public park, and a riverside pathway. In 1995, construction of Washington's Landing commenced. This development, by Montgomery and Rust, includes upscale townhouses (prices ranging from $139,000 to $560,000) and an office park flanked by a rowing club, tennis courts, and a marina.

Reducing Infill and Redevelopment Costs

Infill development and redevelopment benefit significantly from many cost-reduction incentives offered by federal, state, and local governments. Such programs help to overcome the high costs of recycling old structures and properties for new uses and the high costs of developing affordable housing and commercial space in cities. Federal incentives include tax abatements and other types of subsidies provided through enterprise zones and empowerment zones to spur in-city development. Federal tax credits for historic preservation and for the production of low-income housing are among the most effective incentives for infill and redevelopment. Effective state and local incentives include tax abatements, low-interest construction financing, and infrastructure investments.

Housing Production and Demand

Many cities have established a variety of programs to reduce the cost of developing new or rehabilitated housing in infill and redevelopment areas. Some such programs are oriented primarily to low- and moderate-income housing and others are oriented to market-rate or mixed-income housing. Other housing programs in cities focus on the demand side of the equation, offering mortgage assistance to homebuyers.

Property tax abatement has become a housing program in some communities. The postponement or reduction of property tax payments for new development is a time-honored technique for attracting economic development (employment-generating land uses). But the use of tax abatements to spur residential redevelopment has grown in recent years.

Baltimore's PILOT (payment in lieu of taxes) program, for example, is being used to encourage developers to adapt high-vacancy downtown office buildings for residential use. Authorized by the state legislature in 1998, the PILOT program allows the city to freeze property taxes on upgraded buildings at pre-renovation levels for a negotiated period of time. In return, developers agree to pay the city a percentage of the project cash flow or residual value once the renovated building is occupied. Paralleling the city's tax abatement program, a state program enacted also in 1998 provides gap financing for the adaptive use of office and commercial space as housing in designated areas.

▶ A mix of residential, retail, and office uses has been developed at Washington's Landing near downtown Pittsburgh, on a cleaned-up brownfield site.

A tax abatement program in Seattle providing a ten-year tax exemption on new and rehabilitated rental housing is representative of programs in many other U.S. cities. Aimed primarily at stimulating the development of market-rate units, this program also requires a percentage of the units in tax-abated buildings to be rented at rates affordable by families with incomes less than the median household income for the region. Seattle is targeting nine neighborhoods for use of the program. Eleven rental developments totaling 673 units were approved for the tax exemption in 1999, the first year of the program.

For almost a decade, Cincinnati has been making what it calls "housing round" investments in the construction and rehabilitation of housing. Using city funds and federal community development block grant funds, the city awards developers grants and loans for housing projects based on annual requests for proposals issued by the city's housing agency. Developers are expected to partner with community groups and nonprofit developers. Housing round investments in rental projects are in the form of loans with repayment expected from rent returns; investments in for sale projects are in the form of grants with some reimbursement required if sale prices rise above expected levels. In 2000, this program awarded $1.35 million in loans and grants, and in the three years before 2000, it helped fund the development or renovation of 328 housing units.

In Dayton, Ohio, the city provides homeowners with housing improvement loans up to $100,000. The loans can be forgiven after ten years if the owner remains in the house. In Sacramento, homeowners can take advantage of low-interest financing provided by the city for improvements to historic houses (in a program called Fainted Ladies Home Improvement Program). Up to $50,000 is available for owner-occupied, single-family houses; from $25,000 to $250,000 per unit is available for multifamily projects. The Fainted Ladies program is funded through a tax-increment financing district, which allocates increases in property tax revenues to the renovation fund.

The New Homes for Chicago program takes a variety of approaches to its goal of encouraging the construction of single-family and two-flat houses and condominiums for low- and moderate-income families (households with incomes below 120 percent of the region's median household income). In addition to reducing lot and construction costs for developers, New Homes provides price subsidies on a sliding scale—from $10,000 for buyers with an income between 81 and 90 percent of median income to $30,000 for buyers with an income below 60 percent of median income. (Chicago also has a similar program that subsidizes the prices of rehabilitated houses.)

Many cities encourage in-town residential development through programs to reduce loan costs for homebuyers. In Seattle, for example, the Hometown Home Loan Program, a joint venture between the city and HomeStreet Bank, provides a variety of favorable loan options to employees of the city, school district, community college district, University of Washington, and other institutions. Hometown Home loan assistance can include reduced interest rates, lower mortgage insurance costs, and reduced closing costs.

City-sponsored programs to reduce loan costs for first-time homebuyers are popular. They are usually established in collaboration with local lending institutions. The Townhomes at Oxon Creek project in Washington, D.C. (see page 127), offers financial assistance to homebuyers through low-interest mortgage loans arranged with local banks, grants from the District of Columbia's home purchase assistance program, recordation and transfer tax credits, and real estate tax abatements for income-eligible first-time buyers.

Market support for infill locations is encouraged by a program in Seattle that allows homebuyers seeking to finance homes located in densely populated neighborhoods served by public transportation to increase the income figure they use for purposes of qualifying for a mortgage by the potential transportation savings they will realize by their location. This type of location-efficient mortgage program is actively promoted by the Center for Neighborhood Technology in Chicago.[14]

Key Public Investments
Infrastructure improvements are a definite need in many neighborhoods suitable for infill and redevelopment. Generations of community development programs have taught governments that key investments can spark private interest in development. One important role of such investments is that they can enhance the financial

feasibility of projects, making them attractive for private funding.

Broken sidewalks and curbs, leaking or undersized water and sewer lines, and other consequences of inadequate long-term infrastructure maintenance and repair are distinct disincentives for investment in many city neighborhoods. To eliminate such disincentives, some cities, including Chicago and Dayton, Ohio, fund infrastructure improvements as part of their housing construction and rehabilitation programs.

Urban renewal projects 1960s style often enticed development by installing complete new systems of streets, water and sewer lines, and other infrastructure. The redevelopment authorities in some cities continue to follow that practice to some degree. In Sacramento, California, for example, the city is contributing about $2 million to pay for sidewalks, street lighting, curbs, some street improvements, and open-space amenities for a project by Post Properties (working with the economic development district authority that plans and manages development around the state capitol building) to develop 175 units of market-rate housing with an integrated parking structure. In addition, the city has arranged $3.4 million in tax-increment financing to aid the project.

Investing $22 million for infrastructure, including a seven-acre park, was one element of the city of Dayton's strategy for encouraging the redevelopment of the Wright-Dunbar neighborhood. Once slated for clearance, the neighborhood contained more than 75 abandoned houses and about as many vacant lots (and fewer than 20 families) when the city scrapped its demolition plan, rebuilt basic infrastructure, and jump-started residential construction and rehabilitation by moving aggressively to acquire and resell abandoned properties. Since 1997, 38 houses have been constructed in Wright-Dunbar and 28 dilapidated houses have been rehabilitated, priced from $165,000 to $220,000.

Cities rarely pass the costs for improving basic systems of infrastructure along to infill developers. In fact, some cities, such as Chicago, even waive impact fees or sewer/water hookup fees for infill projects. Some cities also establish tax-increment financing (TIF) districts for infill and redevelopment sites, which allow infrastructure expenses to be repaid out of the increased property tax revenue

resulting from new development. Chicago makes frequent use of TIF districts for residential, commercial, and industrial infill development. Houston and San Antonio designate infill sites as tax-increment reinvestment zones and use increases in property tax revenues from those zones to repay developers for the front-end costs of infrastructure improvements.

Many cities look for key investments that will provide important services for new development on infill sites. Often that investment is a parking garage. Bethesda Row in Bethesda, Maryland (see page 129), is an essentially private redevelopment project that was built around a county parking garage that the developer deemed absolutely critical to the project's bottom line.

Recognizing that revival of one of downtown's key retailing areas depended on parking availability, the city of Seattle invested $73 million to fund the six-story underground parking facility developed for Pacific Place in Seattle (see page 126), a retail and entertainment complex that includes Nordstrom's (renovated) flagship store. Pacific Place's developer constructed the garage for later purchase by the city. Norm Rice, then-mayor of Seattle, called the Pacific Place plan "the biggest revitalization effort in downtown Seattle since we rebuilt from the Great Fire" (which occurred in 1889).[15]

Support for Community Development Organizations

The involvement of nonprofit community development organizations, including community development corporations (CDCs), is critical for many infill and redevelopment projects. The central role of most CDCs is to stitch together financing for development projects. Another essential role played by such organizations is to bring neighborhood residents into the decision-making process for development projects. Many CDCs fund or operate a variety of social services, housing improvement programs, economic development programs, and neighborhood conservation programs. CDC coalitions are often seen carrying out political advocacy in city halls and statehouses.

CDCs generally are funded in part by state and local government grants and loans (some of them channeled from federal sources) and they also receive support from national and local foundations and business corporations. Local banks are also an important source of funding because of the federal Community Reinvestment Act, which requires banks to make loans to such groups for the construction and rehabilitation of affordable housing.

CDCs have assumed essential roles in infill and redevelopment processes in communities throughout the United States. Many city governments work closely with such organizations in encouraging and implementing infill development.

Cleveland's Lee-Harvard shopping center renovation project (see pages 135–136), for example, included two nonprofit community development organizations on its development team and received patient low-interest loans from several others. CDCs, of which there are more than 2,000 in the United States, are active in almost all cities with populations above 100,000.

Many CDCs are established to work in specific neighborhoods. Often they also work together in networked arrangements and coordinating entities have been established in many communities.

A number of nonprofit economic development advocacy organizations on the national level, such as the Local Initiatives Support Corporation (LISC), the Enterprise Foundation, and the Community Redevelopment Corporation, help to raise equity capital for infill development and redevelopment projects by arranging syndication of the federal low-income housing tax credits and historic-preservation tax credits described in the following section and by providing grants, loans, and technical assistance to local CDCs.

Tax-Credit Programs

In the opinion of some observers, the federal tax credits offered for historic-preservation projects and for low-income housing projects are the most important generators of adaptive use and redevelopment in cities today. Both tax-credit programs were established in the 1986 tax reform act.

The historic-preservation tax credit allows 20 percent of the amount spent in a certified rehabilitation of a certified historic structure to be credited against taxes owed by individuals and corporations. (The rehabilitation of a nonhistoric building built before 1936 qualifies for a 10 percent credit.) The tax-credit program is administered by the National

Park Service (U.S. Department of the Interior), the Internal Revenue Service, and state historic-preservation officers.

Structures are certified as historic by being listed in the National Register of Historic Places or by being certified as contributing to the historic significance of a registered historic district listed in the National Register, which includes state and local historic districts. Owners of historic buildings may apply to the National Park Service for listing in the National Register. Owners of buildings located in historic districts may apply to the state historic-preservation officer for certification and the National Park Service makes the final determination based on established standards.

The National Park Service also determines certification of rehabilitation actions according to the Secretary of the Interior's Standards for Rehabilitation, which generally require retention of the historic character and distinctive features of the property. The preservation actions taken in the reuse of the Cotton Mill in New Orleans as apartments (see page 122) and the Bass Lofts high-school conversion project in Atlanta (see page 122) show the types of actions that may be necessary in a historic-building reuse project to retain designation as a historic property and earn tax credits.

Made permanent by Congress in 1993, the federal low-income housing tax credit is the nation's most productive program for the construction of affordable rental housing. It has generated a total of about 1 million affordable units, mostly for house-

▲ **Dayton, Ohio's Wright-Dunbar neighborhood has been revitalized with the renovation of existing housing and the construction of new housing on vacant lots. The look and feel of the old neighborhood has thus been recreated.**

holds with incomes below 60 percent of the area's median family income. Because the tax credit can be used for projects in which as few as 20 percent of the units are reserved for low-income households, many housing projects using tax credits are mixed-income projects.

Typically, 30 to 40 percent of the financing for affordable housing projects comes from equity raised by syndicating tax credits. The tax credits run for ten years, and investors line up to acquire them, thus providing developers with front-end equity outside the traditional loan market and reducing their mortgage loan requirements. This favorable financing makes it feasible to restore the historic character of buildings.

States receive an annual allocation of low-income housing tax credits equal to $1.25 per capita. (Additional credits from a national pool of unused credits are also made available to states.) States reallocate their available credits according to published priorities and competitive criteria, and they are required by federal law to set aside a minimum of 10 percent of the credits for projects that involve nonprofit organizations. Developers may combine low-income housing credits with historic-preservation credits to leverage additional investor equity.[16]

Three-quarters of the rental units at the Belmont Dairy adaptive use project in Portland, Oregon (see pages 22–23), are affordable. Some financing came from the sale of $8 million in low-income housing tax credits to Fannie Mae, whose American Communities Fund invests equity in infill housing projects in neighborhoods that have difficulty attracting financing. Other funding for Belmont Dairy came from local banks, the Network for Oregon Affordable Housing, several city agencies—the Development Commission, the Livable City Housing Council, and the Office of Transportation— and the state's special transportation project funding program.

Marketing In-City Living and Locations

Over the years, cities have become adept at marketing their communities to employers and commercial and industrial developers. The economic development departments in many cities have deployed a battery of incentives to generate interest in in-city locations. Only recently, however, have cities begun to act in entrepreneurial ways to attract residential development.

Some cities like Seattle and Denver have made use of the bully pulpit of the mayor's office to sell developers and builders on in-city locations. Other cities have embarked on campaigns to introduce residents of the region to the benefits of in-city living. A number of cities support research and studies to help define markets for in-city housing and provide other information useful to developers.

Mayoral summit meetings have been used effectively to raise community consciousness about opportunities for housing in cities. In one of his first actions as mayor of Seattle, Paul Schell, a residential developer, convened the 1998 Seattle Housing Summit. The meeting brought together more than 600 developers, bankers, neighborhood activists, consultants, advocates for the homeless, and residents to explore housing issues and brainstorm ideas for increasing the city's supply of market-rate and affordable housing. Several housing initiatives and programs came out of the summit, including the establishment of a housing coordinator in the mayor's office.

Mayor Wellington Webb of Denver convened a downtown summit in 1991 to identify the most important strategies for revitalizing downtown and he led the discussion on housing as a key revitalization strategy. Later, the Downtown Housing Office was established to gather and distribute information on properties, market conditions, and available public financing tools. City agencies, including the urban renewal authority, were urged to funnel financial resources into downtown housing and funding earmarked for historic preservation was targeted for housing. In 1995, Mayor Webb convened a second summit, which was devoted entirely to housing.

Traceable to this summit are the city's General Housing Plan establishing housing goals and an inclusionary zoning ordinance requiring developers to include affordable housing units in major projects. According to Jennifer T. Moulton, director of the city's Community Planning and Development Agency, the summit played critical roles in helping to form a public consensus and in helping to coordinate city responses to housing needs in the downtown core and surrounding neighborhoods. Between the first summit in 1991 and the end of 2000, more than 6,600 housing units were completed in the nine residential neighborhoods of downtown Denver, and, as of the end of 2000, another 1,600 units were under construction and 4,600 units in planning.[17]

Many other instances of mayoral leadership in efforts to stimulate the development of infill housing development exist. In Houston, Mayor Bob Lanier made residential reinvestment a top priority of his administration by initiating a neighborhood conservation program in 1996. His successor, Mayor Lee P. Brown, has launched a public/private collaboration to increase housing construction and homeownership in the city. Mayor Richard Daley of Chicago has vigorously supported expansion of that city's housing infill and redevelopment programs. In Cincinnati, Mayor Roxanne Qualls worked with builders, lenders, and housing advocates to forge a public/private partnership for boosting housing construction and rehabilitation in the city.

Formed in 1996, the Cincinnati Homeownership Partnership seeks homeownership opportunities for middle-income as well as low- and moderate-income residents. It works imaginatively to market the virtues of in-city neighborhoods to homebuilders and homeseekers. Among its many activities, it channels mortgage credit certificates issued by the state housing finance agency, manages a first-time homebuyer financing program, and

coordinates a Freddie Mac–sponsored alliance of lenders and housing counseling agencies.

Through its Homeownership Center, the partnership's marketing activities include a Web site and a real estate agent training program. The Web site (and a printed report) provides detailed information on the city's 51 neighborhoods, including their history, demographics, types of housing, and special features such as parks and museums. (The address is: www.cincinnatihome.org.) The Web site includes a guide to obtaining home loans, a user-friendly loan prequalification application, and a list of real estate agents who have completed the partnership's training program. The initial training program involved 81 agents selected from 200 applicants. Training includes tours of city neighborhoods, visits to local schools so that agents may evaluate school quality firsthand, and lectures on the city's history and development trends. The partnership endeavors to keep the trained agents informed about upcoming projects of interest.

In a number of cities, home showcases have been mounted, modeled after the home-a-ramas that many suburban homebuilder associations sponsor. Showcases provide potential builders and homebuyers an opportunity to see real products in their neighborhood context. The Greater Cincinnati

◀ Cincinnati's first CiTiRAMA, a home showcase to market in-city living, included 13 new market-rate housing units on a site assembled by the city in a historic district. The new housing features historic design elements.

Home Builders Association puts on an in-city showcase, CiTiRAMA, annually. The association allocates lots for the houses included in the showcase by lottery to builders that have submitted proposals. These lots are on city-owned sites and the city assists in providing infrastructure improvements. The association selects a developer/coordinator and contracts with the selected builders to satisfy program guidelines and schedules. In its first four years, the CiTiRAMA program made 71 lots available for houses priced at $135,000 to $225,000, all of which have been sold and have appreciated in value.

Commissioning studies and plans for the purpose of stimulating and guiding residential construction in cities can be a powerful marketing tool. Mayor Michael B. Coleman of Columbus, Ohio, for example, requested the Capitol South Community Urban Redevelopment Corporation to undertake a study to determine the market feasibility of developing market-rate housing in downtown. Identification of market demand, it was hoped, would attract builders. Capitol South, a 501(c)(4) corporation created in 1975 to redevelop the area south of the state capitol, used a discretionary fund to commission a multifamily housing analysis by a Columbus-based firm with national experience in housing market studies. The study, which was completed in late 2000, concluded that the down-

town market can support the construction of 500 to 860 multifamily units annually, both rental and condominium and at all price ranges, and 100 to 200 single-family houses annually.

By developing plans for stimulating and guiding housing development, cities can show their commitment to supporting housing. And such plans can help cities market in-city locations to builders and in-city living to homeseekers. San Antonio and Sacramento provide examples.

Housing deterioration and disinvestment in San Antonio's city center pushed the mayor and city council to create the 24-member public/private Community Revitalization Action Group (CRAG) in 1998. CRAG was charged with identifying barriers to revitalization and opportunities for development, as well as recommending means for revitalization, including public/private partnerships. Reliance on market forces was seen as the best way to optimize housing investment in the city center, and CRAG's 38 recommendations, contained in its July 1998 report, focus on providing support for market forces. To follow through on these recommendations, the city allocated more than $1.3 million in its FY 1999 budget, $3 million in FY 2000, and $5.1 million in FY 2001. Activities in the first year of implementation concentrated on providing information to builders and the public.

Sacramento's central-city housing strategy was approved in 1991. It guides the work of four public agencies that are engaged in promoting infill housing and redevelopment. The housing strategy includes 65 recommendations for actions to boost the production of housing, including a recommendation against the rezoning of residential land for nonresidential purposes.

Promoting Downtown Development

Downtowns are the new success stories in cities across America. From the 1970s through the 1990s (with a pause for the real estate recession of the late 1980s and early 1990s), a tremendous amount of public and private investment changed downtown skylines. Cities poured billions of dollars into government centers, stadiums, convention centers, museums, and performance centers. Development transformed historic districts into people magnets and urban waterfronts into recreational centers. The latest strategies for downtown development and redevelopment put more emphasis on attaining a critical mass of residents to transform commercial downtowns into multiuse, 24-hour downtowns. Living downtown is in fact a growing phenomenon.

Many cities have adopted special programs and policies to support the revitalization of their downtowns. They may, for example, give priority to downtown locations in their decisions on where to site public facilities. Or they may provide density bonuses for the inclusion of residential units in downtown developments. Often the smart-growth benefits of having a diverse 24/7 downtown are given as the stated purpose of such special treatment for downtowns.

Governments at all levels can and do as a matter of policy select downtown sites for public facilities. Their purpose in doing so is to add employment and activity to downtowns. The federal government is directed by the 1976 Public Buildings Cooperative Use Act and executive orders issued in 1978 and 1996 to give first consideration in fulfilling its space needs to historic buildings, central business districts, and urban and historic locations, in that order. States including Maryland, Oregon, Vermont, and New Jersey have issued executive orders and enacted legislation to give preference to in-city locations for new state facilities. Local governments often reinforce revitalization efforts by siting office buildings and other facilities in downtown areas.

Cities can support the growing market for housing in downtowns by providing density bonuses for projects that include housing. Cities such as Seattle and Washington, D.C., encourage developers to add residential uses to commercial projects by giving such projects density bonuses. Orlando's downtown code adds allowable floor area to projects with more than one use, increasing the floor area bonus with each use added to the project. The downtown ordinance for Portland, Oregon, allows developers to triple the maximum floor area by adding residential uses.

Promoting Neighborhood Conservation

The simultaneous revitalization and conservation of older neighborhoods is a time-consuming, incremental, difficult—and worthwhile—process. Some older neighborhoods in many cities and inner suburbs are experiencing a process of gentrification in which outsiders move in and restore and upgrade housing.

Thus far gentrification involves only a small segment of urban housing markets. However, its resurgence in the 1990s confirms that a widespread revival of central land markets is in process. According to a recent study of gentrification trends, between 1992 and 1997 mortgage investment in gentrified neighborhoods (based on eight case study cities) grew more than 2.3 times as fast as the suburban rate.[18]

The regenerative power of market forces still remains to be played out in many urban neighborhoods. Neighborhood residents tend to resist change. Denizens of in-city neighborhoods may rightly view gentrification (itself a patronizing term) as a threat. As it proceeds, renters are evicted to make way for renovations affordable only by outsiders. Rising rents and property values and associated property taxes force renters and homeowners with modest incomes to move out. Many displaced households have little choice of housing in other areas. Local governments often pay little heed to these incremental consequences of market forces.

The HUD-sponsored HOPE VI mixed-income housing projects being developed in many cities and suburbs are an inadequate answer to displacement. HOPE VI projects represent a way of producing affordable and sustainable public housing that contributes to its neighborhood, but most

HOPE VI projects provide far fewer units of low- and moderate-income housing than did the public housing projects they replace.

City housing agencies claim that many of the units being torn down to make way for HOPE VI projects have been vacant and boarded up for many years for lack of funding for renovations and repairs. Housing advocates suspect that the agencies deliberately allowed units in problem projects to deteriorate to reduce management headaches. In any case, as detailed in chapter 5, the supply of affordable housing for low- and moderate-income families continues to decline, forcing millions of households to live in dilapidated and over-crowded units.

Thus, to truly achieve smart-growth goals, local governments and housing producers must determine to supply affordable housing for low- and moderate-income residents being displaced in gentrifying neighborhoods. There is not an easy answer to the dilemma—the benefits of gentrification versus the housing needs of displaced low-income households. Solving the dilemma will take aggressive community programs to build affordable housing, to provide significant financial support for privately supplied affordable housing production, and to require affordable units in new residential developments (through inclusionary zoning, for example). At the same time, action at the federal level to reverse the decline in federal funding for affordable housing production would recognize the increasing crisis in housing for a substantial proportion of the nation's population.

Neighborhood revitalization cannot occur in the same way that downtown revitalization has occurred, that is, without regard to existing uses/users. Neighborhood revitalization needs to be a wholly different process that emphasizes neighborhood conservation (retaining neighborhood character and the ability of current residents to stay in the neighborhood) while attracting infill and redevelopment. Neighborhood conservation requires carefully tailoring revitalization actions to minimize damage to existing neighborhood assets and optimize value added for present residents. It needs to seek what a recent Fannie Mae foundation publication called "just right" neighborhoods.

Revitalizing neighborhoods are "just right" neighborhoods when they are retaining affordable hous-

ing and relieving the market pressures that displace low- and moderate-income residents.[19] Research sponsored by the Fannie Mae Foundation identifies ten "just right" neighborhoods for affordable homeownership in ten U.S. cities. Some of these benefit from targeted efforts to leverage their new market popularity to create mixed-income housing opportunities. Others benefit from the coincidence of public investment and market forces that together are bringing about revival. Some are developing at rather high densities, but most resemble inner suburbs in their density.

The Fruitvale neighborhood in Oakland, California, is a "just right" neighborhood that resembles an inner suburb in its density, but with differences: little vacant land, a great deal of residential over-crowding, and a low homeownership rate (37 percent). Once mostly a working-class Latino neighborhood, Fruitvale has diversified since 1980 with a sizable influx of Asians and African Americans. The Unity Council has been spearheading efforts by the city and other community organizations to revitalize the neighborhood. It has sparked projects to clean up parks and create new parks, offered welfare-to-work programs and business assistance for local business owners, sponsored an annual festival that brings 75,000 visitors, and collaborated with the city to increase housing opportunities.

The Unity Council has been prominently involved in the design and development of a mixed-use center at the neighborhood BART (Bay Area Rapid Transit) rail station. With help from BART and a host of federal and city agencies and nonprofit organizations, the Unity Council is implementing the $100 million development over a ten-year period to include 250 units of affordable and seniors housing, a health clinic, a child-care center, a seniors center, offices for social services, and a library branch.[20]

In Cleveland, the nonprofit Neighborhood Progress Inc. works with neighborhood groups to catalyze housing improvements, improved public services, and economic development—and to make sure that neighborhood revitalization occurs in "just right" ways. NPI is strongly backed by the city government, which established a housing trust fund to help it and other nonprofit housing groups. The housing trust fund is financed by federal community development block grant and other funds, city-issued neighborhood bonds to fund site acquisition and improvements, and a $40 million revolving loan program. Collaborative endeavors involving the city of Cleveland, community organizations, and neighborhood groups have resulted in the construction or rehabilitation of thousands of housing units and several neighborhood shopping centers.

A number of cities, including San Antonio and Houston, provide grant funds to neighborhood-based organizations for making small public improvements—such as sidewalk and curb upgrades, tree planting, and landscaping—in partnership with private interests.

Neighborhood conservation requires leadership and strong commitments from community organizations and local governments over a substantial period of time. At the community level, neighborhood conservation should carefully target neighborhoods in which public investment is most likely to leverage overall improvement. At the neighborhood level, it should seek to cluster public improvements to attain a critical mass of change.

In Baltimore, for example, a city that has long been losing population and seeing many of its neighborhoods decline, the housing department seeks to stimulate neighborhood conservation and reinvestment by focusing housing investment rather than engaging in less effective piecemeal efforts. For example, the department's strategy is to:

▲ target the worst blocks for demolition in order to remove obsolete housing and make buildable sites available;
▲ avoid piecemeal demolition because it devalues adjacent good housing;
▲ target better blocks for stabilization and revival through the rehabilitation of abandoned and vacant buildings;
▲ give priority for housing in rehabilitated buildings to nearby residents in substandard housing who are financially capable of moving to better housing; and
▲ cluster housing improvements and homeownership opportunities to enhance community revitalization, preserve historic neighborhoods, and reduce housing abandonment.

▼ **The Terraces is a mixed-income HOPE VI community in west Baltimore, with both rental and for-sale townhouses as well as a seniors' rental facility. This mixed-density community replaces five high-rise and 20 low-rise buildings in a public housing project.**

The housing department's focused-investment strategy together with the housing authority's program to rebuild much of its public housing stock over time using the HOPE VI model of mixed-income housing is enabling Baltimore to significantly change the dynamics of the central-city housing market while attending to the needs of low- and moderate-income households.

Streamlining Regulations

As noted in the earlier "Issues and Obstacles" section in this chapter (pages 130–133), complex development regulations and lengthy approval procedures in many cities needlessly complicate the development process and raise the cost of infill and redevelopment. Many cities have taken steps to address these regulatory obstacles. A number of specific streamlining techniques and other reforms —similar to those recommended for promoting smarter growth in greenfield communities—offer opportunities for simplifying the development process for infill and redevelopment:

▲ Provide a one-stop center for zoning and building approval that promotes coordination among the different agencies and departments scrutinizing applications.
▲ Assign expediters to keep applications for high-priority projects moving through the approval process.
▲ Reduce the number of agencies, departments, and committees involved in project approval and reduce the number of procedural steps required to review applications.
▲ Limit approval periods to a specified number of days or weeks.
▲ Ensure that regulatory provisions are 1) necessary, 2) clearly written, and 3) consistent with other provisions and requirements.
▲ Adopt rules to guide citizen input at public meetings and hearings.
▲ Train relevant staff members so that they understand requirements and procedures and can provide helpful service to applicants.

The city of Seattle has worked to streamline the permitting process in response to increasing demand for new housing. In particular, it sought to reduce the time required for permit reviews. In April 1998, about 30 percent of construction applications for simple projects were reviewed within 24 hours; by September 1999, 65 percent of such applications were reviewed within 24 hours. The department of construction and land use has decreased the turnaround time for its review of more complicated master use permits by 60 percent compared with average review times experienced during the housing boom in the late 1980s.

Tampa significantly overhauled its project approval process to make it more responsive to fast-paced development. A management consultant was hired to analyze the administrative operations of the planning and building department and to conduct motivational training sessions for all staff members. The formerly dispersed department was consolidated in one (new) building, which is a one-stop permitting center. In addition, the city and the local builders association established a schedule of monthly (now quarterly) meetings to discuss current problems and reach agreement on solutions. Tampa's review process now benefits from a state-of-the-art communications network that links building inspectors in the field, decision makers in the downtown planning and building office, and builders and consultants. This network allows quick decisions on issues that arise during inspections.

Chicago has initiated a self-certification program modeled on one in New York City to allow architects to avoid detailed reviews of previously approved designs, and thus significantly speed up the building permit process for single-family and townhouse construction. When an architect reuses a design that has been issued a permit she or he can sign off on all standards except those for electricity, plumbing, and sewers. Reviews of previously approved designs normally require only two to three days compared with one or more months for complete reviews.

Most building codes are written to guide new construction and are hard to reconcile with the older buildings that provide opportunities for rehabilitation and adaptive use. Rehabilitators are often compelled to undertake massive demolition and reconstruction to meet building code standards for hallways, windows, and other building components. The cost of such improvements may persuade many owners to forgo renovation or to tear down the building.

New Jersey streamlined its housing code for the rehabilitation of existing structures in 1998, making common-sense adjustments that ease the renovation process. The new rehabilitation subcode helped spur a 16 percent increase in housing rehabilitation projects in the state's 16 central cities the first year after its adoption and a 56 percent increase the second year, compared with just a 15 percent increase in rehabilitation projects statewide.

As New Jersey was adopting its rehabilitation code provisions, the U.S. Department of Housing and Urban Development developed and published rehabilitation standards—the Nationally Applicable Recommended Rehabilitation Provisions—as a model for adoption across the nation.

Maryland adopted a rehabilitation code in 2001 that includes an index to state codes that identifies precisely which provisions apply to rehabilitation work. Major rehabilitation projects in the state may still require substantial renovations to meet code provisions, while smaller repairs and upgrading may be required to meet relatively few provisions. Other states are contemplating similar streamlining.

Evening the Odds for Infill Development

There is hope that the revitalization of city cores and inner suburbs will spread from a few areas deemed highly desirable in the marketplace to many other parts of older communities. But that will occur only with help from the public sector to even the odds that remain tilted in favor of greenfields development.

Righting the imbalance of public and private incentives that favor greenfields over infill will continue to be a challenge. Federal, state, and local programs that continue to invest heavily in supporting suburban style development need redirection. The Ohio First Suburbs Consortium, a coalition of inner-ring suburbs, for example, thinks that state funding for highways and other facility improvements is stacked against inner suburbs. The consortium has been working with only partial success to capture some of the flow of state funding to Ohio's outer suburbs. This situation is found in most regions: elected officials generally find it easier and politically more palatable to steer funding to the construction of new facilities in developing areas rather than to the retrofitting of old infrastructure.

But there is some evidence that states are beginning to pay more attention to investment needs in cities. In addition, regional initiatives as described in chapter 8 could overcome some of the barriers to achieving infill and redevelopment in metropolitan areas.

Notes

1. Alexander von Hoffman, *Housing Heats Up: Home Building Patterns in Metropolitan Areas* (Washington, D.C.: Brookings Institution Center on Urban and Metropolitan Policy, 1995).

2. Michael D. Beyard and Michael Pawlukiewicz, *Ten Principles for Reinventing America's Suburban Strips* (Washington, D.C.: ULI–the Urban Land Institute, 2001).

3. Michael A. Fletcher, "More Retailers Are Sold on Cities," *Washington Post*, 5 March 1999, pp. E-1, E-10.

4. U.S. Department of Housing and Urban Development, *New Markets: The Untapped Retail Buying Power in America's Inner Cities* (Washington, D.C.: July 1999), p. v.

5. Ibid., p. vi.

6. For a description of off-the-shelf projects that lenders are most willing to finance, see Christopher Leinberger, "The Connection between Sustainability and Economic Development," in *The Practice of Sustainable Development*, ed. Douglas R. Porter (Washington, D.C.: ULI–the Urban Land Institute, 2000).

7. Ibid., p. 56.

8. Real Estate Research Corporation, *Infill Development Strategies* (Washington, D.C.: ULI–the Urban Land Institute and the American Planning Association, 1982), p. vi.

9. Donovan D. Rypkema, "Preserving for Profit," *Urban Land*, December 1998, pp. 68–69.

10. Monica P. Wraga, "Neighbors Mixed about Cabin John Center Renovation," *The Gazette*, 18 April 2001, p. A-43.

11. Myra Mensh Patner, "Recreation Center Still Too Small, Activist Group Says," *The Gazette*, 18 April 2001, p. A-4.

12. Charles Lockwood, "Suisun City, California," *Urban Land*, May 1995, pp. 20–26; and Suisun City homepage (Waterfront Projects) at: www.suisun.com.

13. J. Terrence Farris, "Barriers to Using Urban Infill to Achieve Smart Growth," *Housing Policy Debate*, v. 12, no. 1, 2001, pp. 1–30.

14. See Kim Hoeveler, "Accessibility vs. Mobility: The Location Efficient Mortgage," *PAS Memo* (a special edition entitled *Public Investment*), September 1997.

15. For details on the planning and phased construction of the project, see Terry J. Lassar, "Bridging a Building Boom," *Urban Land*, February 2000, pp. 50–54.

16. For information on low-income housing tax credits, see Susan Hobart and Robert Schwarz, "The Low-Income Housing Tax Credit," *Urban Land*, November 1997, pp. 48–51, 78–80.

17. Jennifer T. Moulton, *Report on Downtown Housing Progress* (Denver: Community Planning and Development Agency, October 1999).

18. Elvin K. Wyly and Daniel J. Hammel, "Islands of Decay in Seas of Renewal," *Housing Policy Debate*, v. 10, no. 4, 1999, p. 761. (The article analyzes the phenomenon of gentrification, the changes in housing policy that have promoted it, and its consequences for meeting affordable housing needs.)

19. Elvin K. Wyly et al., "Learning from 'Just Right' Neighborhoods," *Building Blocks* (Fannie Mae Foundation), winter 2000, p. 3.

20. Ibid., p. 6.

Mobilizing Support For Smart Growth

8

Smart growth may be a desirable objective, but achieving it will be neither easy nor inevitable. Smart growth requires fundamental changes in development processes and in public programs and regulations that, up to this time, have produced less than fully satisfactory forms of urban development. By necessity, smart growth will have to proceed by incremental steps rather than wholesale shifts in development processes—and this will take time.

More than time, smart growth will require strong political will, targeted investment, and developer determination to take up new ways of development. Official and community expressions of support for smart-growth principles are not enough. And debates over the fine points—how much density? what conditions make transit feasible?—are inevitable. But the real challenge smart growth poses is one of will: Can the stakeholders—elected officials, developers and associated businesses, and community spokespersons—summon up the dedication that will be required to alter the basic processes of community development?

The blind faith in the ideals of smart growth indulged in by many of its advocates has inspired criticism of smart-growth advocacy. Whether their dissent is based on opposition, cynicism, or pessimism, critics sound a note of healthy realism. Naysaying raises the ultimate issue: Can enough support for the goals of smart growth be won to make a difference? To put the question more positively:

What conditions must be met for progress toward the goals of smart growth to occur?

Donald Priest, a developer and former head of research at ULI, thinks that smart growth could backfire.[1] There is considerable evidence, he says, that higher-density development will attract a significant number of residents only if it is well executed and properly serviced with transportation infrastructure. The difficulty is not a lack of market support for higher densities but the inadequate, rundown condition of transportation infrastructure, both road and rail, in almost every metropolitan area. "These problems can be remedied," says Priest, "but remedies will require major up-front capital investment." In his view, the public support necessary to raise sufficient capital for transportation is the Achilles heel of smart growth. Highway funding is beset by fiscal conservatism (and highway proposals face environmental barriers) and transit funding needs considerably more voter support than it has received so far.

Furthermore, noting that smart growth depends on land use decisions that reflect a regional perspective and that the concept of regionalism has been expounded for decades with little effect, Priest concludes that "today there are few signs that the delegation of significant land use powers to regional agencies is the wave of the future." At the local level, says Priest, the balance of power is firmly in the hands of interests who do not see growth as an inherently good thing. NIMBY resistance eventually will slow growth in most jurisdictions, he says, "and most smart-growth programs implemented at the local level will inevitably morph into slow-growth strategies." Ultimately, says Priest, the failure of existing jurisdictions to accommodate the development necessary to serve an increasing population will continue to force growth to outlying areas.

Richard Ward, president of Development Strategies Inc. in St. Louis, Missouri, sounds similar cautions about the prospects for smart growth, as follows:[2]

▲ There is no reason to believe that there will be significant progress in causing metropolitan regions to think and act as a unit in addressing growth challenges.

▲ Despite increases in gasoline costs, Americans remain committed to automobile travel and consequently they support development patterns that favor that means of travel.

▲ Investment in transit systems has produced new systems that for the most part consist of single lines that are incapable of adequately serving transit-dependent life styles.

▲ With few exceptions, regulatory reform has been unsuccessful in creating a more favorable permitting process for smart development.

These are hard realities—and they are realities—to deal with. They challenge all people involved in community development to make substantial changes in their personal living and travel choices and in their professional or institutional behavior. Particularly important is to make progress toward the four major conditions necessary to make smart growth work:

▲ a positive political climate sufficient to overcome NIMBYist opposition to compact, multiuse forms of development;

▲ sufficient support for balanced programs of transportation improvements to reduce growing congestion and provide greater access to a variety of travel modes;

▲ effective regional decision-making processes for the resolution of regional issues such as transportation investment priorities and environmental protection; and

▲ a regulatory climate that does not unduly constrain innovative approaches to meeting smart-growth goals.

Can society muster the will to make change happen, accepting that it will take effort and time, two precious commodities in today's world. Achieving the principles of smart growth will take leadership, innovation, and collaboration. Leadership needs to focus on smart-growth goals and how to reach them. Innovation is needed in the business of development and in the public guidance of development. Collaboration among all the players involved is needed to determine the shape, location, and character of community growth and change.

This chapter focuses on ways to mobilize the support and secure the commitments necessary to make smart growth work, in particular on ways to usher in the four conditions needed to make smart growth work. Based mostly on discussions in the previous chapters, the many kinds of tools that could be useful are summarized in a table. Two smart-growth process issues are explored: 1) effective regional guidance (supported, it is to be hoped, by state actions) and 2) collaboration at various levels for building consensus on smart-growth initiatives. Rating systems and scorecards that can be used to evaluate the smartness of development projects and policies and to generate endorsements for smart projects are described. The book concludes with action punch lists for developers, public officials, and civic organizations—lists of who must do what to make smart growth work.

A Toolkit of Smart-Growth Actions

This book has described policies, programs, regulatory devices, developer location choices, project designs, and other initiatives that have generated forms of development reflecting smart-growth principles. Figure 8-1 summarizes these tools for smart growth.

Many of the tools in this toolkit are rather traditional, and some of them are applied almost routinely in some communities—but not necessarily to promote smart growth. To meet smart-growth goals these tools may need sharpening or customizing or more forceful use. For example, planning in advance of growth to improve the policy and regulatory climate for mixing uses or conserving open space is a tried-and-true approach, yet it requires thoughtful definitions of program goals and recognition of specific points of leverage in the development process to generate desired results. If

Figure 8-1 Tools for Smart Growth

	Compact, Multiuse Development	Housing Diversity And Affordability	Open-Space Conservation	Multimodal Transportation	Community Livability
Federal Tools	HUD HOPE VI projects DOT transit joint development guidelines for development around transit stations EPA brownfields cleanup programs	HUD HOPE VI projects Other low- and moderate-income housing assistance programs CRA Low-income housing tax credits Historic-preservation tax credits	Funding for open-space acquisition and protection (including the Land and Water Conservation Fund) Maintenance and expansion of national parks, forests, wildlife refuges, wilderness areas, scenic rivers, and so forth Regulatory protection for wetlands, wildlife habitat, and other open areas	DOT capital funding for transportation TCSP and CMAQ special funding for transportation-related improvements DOT transit joint development guidelines for development around transit stations Requirements for state SIPs and regional MPO plans and TIPs DOT demonstration projects TRB research projects and publications	Education funding Economic development assistance Water supply and wastewater treatment funding Health and welfare programs Siting rules and guidelines for federal facilities
State Tools	Requirements for locally designated growth areas Capital funding targeted to growth areas Highway-access controls Recognition of local growth management policies in siting state facilities	Housing finance assistance Tax-abatement programs Neighborhood conservation programs Fair share housing requirements New or model rehabilitation codes	Maintenance and expansion of state parks, forests, recreation areas, and so forth Funding for open-space acquisition and protection, including greenways and farmland Authorization for the public acquisition of less-than-fee interests in property for open space. Grants and authority for local open-space acquisition programs, including farmland preservation Requirements for local government protection of sensitive lands, for example through designation of urban and conservation areas Authorization for TDR	Prioritization and management of federal and state funding for transportation improvements Management of transit systems (in some states) Highway- and road-design standards and transit guidelines MIS and other studies to determine transportation improvement needs and priorities Access controls on new and improved highways Requirements for links between transportation funding and appropriate land uses	Education funding Economic development assistance Water supply and wastewater treatment funding Health and welfare programs Siting rules and guidelines for state facilities Coordination of state agency programs Targeting funding for local facilities to designated growth areas Support for regional intergovernmental coordination Promotion of regional development planning

figure 8-1 continued on next page

Figure 8-1 Tools for Smart Growth (continued)

	Compact, Multiuse Development	Housing Diversity And Affordability	Open-Space Conservation	Multimodal Transportation	Community Livability
Local Government Tools	Planning policies and zoning regulations to promote compact, multiuse development	Planning and zoning to promote housing diversity and affordability	Funding for open-space acquisition and conservation	Regional transportation policies and plans	Planning and regulations to promote project designs that connect community components
	Waiver of exactions for smart projects	Targeting housing redevelopment and renovation for federal and state grants and loans	Planning policies to optimize the use of natural assets, such as waterfronts and scenic views	Standards and requirements for subdivision streets	School siting and design standards that emphasize school/neighborhood relationships
	Infill and redevelopment programs, including brownfield reuse	Assembly of tax-delinquent properties for residential reuse	Promotion of TDR programs	Streetscape improvements programs	Zoning to allow neighborhood-based employment
	Minimum density requirements	Protection and revitalization of historic neighborhoods	Zoning to conserve open space and farmland	Zoning and infrastructure funding to promote transit-oriented development	Support for the expansion of existing businesses
	Cluster subdivision provisions	Redevelopment and revitalization of residential neighborhoods	Requirements for open-space conservation in subdivisions	Zoning to promote walkable and transit-friendly neighborhoods	Provision and maintenance of high-quality services
	Density bonuses for mixed uses	Abatement of taxes for infill housing	Impact fees for open-space conservation	Shared-parking requirements	Siting of public facilities
	Expedited approvals for smart projects	Marketing and educational campaigns for infill housing		TDM and congestion management programs	
		Affordable or employee housing requirements for new development			
		Waiver of fees for affordable housing			

policies and regulations are adopted to promote compact or clustered development, they must incorporate procedures for considering the compatibility of proposed projects with surrounding development. For another example, a metropolitan transportation planning process takes place in most regions, but to become an effective tool for smart growth, regional transportation planning generally needs to be redirected to truly integrate decisions on transportation improvements with local land use policies.

The tools included in figure 8-1 are just some of the tools that could be useful—a starting point. Many

	Compact, Multiuse Development	Housing Diversity And Affordability	Open-Space Conservation	Multimodal Transportation	Community Livability
Developer Tools	Cluster designs Multiuse programming Site selection to add uses and compactness to development in surrounding areas Expertise in smart forms of development	Participation in HOPE VI and other affordable housing programs, including low-income housing tax credits Adaptive use of old buildings for housing Participation in promotional campaigns for housing in redeveloping areas Site selection and project design to relate housing to employment and service uses Expertise in renovation and historic restoration	Design of projects to conserve natural features and open-space systems Use of natural systems for drainage and wastewater treatment Minimizing of impervious surfaces in appropriate locations Set-asides of parks and other open space	Site selection based on the availability of transportation systems Design of projects to encourage walking, biking, and transit use TDM programs Design of projects to allow shared parking	Incorporation of amenities and civic uses in projects Place-making project designs Design of projects to provide connectivity to the surrounding community and natural systems
Nongovernmental Organization Tools	Educational campaigns for compact, multiuse development Support for proposals to develop compact, multiuse projects CDC participation in compact, multiuse developments	CDC participation in housing renovation and redevelopment projects Local financial institution participation in low-cost mortgage programs (according to CRA) Fannie Mae and Freddie Mac housing assistance programs Homeownership counseling	Conservancy and land trust purchases of open space Conservancy and land trust protection of open space Support for open-space purchase by state and local governments	Research and education on ways to improve mobility in urban development Support for consensus-building for the funding and construction of multimodal transportation systems	Support for livable features in proposed developments Extension of civic service networks to developing and redeveloping areas Provision of cultural amenities—cooperatively with developers and residents

Acronyms used in table: CDC (community development corporation); CMAQ (congestion mitigation and air quality improvement); CRA (Community Reinvestment Act); DOT (U.S. Department of Transportation); EPA (U.S. Environmental Protection Agency); HOPE VI (a HUD housing program); HUD (U.S. Department of Housing and Urban Development); MIS (major investment study); MPO (metropolitan planning organization); SIP (state implementation plan); TCSP (transportation and community and system preservation); TDM (transportation demand management); TDR (transferable development rights); TIP (transportation improvement program); and TRB (Transportation Research Board).

federal tax policies and funding programs play a significant role in shaping community growth, and those policies and programs affecting housing affordability, economic development, transportation improvements, and other major components of community life must be changed where warranted in response to the challenges posed by smart growth. States have a decisive role to play, particularly in regard to prioritizing and channeling federal and state programs and funds to promote smart development.

Local governments and regional agencies are on the front line of smart growth, able to promote it or put obstacles in its way by means of planning, regulatory requirements, and various programs. Developers and other private sector participants in the development process have an obviously important role to play in smart growth based on their control over project locations, project design, and development programming. Civic and special-interest organizations also play key roles as advocates and watchdogs, participants in development and conservation, and sponsors of research and education.

The Regional Imperative

Many aspects of smart growth—including, for example, integrated transportation and land use planning, the conservation of sustainable open space, and the attainment of a jobs/housing balance—are most logically approached from a regional perspective. A regional forum for prioritizing and targeting investment is conducive to smart growth. Smart growth's regional imperative arises partly from the fact that regions are becoming "the premier unit of competition in a global economy."[3]

Many of the goals of smart growth—reducing the outward spread of new development, promoting better use of existing urbanized areas, and creating more connected communities—reach across jurisdictional boundaries within regions. Regional organizations should be in a position to guide local planning to reach regional as well as local smart-growth goals.

In the Washington, D.C., area, for example, a federal planning agency formulated a regional wedges and corridors strategic plan in the 1960s. This plan laid the policy foundation for the comprehensive plans of a number of local communities—including Arlington County, the city of Alexandria, and Montgomery County—that are now focusing development around transit stations in the region's rail corridors. In the Portland, Oregon, region, Metro, the regional planning and service agency, and Tri-Met, the regional rail agency, have worked closely with local governments to orient development patterns to the emerging rail system.

Smart growth will be the beneficiary if regional agencies become more active players in determining development strategies and setting standards for balanced and equitable urban growth. This section discusses promoting smart growth through mechanisms for regional collaboration and the range of approaches used in metropolitan regions. It also discusses the role of regional organizations in establishing and protecting regional open-space systems and in reducing fiscal disparities within metropolitan regions.

Promoting Smart Growth Regionally

In terms of making smart growth work, there is no substitute for the forward thinking and day-to-day coordination that regional organizations can provide. The regional context that makes regionalism so imperative is the plenitude of local governments, including special taxing districts, in control of much of the development process, each empowered to act independently in determining and achieving its self-defined objectives. In the spirit of rugged individualism, these local governments tend to be competitive and wary of collaborative actions. Often they are beholden to landed interests that stand to profit from local development. Local governments are fundamentally uninterested in envisioning goals for metropolitan growth, much less in carrying out regional strategies. Thus, reaching agreement on regional solutions is likely to be difficult.

Few regional organizations have yet been very effective in guiding metropolitan development in ways that might achieve smart-growth objectives. Many lack the statutory authority to adopt metropolitan strategies and few have the regulatory powers to implement them. Local governments zealously guard their sovereign prerogatives by constraining the planning and management capabilities of regional organizations. State attitudes toward regionalism and the role of regional agencies have not helped much. In fact, most state growth management programs have paid little attention to metropolitan development issues.

In many metropolitan areas, regional agencies exist primarily as a forum for exchanging information and cooperating on various endeavors of mutual interest—not unworthy functions but far short of strategic planning for metropolitan development. As consultant William Dodge observes: "We still consider regional governance on an ad hoc basis. We seldom think about future visions for governing our regions. Equally rarely do we design and implement collaborative strategies for achieving them."[4]

Nevertheless, the importance of a regional approach is widely recognized. The National Governors Association, for example, in a report on smart growth, said: "the best solutions for growth problems must be regional in scope.[5] Without a regional blueprint for smart growth, local solutions to growth issues will be piecemeal and likely to fall short of success.

A variety of mechanisms exists for effectuating collaboration among local governments—including regional organizations formed by states, regional councils formed voluntarily by local governments, and metropolitan planning organizations mandated by federal legislation in the 1960s to plan transportation systems and investment in large metropolitan areas. There are organizations sponsored by business groups to promote economic development across local jurisdictional boundaries, such as the Allegheny Conference in Pittsburgh and the Bay Area Council in San Francisco. There are metropolitan service districts and authorities, entities established to manage regional public facilities such as transit systems, airports, and sewer systems.

There is the Regional Plan Association, an independent nonprofit entity established in 1922 that addresses planning and implementation issues in metropolitan New York covering parts of three states—New York, New Jersey, and Connecticut. There is the Metropolitan Planning Council of Chicago founded in 1934 by business and civic leaders to promote and implement sensible planning and development policies for its region. And there is the Metropolitan Council in Minneapolis-St. Paul, established cooperatively with the state to provide planning and management services (covering transportation and airports, sewers, water, parks, and low- and moderate-income housing opportunities) for the Twin Cities region.

Some recent regional actions illustrate the range of approaches being implemented:

▲ the Regional Plan Association's participation in successful multistate efforts to fund the purchase of major open-space preserves in the northwestern sector of the region;[6]

▲ the publication of the Regional Plan Association's third regional plan;[7]

▲ the emergence of the First Suburbs Consortium, a government-led advocacy coalition of older suburbs in Ohio dedicated to fighting urban sprawl and achieving greater state investment in existing cities and suburbs;[8]

▲ a movement among state and local public officials and the business community in southeastern Massachusetts to establish a voluntary, regional strategic development program through a system of interlocking interjurisdictional agreements;[9]

▲ a federal/state/local program in southeastern Florida to stimulate infill and redevelopment in the urbanized corridor to relieve pressure for development that would adversely affect restoration of the Everglades;[10]

▲ the efforts by the Greenbelt Alliance, a San Francisco Bay Area citizens land conservation and urban planning organization, to retain a greenbelt of 3.75 million acres around the urbanized region that would channel future growth and reinvestment to existing urban areas;[11]

▲ the involvement of the Treasure Valley Partnership, a forum of local elected leaders in the Boise, Idaho, region that meets regularly to discuss and resolve regional issues and fashion regional solutions to future infrastructure needs;[12]

▲ the adoption in 1997 by the Denver Regional Council of Governments of a metropolitan vision and plan that lays out a long-range growth strategy and calls for governments within the region to voluntarily contain development within a designated growth area;[13] and

▲ the promotion of economic development in the St. Louis metropolitan area by the Bi-State Development Agency and that agency's management of the construction, operation, and expansion of a regional rail-transit system.[14]

These examples demonstrate that regional organizations offer substantial hope for promoting smart growth. State support for smart growth can provide a useful policy context, but it is regional organizations, many of which are gaining in vitality and credibility, that are most ideally placed to conjure up the kind of intergovernmental collaboration that is needed. Smart growth involves various tradeoffs, or a balancing of various goals—development, environmental quality, and social and economic well-being. Striking that balance requires strong intergovernmental commitment at the regional level.

Most regional organizations are knowledgeable about local issues and experienced (if not fully effective) in fostering cooperation among local governments. They can obtain and provide credible information on metropolitan growth issues and work with local governments to define regional needs, fashion regional strategies, assess the mutual and regional compatibility of local development plans and decisions, and manage key regional services. Whatever their authority—state authorization, intergovernmental agreement, or voluntary association—regional organizations are likely to have their ear to the ground politically and to know what's in the development pipeline.

Furthermore, what regional organizations do—the actions they take—must be conceived as (and perceived as) adding value to the growth and development process rather than as imposing irrelevant and perhaps costly burdens on the process. Regional organizations can add value in integrating planning for transportation and land use and in balancing the growth of jobs and housing, for example. They can also take a significant role in conserving open space and mitigating the impacts of growth, as described in the following sections.

Preserving Regional Open Space

To recognize—as is increasingly the case—the value of integrating open space into urban and urbanizing areas and the value of preserving large natural and farmland areas on metropolitan fringes is to recognize the value of a regional outlook in identifying, planning, and preserving open space. For small cities, counties generally can stay on top of open-space planning, but for large multicounty metropolitan areas, the leadership and resources of a regional organization are a necessity.

Portland, Oregon's Metro plans and conserves outlying regional open spaces. So do the New York region's Regional Plan Association and several other regional agencies. Many urbanizing counties as well lead open-space preservation efforts. Counties around Chicago, for example, are acquiring forest preserves. Maryland counties are using various tools—the state's Rural Legacy program, county park acquisition programs, and restrictions on the development of rural land—to piece together sustainable open-space corridors.

A regional perspective permits implementation of a strategy that links development in designated growth areas to conservation in designated rural areas. In some metropolitan areas, regional mitigation banks have been established to accumulate open-space contributions by project developers for the preservation of wetlands, forests, habitat, and other natural features being displaced by development in urbanizing areas. Such banks can be established by public agencies, utilities, or private firms.

Two Oregon cities, Eugene and Springfield, exemplify the benefits that can be obtained through interjurisdictional cooperation. For an area within both those cities that is slated for industrial development, 1,019 acres of wetlands is being managed as a wetlands mitigation bank under a plan drawn up in 1992 by the city of Eugene. Jointly managed by the city, the federal Bureau of Land Management, and the Nature Conservancy, the bank accepts land purchased by public agencies and private developers who need to replace wetlands adversely affected by development.

The Trust for Public Land and the Florida Game and Freshwater Fish Commission are collaborating in a statewide mitigation program for losses of upland habitat, involving two mitigation land banks established by the trust and financed by fees paid by developers of projects with regional impacts. In 1999, King County, Washington, established a wetlands mitigation banking program as a better alternative to individual, small mitigation efforts scattered around the county. A private banking program run by the Mile High Wetlands Group serves mitigation needs in the Denver region.

Transfer of development rights (TDR) programs in which rural development rights are sold and used in designated urban areas also lend themselves to regional applications. Certain highly valued conservation areas such as the New Jersey Pinelands and the Lake Tahoe region of California and Nevada use TDRs to preserve open space. Although TDR programs generally have not operated across jurisdictional boundaries, several counties have instituted successful, large TDR programs to preserve farmland and other open space. Montgomery County, Maryland, is well known for its use of TDRs to protect farmland. Riverside County, California, requires the developers of sites in urbanizing areas to purchase conservation credits, and the revenues are used to conserve open space.

Regional agencies could make more use of similar programs linking development to the protection of open space to guide growth and protect open space.

Supportive State Actions

What can states do to promote smart-growth actions by local jurisdictions? The National Governors Association recognizes the opportunities that states have to "improve statewide planning to enhance and shape economic development, protect natural resources, and preserve each community's quality of life."[1] The association has compiled a list of potential supportive state actions based on programs already underway in some states. These actions emphasize the leadership role that states can take in three areas—leadership and public education, economic investment and financial incentives, and government collaboration and planning strategies.

Leadership and Public Education

▲ Articulate a statewide vision for growth and quality of life that meets the goals of citizens, local governments, and private organizations.

▲ Produce and provide access to information— of use to the general public, state and local agencies, and interest groups of all types— documenting trends in the use of land, infrastructure needs and conditions, open-space conservation, and other issues connected with growth.

▲ Create tools to support local actions, including grants, technical assistance, and sources of information that spur local and private initiatives.

▲ Foster collaboration on growth strategies by encouraging, supporting, and even leading efforts to improve decisions about growth.

▲ Enlist state agencies to support statewide development goals through better coordination of their planning and action programs.

Economic Investment and Financial Incentives

▲ Target state funds to support statewide development goals—such as guiding growth into designated growth areas and reinvigorating existing neighborhoods and business centers.

▲ Revitalize town centers and neighborhoods through financial and technical assistance, tax abatements and tax credits, and other programs.

▲ Integrate brownfield redevelopment efforts with broader initiatives for community development and redevelopment.

▲ Acquire and encourage the preservation of contiguous land areas that make up green infrastructure and regional green spaces.

Government Collaboration and Planning Strategies

▲ Recognizing that the ability of local governments to deal with some regional issues is limited, help them coordinate infrastructure investments, enforce compliance with local plans, provide planning resources, involve the general public in setting goals and priorities, and remove regulatory barriers.

▲ Reduce barriers to development in targeted areas by, for example, adopting "smart" codes and proactively preparing sites for development.

▲ Require local planning and provide goals and standards to promote smart-growth planning by localities.

▲ Assume authority over local development decisions in those rare cases that require state intervention to override inadequate local controls.

Examples of state efforts to promote smart growth include New Jersey's commitment to put new life into its state plan and dramatically increase funding for the conservation of open space, Maryland's Smart Growth program targeting capital investments to designated growth areas, Georgia's smart-growth toolkit Web site, Illinois's main street revitalization program, Wyoming's program to educate landowners about conservation options, state construction codes in New Jersey and Maryland tailored to infill and redevelopment, the new Office of Smart Growth in the Colorado Department of Local Affairs, the Envision Utah initiative (see pages 163–164), and the executive orders issued by a number of governors (Maryland, Washington, Oregon, and other states) to urge state agencies to make more effective use of state resources in developing smart communities.

Note

1. Joel S. Hirschhorn, *Growth Pains: Quality of Life in the New Economy* (Washington, D.C.: National Governors Association, 2000), p. 2.

Compensation for Development

Compensatory mechanisms for development impacts across jurisdictional boundaries are a tool for smart growth to the degree that they discourage fiscal zoning and development decisions that ignore nonlocal impacts. Fiscal zoning lures land uses that generate high tax revenues, such as shopping centers and office buildings, while it leaves little room for land uses that generate net spending by city governments, such as affordable housing. The kinds of development favored by fiscal-impact analysis often produce effects in neighboring jurisdictions—traffic, employee housing, and other conditions—that require public expenditures.

Tax-sharing arrangements can help. The Metropolitan Council of the Twin Cities (Minneapolis-St. Paul) administers a regional tax-sharing program that earmarks 40 percent of property tax increases from new development for a regional pool. Funds in the tax pool are distributed to jurisdictions according to population and other factors. Although this approach has been widely admired as a useful means of balancing fiscal disparities, other metropolitan regions have not adopted it.

Some states help to equalize fiscal disparities among jurisdictions by collecting a state tax and distributing it to local jurisdictions according to need.

Another mechanism is the regional evaluation of developments with multijurisdictional impacts, called developments of regional impact (DRIs) in some states. Such evaluations can determine fiscal impacts and findings of impact can activate interjurisdictional compensatory mechanisms. Several regional organizations, including the Atlanta Regional Commission, the Metropolitan Council (Twin Cities), and all Florida regional planning agencies, are empowered to review DRIs and recommend measures to mitigate their impacts, but these agencies have relatively little power to enforce mitigation measures.

A possible compensation mechanism that might be more acceptable to local jurisdictions is agreements among local jurisdictions that provide for compensation for the impacts of certain kinds of development near jurisdictional borders. Regional agencies could formulate a model agreement for use by local governments, including definitions of developments that would trigger compensation, methods for measuring impacts, and types of compensation.

Collaborative Approaches

A solid commitment to smart growth on the part of many people and groups with a stake in community growth and change is what will make smart growth work. And securing widespread commitment means accommodating widespread interests. Smart growth must be approached collaboratively.

Community planners have a great deal of experience with consensus building and collaborative planning. This experience arises out of long-range community planning and other growth management efforts; efforts to deal with regional issues, such as air quality or economic development; efforts to resolve disputes over specific development projects in specific neighborhoods; and efforts to meet the planning-process requirements in such federal programs as transportation funding. This experience provides lessons in how to seek advice from a broad constituency of interests and how to make decisions through a collaborative process.

The collaborative approaches discussed in the sections that follow illustrate consensus building for comprehensive plans and other public initiatives, intergovernmental collaboration, and smart-growth ratings for securing community support for projects that incorporate smart characteristics. The work of the Santa Ana River Watershed Group, a multiparty, multitask entity that has had considerable success in dealing with regional issues, is discussed.

Building Consensus on Public Initiatives

Policy planning and implementation for community development generally takes place in a context of broad participation. Rarely is a major policy decision made without the input of specially constituted committees, task forces, and blue-ribbon groups and without feedback from numerous community and neighborhood meetings. Broad participation in planning and implementation helps educate civic leaders and the general public on issues of community growth and change and can forge consensus on desirable future courses of action, whether regulatory or programmatic in nature. Some widely used approaches to building consensus are described in the following sections.

Visioning Exercises

Visioning or goal-setting exercises have been conducted in many communities (and some regions) to guide the subsequent preparation of a general plan or zoning ordinance. Participants, usually representing a cross section of community interests, are asked to agree on the most desirable character of the future community or on objectives for the future development of the community. The focus of a number of visioning exercises has been on the broad goals of smart growth applied to specific regional or local concerns and conditions. In a typical visioning process, meetings may occur monthly and occasionally weekly for several months or even years, discussions are guided by trained facilitators, and the group is divided into committees and subcommittees to pursue solutions to specific issues.

The strategic program developed by Long Beach, California, in the 1980s to promote economic recovery and improve quality of life serves as an example of such a process that is notable for its long-standing value in directing community development. Long Beach fell on hard times when defense industries closed down in the 1960s, and its downtown, waterfront, and inner neighborhoods spiraled downward.

In 1984, city leaders organized citizen task forces to draft suggestions for improvements in transportation, economic development, housing and neighborhood development, infrastructure, quality of life, education, and human services. Working for almost two years, the task forces identified current problems and issues in each area of concern, framed appropriate policies, and recommended specific actions by the city to implement the policies. A strategic plan was the result. It contained 98 recommendations for action: the reorganization of city departments, the refocusing of some city programs, the establishment of new development plans and programs, the creation of new organizations for implementing housing and neighborhood improvements, more financial support for the construction of public facilities, and so forth.

The city council adopted 15 general policy statements that signaled the city's intent to pursue the strategic plan's economic and social objectives. Annual reports were prepared to indicate progress toward the completion of projects and achievement of administrative changes. The first strategic plan and others that followed have promoted and guided community development efforts over many years. Results include a rebuilt downtown, rejuvenated waterfront, and redevelopment and renovation in Long Beach.

In 1995, Flagstaff, Arizona, undertook a similarly comprehensive effort to try to come to terms with the rapid growth and associated economic, demographic, and social dislocations of the 1980s and 1990s and to try to get out of the crisis mode that characterized the city's responses to these changes. The Flagstaff 2020 visioning process sought to build a community vision around shared purposes and to use this vision as a proactive foundation for guiding community growth and change.

The visioning process was designed by a management committee that included representatives of five public entities and four private organizations and a private citizen. A project management team composed of city, county, chamber of commerce, and Grand Canyon Trust representatives met regularly to provide day-to-day oversight of the management committee's activities. A project coordinator and a facilitation consultant were hired.

The ideas and comments received during numerous public visioning meetings and surveys were evaluated and consolidated by a task force made up of 37 people representing a cross section of community interests. The task force's draft vision statement was reviewed in 50 public meetings before being finalized in June 1997. Seven action teams were assigned the task of identifying five-year and one-year (early success) actions for implementing the goals and strategies in the vision statement. Some 5,000 citizens took part in Flagstaff 2020, not including hundreds of students who participated in youth visioning programs. To keep people informed, three newspaper inserts were published and distributed to more than 23,000 households in greater Flagstaff.

The Flagstaff 2020 vision document describes goals and actions for strengthening and sustaining community ties, improving housing and livability, protecting the environment, fostering human development, managing growth, promoting family life, promoting health and safety, and providing economic opportunity. Under the "protecting the environment" rubric, for example, 14 goals from healthy forests to low-impact recreation are stated along with various recommended actions. Actions recommended to promote environmentally sensitive lifestyles, for example, include learning about and practicing environmental lifestyles, establishing community gardens and adopt-a-tree programs, revising building codes and zoning to provide incentives for energy-efficient buildings, and using a market-pricing system for resource consumption.

Envision Utah is an example of a visioning process at the regional scale. This process for rethinking regional development in the Greater Wasatch region (Salt Lake City) was set in motion in 1997 by the Coalition for Utah's Future and began with formation of the Utah Quality Growth Public/Private Partnership, a group of more than 100 community leaders. The partnership's job was to come up with a growth scenario that could guide development, focused especially on the rapid growth taking place in the Greater Wasatch region. A survey of residents on the values they held for their communities kicked off the Envision Utah process.

Over almost two years, a series of more than 100 workshops and meetings allowed residents to identify their desires for regional development. The workshops (see under "Charrettes" on page 165) fed ideas into four growth scenarios depicting conventional and more compact patterns of development. The scenarios were tested for fiscal, environmental, and other impacts, and then in 1999 they were configured into a single regional plan, the quality growth scenario. The quality growth scenario now guides the community development actions of cities and suburban communities in the region, as well as state actions.[15]

Visioning can be a useful tool for defining and expressing goals, but it works best when structured to produce concrete recommendations that can be folded into planning and implementation programs already in place. Visioning efforts are often misguided in championing wide participation and interaction to achieve broad consensus rather than seeking the production and implementation of specific action plans.

The Atlanta Regional Commission (ARC) recently evaluated the results of that region's Vision 2020 process from July 1991 through September 1995. It found that much of the visioning process was "very effective in promoting interpersonal interaction on topics it identified as important," but that it "yielded few clearly significant, immediate results from its list of action initiatives, produced no plan capable of providing 'a roadmap to the vision,' and required the commitment of $4.4 million."[16]

Among the mistakes of the Vision 2020 program, according to the ARC study, are that it set process objectives rather than outcome goals, required consensus without a means of stimulating compromise and change, and de-emphasized substantive planning expertise without providing an alternative standard and without providing a credible alternative source of data. Thus overall goals were blurry, timeframes for action undefined, proposals not well evaluated, and participation spotty over the lengthy process. Furthermore, how the Vision 2020 conclusions were related to ongoing local and regional planning programs was not fully explored or made explicit.

Small-Area Planning Committees

Development or revitalization planning for smaller areas such as neighborhoods, business districts, historic districts, and transportation corridors is also frequently a collaborative group effort. These groups often are asked to agree on goals for the development of the area under consideration and to make specific recommendations about the character and location of the major components of development. Rather precise goals and even detailed designs can emerge from this process.

For example, the development of Bethesda Row and associated transit-related projects in Bethesda, Maryland (see page 129), were implemented according to a sector plan that had been prepared by a community planning committee for the commercial center. Appointed by the county planning board, the committee members represented a broad continuum of interests. After lengthy discussions, the committee agreed on a plan that included specific goals and design guidelines for development in the commercial center.

In Charlotte, North Carolina, the region's 14 chambers of commerce were convinced that the region required a multimodal transportation system, so they worked to establish the public/private Business Committee for Regional Transportation Solutions to promote planning, funding, design, and development of a coordinated regional system of highways and transit. In particular, the group has worked closely with state, county, and city officials to back planning for rail-transit facilities in five corridors and for designing and implementing transit-supportive development patterns near proposed station areas. (The Business Committee for Regional Transportation Solutions also sponsored ULI advisory panels to recommend appropriate land use patterns and actions in each of the five corridors and a concluding symposium to educate the community about the findings and recommendations of the panels and encourage a dialogue about transportation and land use strategies in the region.)

The sponsors of small-area planning committees and ad hoc task forces can be city councils, planning commissions, or many other entities. Their purview can be equally varied, from the streamlining of development regulations to the creation of a regional parks authority or transportation authority, the resolution of an interjurisdictional land use dispute, or the establishment of a mixed-use zoning district. Although they may begin with vision and goal statements, such task-oriented groups typically produce detailed recommendations as well. In some communities, ad hoc task forces and committees have become a fairly standard way of addressing special concerns, and at any given time several such groups will be in the process of investigating and making recommendations on various subjects.

Charrettes

A charrette is an effort concentrated in time to understand conditions and issues, define development goals, and propose courses of action. Charrettes engage a broad array of residents and special interests and have become a popular method for reaching consensus on future growth and change, particularly in relatively small, contained areas such as small towns, neighborhoods, and business districts. Led by professional facilitators (who frequently are planners or urban designers), charrettes are carefully organized to proceed from a discussion of general concerns and objectives to participants' recommendations for specific plans, designs, and actions. Charrette meetings may be scheduled to last only over a single weekend or they sometimes may involve several two-day sessions over a month or two. Whatever the format, the emphasis is on intense, focused deliberations that can produce results within a short time frame.

For example, the Treasure Coast Regional Planning Council (covering Palm Beach, Indian River, Martin, and St. Lucie Counties in southeastern Florida) managed a series of charrettes in the mid- to late 1990s in small communities along the coast to define desirable components of future development in the town centers. Each charrette took place over a weekend or two, sandwiched by prior studies and follow-up detailed design work. They proved highly popular among townspeople and produced some interesting new ideas for parks, waterfront uses, business area improvements, and other aspects of town center development. Many of these ideas were incorporated in later revisions of communities' comprehensive plans and zoning ordinances.

Envision Utah (see "Visioning Exercises" on pages 163–164) organized a series of workshops similar to charrettes to encourage people to plan the future course of development in the region. In the first workshop, for example, participants were given regional maps and stacks of chips representing the amount of land required for future growth, and they were asked to put the chips on the map where development should occur. (Depending on the subarea, from almost half to more than three-quarters of the chips ended up on infill and redevelopment sites.) Additional workshops further defined the character and location of projected development, eventually leading in the second year of the effort to a regional plan for the Salt Lake City area.

Intergovernmental Collaboration

Local governments hold the power to plan and regulate development. The limitations of this jurisdictional focus have become all too evident. Local communities operate within a regional context of economic, social, and environmental forces—and sometimes within a state, national, or even global context. Economic, transportation, environmental, and other systems transcend local boundaries, are interrelated, and involve a complex network of public entities. Smart-growth advocates recognize the interrelatedness of urban systems and their transcendence of local boundaries, and endeavor to spread the word. For smart growth to work, collaboration among the many agencies and departments engaged in making communities livable is essential—essential although difficult.

Relationships between local governments and the federal establishment tend to make the difficulties of intergovernmental collaboration evident. A large part of the problem has to do with the consciously narrow focus of many federal agencies. Their missions are hard to decipher—defined by Congressional mandates, agency regulations, and court cases—and colored by the attitudes of whatever administration is in power and the attitudes of long-time agency professionals. Even departments and agencies within the federal establishment and offices within single agencies and departments may fail to collaborate with one another. Cooperative endeavors between federal agencies and nonfederal governmental entities are the exception rather than the rule, despite what agencies may say about the value of collaboration and the frequent willingness of individual staff members, especially in the regional offices, to be involved in collaborative ventures.

There are three federal planning processes for areas of special concern that offer opportunities for collaboration:

▲ **Advance identification of wetlands.** Under Section 230.80 of the EPA 404(b)(1) guidelines, EPA and the U.S. Army Corps of Engineers may carry out studies and, in advance of application for permits, designate wetlands as suitable or unsuitable for disposal of dredged or fill material.

▲ **Special-area management plans.** To protect natural resources and allow reasonable coastal-dependent development in specific areas, the 1980 amendments to the Coastal Zone Management Act allow the Corps, in conjunction with federal, state, and local resource agencies, to develop special-area management plans (SAMPs) that contain comprehensive statements of policies and criteria to guide land use.

▲ **Habitat conservation plans.** Under the Endangered Species Act, the U.S. Fish and Wildlife Service can approve habitat conservation plans that allow some development to occur on land that is habitat for endangered species, if the development will not substantially reduce the survivability of any endangered species.

These three planning mechanisms attempt to balance conservation with development in a way that reduces future conflicts, improves the predictability of potential development, and protects important natural areas. Also, all three mechanisms involve processes requiring close working relationships among federal, state, and local agencies, developers, and special-interest groups.[17]

State agencies are little better than federal agencies in working collaboratively among themselves but they are more apt to join in collaborative enterprises with local governments, perhaps because of proximity. State agencies typically develop local constituencies across the state, which may stimulate collaborative undertakings. Administering growth management laws routinely involves state agencies in a dozen or so states with local planning and development authorities.

The Maryland Rural Legacy program represents an effective approach to state/local collaboration. Authorized in the state's 1997 Smart Growth legislation, the Rural Legacy program provides state funding for local acquisition of conservation easements to preserve open space. Local governments compete for funding by proposing projects that meet state goals for protecting areas large enough to preserve multiple natural qualities of value. The state especially welcomes collaborative proposals from two or more local governments, for example to preserve extended natural corridors, and proposals that incorporate other conservation funding to augment the Rural Legacy funds. In the first three years of the program, the state committed approximately $100 million in grants to conserve 47,000 acres of land.

Collaborative Planning for Private Projects

For private projects today, particularly for large projects, the developer's collaboration with government agencies, community interests, and special interests on program and design details is a fact of life. Neighborhood and community groups are likely to want to especially examine less conventional project proposals that adhere to smart-growth principles. NIMBYism is one component of activism toward development in many communities, but another component is the public's interest in assuring development that in character and quality adds to—and does not detract from—neighborhood and community livability and value. A 1994 ULI publication sees collaborative project planning as stemming from several changes:

> No longer is it possible to consider the public and private sectors as independent actors. Tight budgets have caused public agencies to act simultaneously as regulators of and partners in private development; interest groups have become stronger and more sophisticated; and the diversity of participants has increased.[18]

Public involvement in development decisions need not be adversarial. A collaborative approach allows private developers and public officials to focus their energies on planning the development rather than on outwitting their opponents. And, to the extent that collaboration reduces project delays and risks and assures a more orderly development process, overall project costs may be contained.

Engaging in collaborative discussions about proposed projects is especially important in the following circumstances:

▲ The proposed project raises complex issues that need detailed examination to be resolved.
▲ The issues are negotiable. In other words, established policies and regulations allow some leeway.
▲ The project affects or involves many parties or more than one local jurisdiction.
▲ The parties and jurisdictions are willing to participate in collaborative planning.

When time is of the essence, when fast action is required and the time to work through tough problems is not available, collaboration is a less feasible option. But frequently time itself can be stretched in time-constrained situations and decisions postponed—to allow constructive discussions among the interests to take place.

Developers can do missionary work to advance their interests, seeking out public support for their developments. Even before they apply for permits, they can talk with community leaders to determine community attitudes toward development and identify potential issues. They can organize neighborhood meetings to describe proposed projects and obtain feedback. Such meetings provide opportunities to work out compromises before attitudes become hardened and issues become crises. Developers can identify what neighborhood or community concerns might be addressed or resolved by their projects. They can supply the community with credible facts and figures before damaging rumors start.[19]

Effective collaboration on smart development proposals hinges most clearly on public officials having done their job in establishing a positive policy context for smart development. Clear and repeated signals from public officials that they support smart types of development will allay developers' worries about the possibility of collaborative discussions becoming contentious rather than constructive.

The major expansion of the 1950s Prudential Center in downtown Boston involved the kind of collaborative approach that increasingly is required for development. In the mid-1980s, Prudential Development wanted to act on the market opportunity to add some 3 million square feet of office and retail space to the 7 million-square-foot Prudential Center. The developer planned to transform the aging center into a destination complex that could compete with its highly successful neighbor, Copley Place, and to improve street and pedestrian access within the redeveloped complex.

When the plan was announced, local residents raised major concerns about potential impacts on adjacent neighborhoods. Mayor Kevin White stepped in to recommend a new planning approach that eventually involved 22 neighborhood, civic, and business groups empowered to establish guidelines, evaluate design concepts, and assess impact mitigation. Robert Walsh, Prudential's chief representative in the planning process, explained Prudential's willingness to take this new road: "For us to leverage our investment, we had to create greater density and for that we needed to work with our neighbors."

The developer reconstituted the planning team to include firms experienced in inclusive design processes. The mayor, the Boston Redevelopment Authority, and the developer combined to launch PruPAC, the collaborative planning group. A facilitator was hired to promote an open dialogue among the participants. Hundreds of meetings took place, some with the whole group and others with key individuals and task groups.

The plan that took shape accomplished the developer's principal objective of expanding the asset base of the center, although at a smaller scale than first designed, and added community value by fostering connections with adjacent areas and strengthening existing assets. The expansion was designed to create a lively and accessible mix of uses, to constitute a memorable addition to the city, and to integrate Prudential Center into the surrounding neighborhoods.

The final expansion plan included 1.8 million square feet of new office space, residential buildings, a new retail area, and an enclosed pedestrian walkway connecting to the existing retail arcade— an investment totaling approximately $1 billion.[20] PruPAC has continued to guide decisions on project design and changes. In the summer of 2000, it approved changes in the master plan to allow development of a hotel. Prudential's willingness to participate in this lengthy process was a key to a successful project.

Smart-Growth Ratings and Scorecards

Project rating systems and endorsement systems can be an innovative tool for securing community backing for proposed developments that advance smart growth. Some communities have used rating systems for many years to guide permitting decisions. Some communities use more recently adopted community indicators to gauge their progress toward smart growth.

Indicators in this context are shorthand, measurable data points used to assess important community conditions and qualities related to smart growth, such as the net density of new development, transit ridership, acres of conserved open space, and the number of affordable housing units. By tracking changes in the indicator measurements, community leaders can determine which programs are working to meet smart-growth goals and which need strengthening or redirection.[21]

The city of Austin, Texas, uses indicators contained in a Smart Growth Matrix that was adopted in 1999 to assist the city council in analyzing development proposals in its designated desirable development zone. The desirable development zone includes downtown and the urban core and certain neighborhoods. Projects that significantly advance the city's goals (chiefly its infill and redevelopment goal) may be offered financial incentives to offset the high cost of developing in built-up areas.

The Smart Growth Matrix is contained in a 23-page application package. Eleven types of project characteristics are evaluated and points awarded up to a maximum number of points for each characteristic:

	Maximum Number Of Points
Location	87
Neighborhood planning and design reviews	85
Critical mass (density)	24
Land use	110
Support of other agencies	24
Urban design	44
Multimodal transportation elements	123
Parking	38
Housing affordability	20
Local economic effects	34
Sustainable building practices	46

For each of these characteristics, the matrix spells out criteria and standards, which are assigned weights and a maximum number of points. Evaluators multiply points awarded by weights to arrive at scores for each criterion or standard. For example, a project's location in the desired development zone earns points if the location is consistent with a transit-station-area plan and gains points if it is close to a bus stop. A project can earn up to 45 points for a downtown location, 28 points for a location in the urban core, and 12 points for a location in the desired development zone. For a lo-

cation in an area of economic need or in an untested (trail-blazing) market area, projects can earn up to 42 additional points. For another example, a project can earn points for its multimodal transportation elements if it offers an interface with or proximity to transit (three points) or pedestrian-friendliness (up to 24 points).

Up to 635 total points are available. A project must obtain more than 225 points to merit approval. The number of points above 225 will determine the extent of financial incentives offered by the city, such as fee waivers and infrastructure funding.

Use of Austin's smart-growth rating system is at the option of developers, who presumably are attracted by the potential financial incentives. By mid-2001, 11 projects had been evaluated using the matrix, and eight had been approved, mostly for fee waivers. That amount of activity may seem insignificant but in fact it represents investment totaling more than $350 million. According to George Adams, the city's chief administrator for the rating process, another eight projects are going through matrix evaluations as of late 2001.

But indicators and Austin's Smart Growth Matrix represent top-down measures of the quality of proposed development. Typically, indicator programs are administered by the jurisdiction's planning staff. A number of environmental and urban advocacy organizations—such as San Francisco's Greenbelt Alliance and the 1000 Friends of Washington—have suggested a more collaborative approach to evaluating the smart-growth qualities of proposed development.

This approach is called endorsement rating. Endorsement rating programs are structured to provide a means for community groups—and developers—to do two things: 1) evaluate the extent to which proposed developments meet smart-growth goals and 2) obtain support for projects that score high on the evaluation. The sponsors of smart projects need all the help they can get given the fact that such projects—compact, mixed-use, transit-focused, and affordable—often encounter the stiffest opposition from neighbors as well as higher-than-normal regulatory hurdles. Endorsement ratings help developers as well to discover what project qualities their potential supporters consider important.

Endorsement rating systems are intended especially for the use of nongovernmental special-interest groups and civic groups that seek assurances that proposed developments advance smart-growth principles. One recent example is the Smart Scorecard for development projects formulated by planners Will Fleissig and Vickie Jacobsen in collaboration with the Congress for the New Urbanism (CNU) with funding from EPA.[22]

The Scorecard, the latest draft of which was completed in January 2002, is intended to help all the parties that are involved in project decisions—elected local officials, developers, investors, neighborhood groups, and project designers—make better decisions. It contributes to better decisions by fostering more effective communication about the common objectives of communities and developers. The Scorecard's authors hope that by using it communities will be able to find the point at which community goals, site opportunities, and economically viable development intersect. Communities using the Scorecard can determine the emphasis to be given various criteria.

The Scorecard evaluates ten critical project characteristics (the percentages state the share of the total score for each characteristic):

	Share of Total Score
Proximity to existing and future development and infrastructure	15%
Mix and balance of uses	12%
Site optimization and compactness of development	12%
Accessibility and mobility choices	12%
Community context and site design	10%
Fine-grained block, pedestrian, and park network	10%
Environmental qualities	8%
Diversity of uses	8%
Reuse and redevelopment options	7%
Process collaboration and predictability of decisions	6%

For each of these project characteristics, the Scorecard identifies critical factors and possible measures of those factors. For example, to evaluate the first characteristic—proximity to existing and future development and infrastructure—the following critical factors are to be measured:

▲ distance to roads, water service, and sewer service;
▲ walking distance to transit;

▲ for residential development, proximity to services (grocery shopping, convenience retail, personal services, schools, daycare, recreation centers);
▲ for commercial development (including employment uses), proximity to housing, restaurants, entertainment;
▲ time before additional support services become available; and
▲ location within designated development or redevelopment areas.

Each critical factor is rated according to specific measures. The project is awarded points for each factor depending on its rating as excellent (four points), preferred (three points), acceptable (two points), or minimal (one point). For the critical factors relating to proximity just listed, for example, the first four factors are rated in miles, with adjacency earning four points (excellent), less than one-third mile earning three points (preferred), one-third to one-half mile earning three points (acceptable), and one-half to one mile earning one point (minimal). The fifth factor on this list is rated in years, with before two years earning four points (excellent) and six to eight years earning one point (minimal). No measures are provided for the sixth factor, because a site is either in a designated area or not in one.

The Scorecard also lists city responsibilities for each of the project characteristics. City responsibilities for the proximity characteristics, for example, include adoption of a capital improvements program tied to comprehensive and district plans, a transportation master plan, a water management master plan, a stated policy not to subsidize infrastructure for leapfrog projects that require the extension of infrastructure outside service areas, and the designation of mixed-use village centers near residential areas.

Special-interest groups interested in endorsing a proposed project can use the Scorecard to evaluate how well it satisfies smart-growth objectives. The Scorecard can be adapted to meet the information and rating needs of specific organizations. For example, it was used by the Home Builders Association of Metropolitan Denver to create a Green Builder Scorecard for master-planned communities.

In late 2001, the Chesapeake & Potomac Regional Alliance (CAPRA), a Washington, D.C., area nonprofit regional action alliance working toward a better regional future, issued a three-part project rating method that is somewhat less complex than the CNU Smart Scorecard.[23] CAPRA proposes that this method be used as an endorsement tool for projects that meet smart-growth goals.

The CAPRA method poses a series of questions (see box). Part 1 provides a short-form checklist to determine if a project prequalifies by meeting the most basic criteria of smart growth. Yes or no questions pertain to the project's 1) proximity to existing urbanized areas, town centers, transit stops, and current or planned public water and sewer systems; 2) accessibility by existing roads, and by walking and biking; 3) avoidance of harm to local streams and bodies of water bodies, and minimal effect on wetlands, forests, and agricultural land; and 4) contribution to balance in the mix of local jobs, housing, and services.

If a project passes muster in the part 1 analysis, and an organization wishes to consider further evaluation leading to a potential endorsement, that organization can use part 2 to determine the strategic significance of the project in terms of 1) size;

▶ Draft rating form for proposed projects from the Chesapeake & Potomac Regional Alliance (CAPRA).

DRAFT MODEL

Smart Growth Project Evaluation Chart

PART ONE: Minimum Smart Growth Standards
Yes | No

Projects must meet all pre-qualifying standards to be called a Basic Smart Growth Project.

Location
Is the project within an incorporated city or town and/or 1/2 mile of an existing or planned fixed rail transit stop, a mixed use town center or similar center, or a major bus stop with at least 6 buses during peak hour. — Yes | No

Public Services
Is the site within a current or planned public water and/or sewer service area unless it is within or abutting an incorporated village or town that lacks these services? — Yes | No

Community Connectivity
Will the development either create an addition to an existing community or create a new community? — Yes | No

Transportation
Will the site be served by existing roads and accessible by bikes and pedestrians? — Yes | No

Environment
Will the project do no harm to the stability and water quality of local streams and water bodies? — Yes | No
Does the project create a net loss of less than 1/4 ac. of wetlands or 1 ac. of forest land or agricultural land? — Yes | No

Land Use Mix
Will the land uses proposed help to balance the local jobs, housing, services mix within a 1/2 mile of the site? — Yes | No

PART TWO: Determination of Strategic Significance
Yes | No | 100

Projects must collect least 50 points of the following to considered for an endorsement review.

Size
Is the project of sufficient acreage (-) and/or building square footage (-) to be significant? — Yes | No | 10

Location
Is the project in a area designated for growth, intensification, or revitalization by the local jurisdiction? — Yes | No | 5
Is the site considered a key development parcel within the community? — Yes | No | 10

Land Use Mix
Will the land uses significantly improve the balance of local jobs, housing, services mix of the community? — Yes | No | 5
Does the project offer significant amounts of affordable housing? — Yes | No | 5
Does the project create a new neighborhood or larger center or support an existing one within 1/2 mile? — Yes | No | 5
Will the mix and amount of development make a significant contribution to encouraging transit use? — Yes | No | 10

Community Benefit
Does the project offer a significant community quality of life benefit such as a plaza, park, school site, etc.? — Yes | No | 5
Does the project offer a significant economic benefit to the community such as jobs, tax base, etc.? — Yes | No | 5

Transportation
Will the project enable the creation, extension, or improvement of public transit in the community? — Yes | No | 10
Will the project make a significant contribution to internal and local pedestrian and bike travel? — Yes | No | 5
Will the project make significant contributions to area roads? — Yes | No | 5

Environment
Is this a redevelopment, intensification, or renovation project on a site with prior disturbance? — Yes | No | 10

Community Participation
Has the developer met with local groups to identify local concerns and desires? — Yes | No | 5

Interest
Has the developer, jurisdiction, or other local interest group requested an evaluation? — Yes | No | 5

Total Score
Percent of Total

2) locational relation to community growth or re-development objectives; 3) mix of uses (including affordable housing); 4) community benefits such as parks, tax base, and transportation improve-ments; and 5) the developer's working relation-ship with local groups.

Projects that collect at least 50 points from posi-tive answers to the part 2 questions can be consid-ered for the detailed analysis presented in part 3. Project characteristics scored during this evaluation include location, density, transportation access, land use mix, community benefits, environmental effects, community connectivity, respect for historic places, respect for existing residents and businesses, and the developer's track record in producing proj-ects meeting smart-growth standards. Projects for which 80 percent of the answers are in the affirma-tive are eligible to receive an endorsement as pro-smart growth and those with a 70 percent score may receive a conditional endorsement. Any proj-ects that are rated 0 in more than one category should not be endorsed.

CAPRA's rating process, like the Smart Score-card, is intended to serve as a starting point for responses to proposed projects. It can be adapted and elaborated as appropriate for local conditions and concerns. CAPRA suggests that the develop-ment and adoption of a uniform rating chart by a coalition of organizations would be the most effective method of endorsement and the most effective way of gaining influence over decision making about development.

CAPRA also believes that the use of its matrix to rate proposed projects can enhance opportunities for dialogue between developers and community groups about project characteristics. The oppor-tunity to gain endorsements through this process will give developers an incentive to revise their proposals to more closely achieve smart-growth goals. At the same time, developers can use the matrix rating system to present the merits of their projects to community groups that might be per-suaded to endorse or actively support them as contributions to smart growth.

The credibility of project ratings and endorsements based on smart-growth ratings will be enhanced if the group leading the process ensures that it is an open process structured to engender a climate of trust and collaboration. Making the process an open one may mean including various members of the community in it. Evaluation processes that result in the credible endorsement of projects that meet smart-growth goals can help gain approval for projects that might otherwise face formidable community opposition.

The Smart Growth Alliance—a collaborative en-terprise to research, identify, and encourage land use development and transportation policies and practices that will support smart growth in the Washington, D.C., region—includes a smart-growth endorsement program. Initiated by the Washing-ton, D.C., ULI District Council, the alliance in-cludes among its partners the district council, the Coalition for Smarter Growth, the Greater Washing-ton Board of Trade, the Chesapeake Bay Founda-tion, and the Metropolitan Washington Builders' Council. A "Smart Growth Alliance Agreement" spells out the mission, objectives, and structure of the alliance. Criteria have been developed for a smart-growth endorsement program, which will recognize project proposals that meet smart growth criteria. The alliance has tested proposed evaluation criteria on several project proposals and is now moving ahead with the endorse-ment program.

Procedures and Issues in Collaboration

Certain steps are important to take in any collab-orative process—whether it is publicly or privately directed and whether it is a community planning effort or a proposed development project. These are as follows:

▲ Define the issues and the desired outcomes. This means assessing the types of concerns likely to be raised by the planning effort or the proposed development project, and clar-ifying the desired results of the process (the indicators of success or failure).

▲ Identify the parties with interests in the plan or project and in the outcome of the process. Interested parties include individuals or groups with authority to make decisions on the matter, with a direct or indirect stake in the decisions, and with the means to influence decisions.

▲ Design an organizational format and decision-making structure. The format and structure should focus on educating participants, instilling a level of trust and respect among participants, and promoting agreement on the goal of re-solving issues and making decisions.

▲ Gather and communicate to participants knowledge of conditions, trends, and existing policies affecting relevant issues.

▲ Work to reach consensus or agreement on specific recommendations, policies, and actions. All agreements forged should be documented.

These steps are important but not easy. Who should be involved, for example, is a question rife with political nuances and practical implications. Frequently, the first draft of a list of participants misses individuals who can play a key role in decisions and whose omission even may render the outcome of the process irrelevant.

Who should be involved hinges sometimes on how likely they are to stick with the process over the long term. The longer the process, the less predictable the attendance of participants. Visioning exercises and comprehensive plan revisions may involve dozens of meetings over many months or even years—and when the planning phase is complete, participants may be reluctant to sign up for follow-up efforts to devise action programs. Participants representing business interests may tire quickly of seemingly interminable discussions, and unless they are directly affected by the results of the process they may drop out. Other participants may drop out because of changes in their personal lives and professional duties.

High dropout rates can necessitate constant adjustments in the process to accommodate and educate replacements. Some turnover among participants involved in community planning is no doubt healthy, but too many fresh faces can mean revisiting previously made decisions. The participants most likely to remain involved over time tend to be representatives of groups with a strong interest in one kind of issue or another. Some are close to being professional meeting attendees and, in the end, their continued participation may lead to decisions unreflective of larger community interests.

In this regard, Debra Stein, author of two ULI books about winning approvals for development, comments that the effectiveness of charrettes as collaborative design processes depends on having "the right people sitting at the table." People opposed to any change rarely cooperate to shape a workable project. Charrettes, she says, "are enjoyable for rational thinkers . . . and lineal thinkers who appreciate the constant refinements and revisions of the design process." But some legitimate stakeholders, notes Stein, often including young and old people, cannot engage constructively in this type of thinking.[24]

Stein points out another weakness of any collaborative process, which is the tendency of many participants to concentrate on protecting the existing quality of their lives and the current character of the community—and to not consider the possible benefits of change and future development. This tendency may account for the underwhelming results of many collaborative exercises in which the recommendations reflect a fixation on keeping things as they are.

An example occurred in Minneapolis some years ago. Planners exploring possibilities for initiating regional rail-transit service proposed using an existing rail line to bring capital costs within a feasible range. They organized a series of discussions involving residents of neighborhoods along the proposed line. One after another, the neighborhood meetings produced great support for rail service. But they also insisted that the new rail line be placed underground to avoid impacts on the adjoining neighborhoods. This solution raised construction costs well above available funding and killed the project. Having failed to imagine that outcome, the planners had neglected to set limits for changes to the proposed project.

Many visioning and planning processes are structured to reach consensus among multiple interests and across multiple issues. Thus, too many of these processes produce little but vague generalizations about future development. It is important to define carefully the expected outcomes of a collaborative process and to formulate procedures to reach them. If agreement on specific policies and detailed action recommendations is desired, consensus (the full commitment of all participants) should not be a goal. Decisions on rules for voting and even dissenting reports should be made early in the process to reflect desired outcomes.

The Santa Ana River Watershed Group illustrates a process consciously designed to avoid many of the problems that are common in collaborative approaches. Initially formed in 1998 to work out solutions to the environmental impacts of about 270 dairy operations and 350,000 dairy animals in the 50-square-mile Chino Basin, the Watershed

Group incorporates a wide array of interests. It soon found reason to broaden its work to encompass issues of urban and economic development.

The Santa Ana River watershed comprises 2,650 square miles extending 80 miles from the San Bernardino Mountains to the Pacific Ocean, including parts of three counties (San Bernardino, Riverside, and Orange) and numerous local jurisdictions (including several water and wastewater utilities). The Watershed Group brought together representatives of the local governments, the dairy and utility interests, environmental organizations, and state and federal agencies to explore issues in the watershed and collaboratively determine potential solutions. This collaborative process was termed "shared governance." It evolved from a need to involve a wide and shifting constituency of interests and to coordinate a variety of local efforts to deal with development and conservation issues.

The fragmentation of interests and goals so often encountered in multiparty processes is not a problem in the Working Group. The Working Group is structured as an open forum of self-selected members who agree to participate in facilitated discussions that sometimes involve a dozen members and sometimes many more. A facilitation team in consultation with participating members prepares draft scoping reports that identify issues and potential strategies for their resolution.

The Working Group does not take formal positions or vote on recommendations. What it does is explore concerns and opportunities for joint efforts, from manure management to habitat conservation to water quality improvements. As specific tasks are identified, they are assigned to task groups that move them forward. This working methodology allows members to articulate views and positions in a context that fosters cooperation and constructive action.

Recently, this process was formalized under a memorandum of understanding signed by the three county boards of supervisors, the Santa Ana Watershed Project Authority (made up of the five major water districts in the watershed), and the Orange County Sanitation District. To add state and federal representatives to this framework, a second memorandum of understanding was signed by the original signatories and key state and federal agencies, committing these parties to

participate in the Working Group and specified initiatives. Funding for the Working Group's efforts has been provided by key participants such as the dairies, local agencies, and EPA and by other public agencies and foundations.

The Working Group has been involved in a dozen or more initiatives over the past three years. Some results of efforts to date include collaborative planning for manure management in the Chino Basin, preparation of a scoping report for a conservation program for 10,000 acres upstream of the Prado Dam, proposals for an information bank for the watershed, and a conservation strategy for protecting the threatened Santa Ana sucker (a fish). A major result is the unprecedented degree of collaboration that has evolved among a wide variety of interests in the watershed.

Commitments Needed

This chapter began by underscoring the need for people and agencies to move past the broad principles of smart growth to change the ways regions, communities, and neighborhoods develop. Everyone involved in community development—developers, builders, urban designers, planners, public officials at all levels of government, and representatives of civic and other interests—needs to commit to the pursuit of smart growth at every step of the community-building process.

This chapter ends with lists of actions that 1) developers and associated professionals, 2) public officials, and 3) special-interest groups can take to promote smart growth—and must take for smart growth to flourish. Unless developers, public officials, and special interests commit to taking these actions—unless they become responsible for pursuing smart growth—smart growth will remain an empty promise. Community developers broadly speaking must commit to taking the following actions, because the success of smart growth absolutely depends on their doing so.

Developers, builders, lenders, planners and designers, and other providers of real estate services must:

▲ Study examples of smart development, learn its nature, and seize every opportunity to adapt, refine, and experiment with applications of smart-growth principles in project locations, siting, design, and construction.

▲ Specifically define and evaluate the costs and benefits of potential smart features in the location, siting, design, and construction of development projects.

▲ Find ways to incorporate considerations of long-term value (operating costs, appreciation, durability) in making decisions about project siting, components, and design.

▲ Seek to physically and functionally connect developments with nearby neighborhoods and to expand the lifestyle, work, and travel choices available within communities and regions.

▲ Find ways to evolve organizational strategies for building and development with the goal of examining potential opportunities for diversifying product lines in terms of scale, form, and uses.

▲ Work proactively with public officials, civic groups, and other organizations to establish a public policy and regulatory context favorable to smart development and to transform widespread antigrowth attitudes into pro-smart-growth attitudes.

Public officials and administrators at all levels of government must:

▲ Using collaborative decision-making processes, define the specific qualities of 1) compact, multiuse development, 2) open space, 3) mobility, and 4) livability that are most desirable for the state, region, and community and adopt those definitions as goals and guidelines for future development.

▲ Incorporate smart-growth principles in the plans adopted to accommodate growth within regions, communities, and neighborhoods.

▲ Incorporate smart-growth principles in capital facilities planning and funding, paying particular attention to the adequacy of funding to meet needs, the location of planned infrastructure investments, and the siting and design of facilities in relation to surrounding development.

▲ Recognize and plan for social and economic needs in smart-growth initiatives and orient social and economic development initiatives to also promote smart growth.

▲ Adopt development policies, regulations, and approval processes that emphasize the importance of high-quality, fine-grained connectivity in the planning and design of neighborhoods, business centers, and development projects.

▲ Program investments in regional components of growth and development—multimodal transportation systems, green infrastructure systems, and so forth—through regional planning and agreements that are collaborative, intergovernmental, and multiparty, and that abide by smart-growth principles.

▲ Prioritize investments by state and regional agencies to support and encourage smart growth at the local level.

▲ Recognize the essential importance of natural and other open land for sustainable environments and for sustainable and livable communities.

▲ Innovate and experiment in promoting smart development, including demonstration projects, zoning and financial incentives, and public/private approaches.

▲ In all decisions regarding growth and development, seek to relate the physical, social, and economic aspects of community development and to broaden living, working, and travel choices.

Civic organizations and special-interest groups must:

▲ Constructively endorse programs, policies, and projects that promote smart growth, taking care to ensure that the endorsements are for programs, policies, or projects that truly represent the interrelationships of smart-growth principles.

▲ Collaborate with private sector developers and public officials to better define the specific qualities of 1) compact, multiuse development, 2) open space, 3) mobility, and 4) livability that should guide supportive actions in each region, community, and neighborhood.

▲ Become educated about development issues, development opportunities, and the development process in order to better inform decisions on opposing or endorsing specific policy proposals and proposed development projects.

▲ Recognize that growth and change occur in all communities and that growth should be accommodated in the smartest way possible.

▲ Conduct research to identify ways in which growth and change can take place with minimal undesirable effects on neighborhoods and communities and with maximum value-added for those same neighborhoods and communities.

▲ For specific areas of special concern, identify in advance of possible development the qualities of growth and change that would be most compatible with existing land uses.

Making good on such commitments will require determination and effort. Proponents of smart growth can benefit from regional thinking and collaborative action to overcome NIMBYist fears and the inertia of business as usual. Naysayers insist that the smart-growth glass is half empty, that its principles are too ambitious to be feasible of achievement. Proponents of smart growth must work on the premise that the glass is half full and capable of becoming fuller.

Smart growth needs us to use existing tools better and to innovate and experiment with new ways of development. Urban development has adapted to changing circumstances since cities and towns came into being. Smart growth means moving again in the right direction, better attuning the built environment to the changing needs of the society and the economy.

Notes

1. Donald Priest, "Smart Growth: The Limits of Existing Policies and Suggestions for a More Pragmatic and Inclusive Strategy" (unpublished paper, June 2001).

2. Richard C. Ward, "How Smart Is Smart Growth?" *Development Strategies Review* (Development Strategies Inc.), summer 2001, pp. 1–3.

3. Kathryn A. Foster, *Regionalism on Purpose*, Policy Focus Report (Cambridge, Massachusetts: Lincoln Institute of Land Policy, 2001), p. 4.

4. William R. Dodge, *Regional Excellence: Governing Together to Compete Globally and Flourish Locally* (Washington, D.C.: National League of Cities, 1996), p. 37.

5. Joel S. Hirschhorn, *Growth Pains: Quality of Life in the New Economy* (Washington, D.C.: National Governors Association, 2000), p. 27.

6. Robert D. Yaro, "Implementing RPA's Third Regional Plan for the New York Metropolitan Region," *Environmental and Urban Issues*, fall 1997, pp. 9–16.

7. Robert Yaro and Tony Hiss, *Region at Risk: The Third Regional Plan for the New York-New Jersey-Connecticut Metropolitan Area* (New York: Regional Plan Association, 1996).

8. See First Suburbs homepage at: www.firstsuburbs.org.

9. Task Force on Growth and Change in Southeastern Massachusetts, *Southeastern Massachusetts: Vision 2020*, adopted February 1999 (Taunton, Massachusetts: Southeastern Regional Planning and Economic Development District, 1999).

10. See South Florida Regional Planning Council and Treasure Coast Regional Planning Council, *Building on Success: A Report from Eastward Ho!* (Hollywood, Florida: report prepared for the Governor's Commission for a Sustainable South Florida by the South Florida Regional Planning Council, December 1998).

11. See Greenbelt Alliance homepage at: www.green belt.org.

12. Douglas R. Porter, *Summary Report and a Synthesis of Recommendations, Treasure Valley Infrastructure Vision and Strategy* (Boise, Idaho: report prepared for the Future Foundation, February 1999).

13. Denver Regional Council of Governments, *Metro Vision 2020*, executive summary (Denver: March 1997).

14. See Bi-State Development Agency homepage at: www.bi-state.org.

15. The Envision Utah process is described more fully in Peter Calthorpe and William Fulton, *The Regional City* (Washington, D.C.: Island Press, 2001), pp. 126–158.

16. Amy Helling, "Collaborative Visioning: Proceed with Caution," *Journal of the American Planning Association*, summer 1998, p. 347.

17. For more information on these federal planning processes, see Douglas R. Porter and David A. Salvesen, eds., *Collaborative Planning for Wetlands and Wildlife: Issues and Examples* (Washington, D.C.: Island Press, 1995).

18. David R. Godschalk et al., *Pulling Together: A Planning and Development Consensus-Building Manual* (Washington, D.C.: ULI–the Urban Land Institute, 1994), pp. 12–13.

19. Useful guides for developers seeking community support are David R. Godschalk et al., *Pulling Together*; and Debra Stein, *Winning Community Support for Land Use Projects* (Washington, D.C.: ULI–the Urban Land Institute, 1992).

20. For a detailed description of the Prudential Center experience, see Charles Tseckares, "The Politics of Development," *Urban Land*, September 2001, pp. 78–81.

21. For a helpful introduction to indicators, see Redefining Progress, *The Community Indicators Handbook* (Chicago: American Planning Association, 1997).

22. Smart Scorecard for Development Projects is available on the Congress for the New Urbanism Web site at: www.cnu.org/cnu_reports/no_formula_ Scorecard.pdf.

23. Chesapeake & Potomac Regional Alliance, *Smart Growth Proposal* (December 2001), available at: www.capregion.org.

24. Debra Stein, "Charrettes: Not Always the Right Answer," *Land Development*, winter 2001, p.4.